HART CRANE

A COLLECTION OF CRITICAL ESSAYS

Edited by
Alan Trachtenberg

D0949812

Prentice-Hall, Inc.　A SPECTRUM BOOK　*Englewood Cliffs, N.J.*

Library of Congress Cataloging in Publication Data
Main entry under title:

Hart Crane: a collection of critical essays.

(Twentieth century views) (A Spectrum Book)
Bibliography: p.
Includes index.
1. Crane, Hart, 1899-1932—Criticism and
interpretation—Addresses, essays, lectures. I. Trachtenberg,
Alan.
PS3505.R272Z673   811'.52   80-25616

ISBN 0-13-383935-4

ISBN 0-13-383927-3 {PBK.}

Editorial/production supervision by Maria Carella
and Louise M. Marcewicz
Cover design by Vivian Berger
Manufacturing buyer: Barbara A. Frick

10 9 8 7 6 5 4 3 2 1

This Spectrum Book can be made available to businesses and organizations at a special discount
when ordered in large quantities. For more information, contact Prentice-Hall, Inc., General
Book Marketing, Special Sales Division, Englewood Cliffs, New Jersey 07632.

PRENTICE-HALL INTERNATIONAL, INC., *London*
PRENTICE-HALL OF AUSTRALIA PTY. LIMITED, *Sydney*
PRENTICE-HALL OF CANADA, LTD., *Toronto*
PRENTICE-HALL OF INDIA PRIVATE LIMITED, *New Delhi*
PRENTICE-HALL OF JAPAN, INC., *Tokyo*
PRENTICE-HALL OF SOUTHEAST ASIA PTE. LTD., *Singapore*
WHITEHALL BOOKS LIMITED, *Wellington, New Zealand*

Contents

Introduction: Hart Crane's Legend

by Alan Trachtenberg

Hart Crane's reputation has been dogged by a peculiar ambiguity. No one denies him a place among the leading poets of his era—Pound, Eliot, Frost, Stevens, Williams—but the exact place remains somewhat obscure, difficult to estimate. He seems not quite at ease in their company—perhaps archaic in his mode of sublime lyricism, perhaps too "personal" and gauche in his thrusting of emotion before the reader. He may seem more at home in the company of Shelley and Keats—a poet of youth who could sing or cry lines like "And so it was I entered the broken world/ To trace the visionary company of love" ("The Broken Tower"). He is not a poet to be taken lightly.

Crane possessed a lavish, original talent, a high capacity for lyricism matched (by a cruel irony) with an eventually fatal incapacity for life. His disorders were colossal: spectacular displays of carousing, wild fluctuations of exultation and despair, periods of sullen depression and violent resentments, and finally suicide in 1932 at the age of thirty-two. No wonder Crane's life has seemed parabolic and legendary: his upper-middle class provincial background (from the Cleveland area, where his father was a successful candy manufacturer); his alienation from the bourgeois demands of his family yet inability to free himself entirely of those demands; the emotional expense of his parents' quarrels, estrangement, divorce, remarriages; his own insatiable needs for love and stimulation—and his sense of difference among many of his friends as a homosexual. New York and his Greenwich Village crowd of artists and writers served as refuge from the family predicament, and the city itself (though in some ways it seemed more to intensify than satisfy his needs) did provide a momentary haven for the nurturing of his talent. Desperately in need of education, for he had not completed high school, he eagerly absorbed the Village atmosphere of literary controversy and experiment. His mature work is very much of the Twenties and New York.

Suicide at sea simply confirmed the legendary cast of Crane's life, and we can detect in the early criticism (much of it from the hands of friends like Waldo Frank, Malcolm Cowley, Allen Tate and Yvor Winters) an anxiety to explain that tragic event, to give it rational meaning as symptom of a larger cultural failure: either the bankruptcy of the visionary Romanticism that was Crane's predominant mode or the inhospitality of America to poetry. Especially since his death Crane has divided readers into camps of intense supporters or detractors, each waving a banner with his face blazoned on it as hero or exemplary villain. Much of the controversy—rehearsed in several of the essays that follow and in no need of summary here— has raged over the poem by which Crane is best known, *The Bridge* (1930). A work of high ambition—nothing less than "the Myth of America"—this sequence of fifteen poems absorbed most of Crane's creative energy between 1923 and 1930 and provided, for better or for worse, the most important focus of his most richly productive years. He was able to publish in the same years *White Buildings* (1926), a book which contains his most astonishingly beautiful and compelling lyrics (along with two major sequences, "For the Marriages of Faustus and Helen" and the incomparable "Voyages"). Critics who view *The Bridge* unfavorably often cite *White Buildings* as representing Crane's genuine talent, the longer poem as a wilful mistake: a mistake perhaps leading to the suicide itself.

Controversies about *The Bridge,* about its supposed optimism or nationalism or mysticism, seem now quite dated—mere echoes that belong more to the record of cultural history than to the reading of poetry. Understandably the poem has loomed as Crane's major statement, chief buttress of his status in the American tradition. But the quarrels have obscured the poem, and particularly the continuity between it and the lyrics of *White Buildings.* Crane first found his true voice in the lyric, and at the same time often conceived of his lyrics as parts of a whole. Although *The Bridge* is the most intricately harmonized of his sequences, the most expansive in scale, in aesthetic intention it is not as isolated from the earlier lyrics as many critics have felt. The longer work is as much a poetic experiment as an "epic" of modern life; in fact its epic meanings are inseparable from its experimental forms. *The Bridge* and *White Buildings* (and the posthumously published poems) all belong to the same enterprise, the same projected world.

It is precisely this world—the world of Crane's imagination—that remains to be explored and mapped: not his poetics alone, his ideological commitments, but the fiber and texture of the world his poems bring into being. It is a world not without peril. In a manner quite different from that of his peers, Crane demands to be taken *personally,* in the double sense of a speaker uttering poems from the immediacy of experience and a reader receiving a new personal experience by that very act. While critics stressing the anecdotal (e.g., stories that he used a blaring victrola and wine as inducements to the muse) have sadly misread the relation of his poetry to his life, Crane insists upon there being such a relation and is set apart by this insistence from Eliot and Stevens. For Crane is an author of spiritual autobiography of a particularly American and modern sort. His is not a world of ideas, or of fine discriminations by the moral intelligence, but a world of encompassing passions and visions, of lavish music and large gesture. At the same time he does not merely recapitulate the older Romanticism but remakes it to accommodate a new tension, a new modern strain upon Romantic aspirations. He is at once traditional and contemporary, Romantic and modern. Emerson's words in "Works and Days" open directly on his motives: "In stripping time of its illusions, in seeking to find what is the heart of the day, we come to the quality of the moment, and drop duration altogether. It is the depth at which we live and not at all the surface extension that imports." The words must be qualified, for Crane's world is one in which depth and surface, moment and duration steadily tug at each other, constantly at odds: a dialectic of opposites in a struggle to free the transcendent without losing the immediate world. The struggle that distinguishes his poetry and works out its proper expression in the displacements of syntax and the "logic of metaphor" is a struggle to attain a vision, a word, a finality of form, something which can be held onto as both alien and immanent in the world of experience. Crane's desire was not to escape time but to find timeless fulfillment within it.

His death preserved the youthfulness of his world; the promise of youth, its absoluteness of desire and desolation of loss, is the condition of his poetry. But what is remarkable, and remarkably slighted in the criticism, is the intensity of *reflection* in the poems. The notorious difficulties of syntax and metaphor might be taken, indeed, as the very form of reflection, a kind of distancing of emotion by mind, of tumult by tranquility. The exultant elevation of language that captures readers is balanced against a controlling sobriety and calm which often suffuse the most rapturous and fulsome lyrics. This "power in repose" flows from Crane's extraordinary compression of meaning and emotion in words that then burst with accumulated implications, to be regathered in a single form.

Consider "Legend," which opens *White Buildings:*

> As silent as a mirror is believed
> Realities plunge in silence by...
>
> I am not ready for repentance;
> Nor to match regrets. For the moth
> Bends no more than the still
> Imploring flame. And tremorous
> In the white falling flakes
> Kisses are, —
> The only worth all granting.
>
> It is to be learned —
> This cleaving and this burning,
> But only by the one who
> Spends out himself again.
>
> Twice and twice
> (again the smoking souvenir,
> Bleeding eidolon!) and yet again.
> Until the bright logic is won
> Unwhispering as a mirror
> Is believed.
>
> Then, drop by caustic drop, a perfect cry
> Shall string some constant harmony, —
> Relentless caper for all those who step
> The legend of their youth into the noon.

As always at his best, Crane invites the reader to several experiences at once: the performance of a voice introducing a book of poems (Whitman's "Inscriptions" comes to mind), enacting by performance rather than explicit statement the kind of book it is; and at the same time, participation in the act itself so that the voice becomes the reader's own performance. The "I" is available to all readers, for the poem speaks of experience in a general way: "realities," "bright logic," "constant harmonies"—all terms without specific referants. Still, the poem enacts and is a concrete event: it enacts the very process of reflecting upon certain events that remain unspecified and wins a point of view toward them, and it arrives unmistakably at a destination: out of suffering (cleaving and burning) and loss (smoke, blood) may come a redeeming gain (a perfect cry). The destination is not the cry itself, but the recognition of its possibility—from chaos and destruction, order and birth. The reader who wins the meaning of the poem thereby wins that possibility, a "bright logic" which fulfills itself not in a summary statement but a constant process.

To win the logic of the poem is, of course, not necessarily to accept it. Translated into behavioral doctrine, the argument of the poem might well seem a Dionysian guide. But the poet seeks no more than (and it is quite sufficient as a demand upon reading) *assent* to the poem itself. His absolutism is not doctrinal but aesthetic. As he put it in a 1925 statement of his creed, "General Aims and Theories": "it seems evident that certain aesthetic experience (and this may for a time engross the total faculties of the spectator) can be called absolute, inasmuch as it approximates a formally convincing statement of a conception or apprehension of life that gains our unquestioning assent." "Legend" asks for belief as poem, not as way of life.

Yet the poem concerns way of life, declares a point of view toward existence, and defends it. It is a "legend" in several senses: an explanatory key to the world of the book it introduces, and to the poet whose "life" constitutes that world. The word "legend" captures Crane's complex sense of himself as already legendary (the subject of stories), and as the maker of legend, of tales that are also explanations. A reading of the poem might begin with these implications of the title, nuances that deepen and accumulate further meanings in the course of the reading. As the poem opens upon silence, it concludes with "a perfect cry" and the attainment of "the legend of their youth." As it opens with a descent or fall ("plunge"), it concludes with an ascending "step into the noon," into the center of the day. Words like *repentence, bends, imploring,* convey notions of religious practice (prayer, confession), which, while overtly rejected ("I am not ready for repentence"), shed further nuances upon "legend," whose earliest meanings included "the exemplary biography of a saint." The poet unmistakably declines conventional holiness—what else is so clear as that "I'm no saint?"—yet the association through the "logic of metaphor," coupled with what may be oblique crucifixion allusions (burning, smoking, bleeding), evokes an analogy between himself and holy men of the past. The poet might achieve "legend," for example, through his own version of saintliness—a version, however, which transvalues all conventional notions. The refusal of repentance is conventionally sin: like the moth before the flame, the speaker brings his suffering upon himself, risks destruction, by giving in to temptation. He will not resist for the sake of an other-wordly definition of saint, but will reconceive the saint as one who submits without regret, who risks a fall, out of belief that here is the only path toward a bright logic, a perfect cry, a constant harmony.

So much is obvious, but only after preliminary readings. Crane's poems do not work by argument alone, but by abundance of implication. Like Pater and Joyce he teases meanings from etymologies, counts his rhythms and stanza structures as elements of meaning (consider how the formality of stanzas one and five frame this poem, how "cry" recovers the suspended rhyme of "by" in line two), and orchestrates literary allusions (Whitman in "shall string some constant harmony," Joyce and Melville in "white falling flakes"). "What I want to get," Crane wrote to Sherwood Anderson in 1922 about Donne's "Expiration," "is just what is so beautifully done in this poem,—an 'interior' form, a form that is so thorough and intense as to dye the words themselves with a peculiarity of meaning, slightly different maybe from the ordinary definition of them separate from the poem." To transmute the ordinary into the extraordinary is not only an intention of method, but also of what might be called theme. In Crane's successful poems idea and act join so completely that the meaning of the poem is not carried by the form but *is* the form. The remark is commonplace enough and may be applied to any successful aesthetic object. With Crane, however, it is true in the special sense that the reader's struggle for meaning is what the poem is "about": corresponding to and illuminating the speaker's struggle for a "bright logic." The lines

It is to be learned—
This cleaving and this burning,
But only by the one who
Spends out himself again,

might be taken as an address to the reader, who must *learn* to read—as well as a reminder to the speaker. And just as the poet declines the conventional learning represented, for example, by the old monitory parable about the moth and the flame, so the reader must learn by submitting himself to the poem, by allowing its words and music to reverberate and declining easy judgments. Crane insists upon his reader's complicity, not merely his attention.

The poem's form emerges with the reader's growing awareness of cunning compressions. We have, in "Legend," a stark assertive address against conventional piety: "I am not ready for repentance." We have, too, a buried argument against a view of human nature—perhaps represented for Crane by his father, who wanted his son to go to college, learn something useful, make a living—that measures "worth" by gain and loss, by cost and profit. The poem subverts and revises these terms of bourgeois morality, converts them to a different currency and thus submits them to ironic criticism. The sexual pun of "spends out" clinches the subversion, just as "caper" discloses that youth is not only fun but in some serious "relentless" way criminal. Equally, Christ and the saints are criminals, and their "legend" is not only a story, tale, myth, explanation, but also, rising from the heart and origin of the term, a word, a Logos: an account and a fulfillment. As we watch meanings exfoliate from meanings—the result of our own activity as readers—we begin to glimpse the making of Crane's form.

Crane wrote in "General Aims and Theories" that he wished "to establish" his poems "as free from my own personality as from any chance evaluation on the reader's part." What preserves "Legend" and such even more private lyrics as "Possessions" and "Recitative" from autobiography pure and simple is the continuous play of meanings qualifying each other. Crane insisted in letters and essays that his so-called obscurities were not gratuitous but integral to the unfolding of the poem, to its freeing itself from both personal reference and from ordinariness. Apparent obscurities compel the reader to reflection upon the process of the poem, mirroring in this way the self-distancing performed by the speaker himself as he plunges and then removes himself from the corrosions of experience. Reflection for Crane is not, as it is for Stevens, an intellectual matter. Instead it is a looking-back, a recovery, an unending effort to glimpse the form or wholeness of past experience: for to catch the glimpse is, for Crane, to win justification and redemption.

Think of the pattern of repetition and retrospection suggested by certain words and phrases in the poem: *re*pentance, *re*grets, twice and twice, souvenir, yet again.

The most potent figure of retrospection and reflection is, of course, the mirror, one of Crane's central images (see especially "Recitative"). It represents his realization of the hold of the Narcissus myth upon him, and his efforts to master its fatal enticements. The opening image of "Legend" immediately encloses the poem within itself, interiorizing it, introducing the peril of solipsism. But Crane manipulates the image so that it also establishes a point of reference outside the poet's consciousness. For the mirror is both interior imagination and the surface that confirms by reflection (or capture) external "realities." The mirror is an instrument for viewing self. It authorizes instantaneous unquestioned belief because of its double-edged mediation, warranting the continuity of self and world that Crane always felt threatened. The poet plunges into experience through the mirror of the imagination, still gripping the other edge, the mirror being, so to speak, an objective lens assuring a position aslant experience from which perspectives may be won. This demanding doubleness works its way into the reader's awareness by the commanding—and by implication terrifying—ambiguity at the outset: is it the mirror itself, as a medium, that "is believed"? Or the images that plunge across its surface? Only if both possibilities can be maintained at once, only if mirror can serve as access to both imagination and world, do "realities" inspire "belief."

Thus the mirror mediates inside and outside, imagination and world. And its magical potency for Hart Crane—its ability to save him for the making of poems—points to perhaps the most telling aspect of his poetic world: its tense divisions between modes of being. Crane stands firmly within what J. Hillis Miller calls "the romantic and symbolist traditions," in which:

> The objects of this world are separated from the supernatural realities they signify, and the consciousness of the poet is separated both from

objects and their celestial models. A poetry based on such assumptions will be a verbal act bringing about a change in man's relation to the world. In uniting subject and object it will give the poet momentary possession of that distant reality the object symbolizes. Such a poetry is the enactment of a journey which may take the poet and his reader to the very bourne of heaven.

Crane's poetry fits this account, with the qualifying remark that in his particular universe unity rarely escapes from chaos; his "visionary company" exists like fragments of a host in a "broken world," which the poet is left to "trace": to follow, to detect, to discern the outlines of.

The tracing of such an outline is suggested in the last stanza of "Legend" in the hint of arcing motion in steps (alternating up and down) along a "string." And here we apprehend the other leading trope, along with mirror, of Crane's world: the bridge. If mirror is the complex reflective act, then bridge is the form of unity, of desire, hope, and promise. It is the constructive shape of "bright logic." Explicit references to bridges appear often in Crane's poem, even before *The Bridge,* but it is not so much as an object, a thing in space, that "bridge" has its place in his world. Rather, the term has the force of a rhetorical figure, signifying a crossing-over from one state to another. Like the priestly function of bridges preserved in the word "pontiff," "bridge" represented for Crane an active mediation between here and there, now and then; it represented an act of fusion, healing, transcendence. The "logic of metaphor" itself, the transformation of ordinary words into extraordinary meanings through new combinations and infusions of new relationships, is a kind of bridging activity: a joining of the discrete into new unities.

The power of the bridge image for Crane, then, resided as much in strictly poetic practices as in religious or cultural aspirations. Larger implications of the image arose for him early in the 1920's, partly in response to Eliot's *The Waste Land* (1922), and partly fostered by friends such as Waldo Frank who encouraged him to expand his horizons from private to historical and cosmic realms. But how Crane arrived at his conception of *The Bridge* is less important than the fact that the project associated him with a group of writers who in different ways shared a common project in the Twenties: to create for modern America a "usable past." The conjunction of Crane's personal project, which we can read so vividly in "Legend," with this larger cultural enterprise, gave rise to much of the controversy, bewilderment, and uncertainty that has marked the reception of *The Bridge.*

The expression "usable past" was introduced in 1918 by Van Wyck Brooks, who urged not only a revision of the literary tradition but a new attention to the energies and forms of popular life, in city streets and in the practical world, that had been excluded by genteel "guardians of culture" as legitimate concerns of art. In "The Culture of Industrialism" (1917), Brooks wrote:

> Our disbelief in experience, our habitual repression of the creative instinct with its consequent overstimulation of the possessive instinct, has made it impossible for us to take advantage of the treasure our own life has yielded.... The real work of criticism, is to begin *low,* [to find and embrace] our lowest common denominator.

Calling on Whitman as a guide to a genuine American art, he concluded in fervent evangelical accents:

> As soon as the foundations of our life have been reconstructed and made solid on the basis of our own experience, all these extraneous, ill-regulated forces will rally about their newly found center; they will fit in, each where it belongs, contributing to the essential architecture of our life. Then, and only then, shall we cease to be a blind, selfish, disorderly people; we shall become a luminous people, dwelling in the light and sharing our light.

The appeal to Crane of such a project was immediate and intense. Here was a method, by enlarging his bridge trope to include the historical and the cultural, by which he might join his own personal struggles for transcendence to that of America as a whole. Thus might autobiography and a "myth of America" become one. How else are we to understand the epic proportions of *The Bridge* except as the poet's quest to find himself in American history—to discover and disclose the poetic self as the center, the redemptive consciousness of the history as a totality?

In one of the influential attacks on *The Bridge,* Allen Tate wrote that "the 'bridge' stands for no well-defined experience....it has no subject-matter....empty and static, it has no inherent content." Surprisingly, Tate seems to miss the fact that the "bridge" of the poem—Brooklyn Bridge—serves as emblem of the bridging event, the crossing-over, the revisionary enterprise in its final form. Crane could not have been more clear about his intentions. "History, fact, location, etc.," he wrote in 1923 to Gorham Munson, "all have to be transfigured into abstract form that would almost function independently of its subject matter." Transfiguration is itself a phase in the act of bridging—it joins one figural meaning to another—and the final achievement of "abstract form" is simultaneous with the accomplishment of bridging itself: for once the form is attained, it will then be possible to see and hold each discrete detail of "history and fact," personal and public event, as connected to all others, as parts of one totality, which can then be named "Bridge": "Thou steeled Cognizance." There is no inherent content precisely because the poem registers a quest, not an arrival, an effort to "trace," not to assert a finished meaning.

I speak of course of the conception of the poem, not its realization. But it is important for new readers to understand the continuity between *The Bridge* and *White Buildings*. They are of the same world, products of the same visionary consciousness. Like all Crane's mature work, the longer poem strives for transcendence, and reckons movingly with failure. Its principle is a broadening of the horizons of the shorter lyrics: the conversion of the ordinary, through vision, into the spiritual—in this case, the raising of America into a new order of consciousness. The ambition itself may seem somewhat embarrassing, if indeed comprehensible at all today, perhaps an instance of what the great Dutch historian Johan Huinzinga described during his visit to America in 1926 as a "higher naivete": the hope he observed for a purely aesthetic transformation of a world already transformed by industrial and corporate capitalism. *The Bridge* does concede a world already technologised, and the hopefulness of the opening prayer in "Proem" ("lend a myth to God") encloses an anxiety that lives irrepressibly throughout the poem (slackening only at points). The poem's "naivete" is "higher" in that it springs from a refusal to surrender to the world as it is, to the sirens of "adjustment," "maturity," progress, heard everywhere in the popular life of the Twenties. Like "Legend" the poem finds that "the only worth all granting" lies in quite another kind of spending and winning than that established on the shores of the river spanned by the bridge. Crane sought a vision, not a new material America; he sought for a place for art, for poetry, for his own world. The poem is hardly "about" Brooklyn Bridge or a literal America in any sense. It translates the bridge into an energy that might perform for the poet a simultaneous possession of self and world. This translation was Crane's version of "usable past," his high alternative to the "normalcy" of the decade. Certainly the luminosity anticipated by Brooks, Crane, and others has long since dimmed, but just as surely the vision of its hope still lives in the poem.

Hart Crane was a severely embattled poet. His world is finally a battleground where art locks in mortal conflict with its enemies. Crane was without secondary defenses; his singer either floats or sinks, and his world either glows in the radiance of vision, or dies in the "muffled slaughter of a day in birth." The body of his work represents ultimate claims for art, a defense on the steepest ramparts. It is on that high ground that he awaits his readers.

General Aims and Theories

by Hart Crane

When I started writing "Faustus & Helen" it was my intention to embody in modern terms (words, symbols, metaphors) a contemporary approximation to an ancient human culture or mythology that seems to have been obscured rather than illumined with the frequency of poetic allusions made to it during the last century. The name of Helen, for instance, has become an all-too-easily employed crutch for evocation whenever a poet felt a stitch in his side. The real evocation of this (to me) very real and absolute conception of beauty seemed to consist in a reconstruction in these modern terms of the basic emotional attitude toward beauty that the Greeks had. And in so doing I found that I was really building a bridge between so-called classic experience and many divergent realities of our seething, confused cosmos of today, which has no formulated mythology yet for classic poetic reference or for religious exploitation.

So I found "Helen" sitting in a street car; the Dionysian revels of her court and her seduction were transferred to a Metropolitan roof garden with a jazz orchestra; and the *katharsis* of the fall of Troy I saw approximated in the recent World War. The importance of this scaffolding may easily be exaggerated, but it gave me a series of correspondences between two widely separated worlds on which to sound some major themes of human speculation—love, beauty, death, renascence. It was a kind of grafting process that I shall doubtless not be interested in repeating, but which is consistent with subsequent theories of mine on the relation of tradition to the contemporary creating imagination.

It is a terrific problem that faces the poet today—a world that is so in transition from a decayed culture toward a reorganization of human evaluations that there are few common terms, general denominators of speech that are solid enough or that ring with any

Reprinted with permission of The Hart Crane Estate.

vibration or spiritual conviction. The great mythologies of the past (including the Church) are deprived of enough facade to even launch good raillery against. Yet much of their traditions are operative still—in millions of chance combinations of related and unrelated detail, psychological reference, figures of speech, precepts, etc. These are all a part of our common experience and the terms, at least partially, of that very experience when it defines or extends itself.

The deliberate program, then, of a "break" with the past or tradition seems to me to be a sentimental fallacy. ... The poet has a right to draw on whatever practical resources he finds in books or otherwise about him. He must tax his sensibility and his touchstone of experience for the proper selections of these themes and details, however,—and that is where he either stands, or falls into useless archeology.

I put no particular value on the simple objective of "modernity." The element of the temporal location of an artist's creation is of very secondary importance; it can be left to the impressionist or historian just as well. It seems to me that a poet will accidentally define his time well enough simply by reacting honestly and to the full extent of his sensibilities to the states of passion, experience and rumination that fate forces on him, first hand. He must, of course, have a sufficiently universal basis of experience to make his imagination selective and valuable. His picture of the "period," then, will simply be a by-product of his curiosity and the relation of his experience to a postulated "eternity."

I am concerned with the future of America, but not because I think that America has any so-called par value as a state or as a group of people. ... It is only because I feel persuaded that here are destined to be discovered certain as yet undefined spiritual quantities, perhaps a new hierarchy of faith not to be developed so completely elsewhere. And in this process I like to feel myself as a potential factor; certainly I must speak in its terms and what discoveries I may make are situated in its experience.

But to fool one's self that definitions are being reached by merely referring frequently to skyscrapers, radio antennae, steam whistles, or other surface phenomena of our time is merely to paint a photograph. I think that what is interesting and significant will emerge only under the conditions of our submission to, and examination and assimilation of the organic effects on us of these and other fundamental factors of our experience. It can certainly not be an organic expression otherwise. And the expression of such values may often be as well accomplished with the vocabulary and blank verse of the Elizabethans as with the calligraphic tricks and slang used so brilliantly at times by an impressionist like Cummings.

It may not be possible to say that there is, strictly speaking, any "absolute" experience. But it seems evident that certain aesthetic experience (and this may for a time engross the total faculties of the spectator) can be called absolute, inasmuch as it approximates a formally convincing statement of a conception or apprehension of life that gains our unquestioning assent, and under the conditions of which our imagination is unable to suggest a further detail consistent with the design of the aesthetic whole.

I have been called an "absolutist" in poetry, and if I am to welcome such a label it should be under the terms of the above definition. It is really only a *modus operandi,* however, and as such has been used organically before by at least a dozen poets such as Donne, Blake, Baudelaire, Rimbaud, etc. I may succeed in defining it better by contrasting it with the impressionistic method. The impressionist is interesting as far as he goes—but his goal has been reached when he has succeeded in projecting certain selected factual details into his reader's consciousness. He is really not interested in the *causes* (metaphysical) of his materials, their emotional derivations of their utmost spiritual consequences. A kind of retinal registration is enough, along with a certain psychological stimulation. And this is also true of your realist (of the Zola type), and to a certain extent of the classicist, like Horace, Ovid, Pope, etc.

Blake meant these differences when he wrote:

> We are led to believe in a lie
> When we see *with* not *through* the eye.

The impressionist creates only with the eye and for the readiest surface of the consciousness, at least relatively so. If the effect has been harmonious or even stimulating, he can stop there, relinquishing entirely to his audience the problematic synthesis of the details into terms of their own personal consciousness.

It is my hope to go *through* the combined materials of the poem, using our "real" world somewhat as a spring-board, and to give the poem *as a whole* an orbit or predetermined direction of its own. I would like to establish it as free from my own personality as from any chance evaluation on the reader's part. (This is, of course, an impossibility, but it is a characteristic worth mentioning.) Such a poem is at least a stab at a truth, and to such an extent may be differentiated from other kinds of poetry and called "absolute." Its evocation will not be toward decoration or amusement, but rather toward a state of consciousness, an "innocence" (Blake) or absolute beauty. In this condition there may be discoverable under new forms certain spiritual illuminations, shining with a morality essentialized from experience directly, and not from previous precepts or preconceptions. It is as though a poem gave the reader as he left it a single, new *word,* never before spoken and impossible to actually enunciate, but self-evident as an active principle in the reader's consciousness henceforward.

As to technical considerations: the motivation of the poem must be derived from the implicit emotional dynamics of the materials used, and the terms of expression employed are often selected less for their logical (literal) significance than for their associational meanings. Via this and their metaphorical inter-relationships, the entire construction of the poem is raised on the organic principle of a "logic of metaphor," which antedates our so-called pure logic, and which is the genetic basis of all speech, hence consciousness and thought-extension.

These dynamics often result, I'm told, in certain initial difficulties in understanding my poems. But on the other hand I find them at times the only means possible for expressing certain concepts in any forceful or direct way whatever. To cite two examples:—when, in "Voyages" (II), I speak of "adagios of islands," the reference is to the motion of a boat through islands clustered thickly, the rhythm of the motion, etc. And it seems a much more direct and creative statement than any more logical employment of words such as "coasting slowly through the islands," besides ushering in a whole world of music. Similarly in "Faustus and Helen" (III) the speed and tense altitude of an aeroplane are much better suggested by the idea of "nimble blue plateaus"—*implying* the aeroplane and its speed against a contrast of stationary elevated earth. Although the statement is pseudo in relation to formal logic—it *is* completely logical in relation to the truth of the imagination, and there is expressed a concept of speed and space that could not be handled so well in other terms.

In manipulating the more imponderable phenomena of psychic motives, pure emotional crystallizations, etc., I have had to rely even more on these dynamics of inferential mention, and I am doubtless still very unconscious of having committed myself to what seems nothing but obscurities to some minds. A poem like "Possessions" really cannot be technically explained. It must rely (even to a large extent with myself) on its organic impact on the imagination to successfully imply its meaning. This seems to me to present an exceptionally difficult problem, however, considering the real clarity and consistent logic of many of the other poems.

I know that I run the risk of much criticism by defending such theories as I have, but as it is part of a poet's business to risk not only criticism — but folly — in the conquest of consciousness I can only say that I attach no intrinsic value to what means I use beyond their practical service in giving form to the living stuff of the imagination.

New conditions of life germinate new forms of spiritual articulation. And while I feel that my work includes a more consistent extension of traditional literary elements than many contemporary poets are capable of appraising, I realize that I am utilizing the gifts of the past as instruments principally; and that the voice of the present, if it is to be known, must be caught at the risk of speaking in idioms and circumlocutions sometimes shocking to the scholar and historians of logic. Language has built towers and bridges, but itself is inevitably as fluid as always.

Introduction to
White Buildings

by Allen Tate

The poetry of Hart Crane is ambitious. It is the only poetry I am acquainted with which is at once contemporary and in the grand manner. It is an American Poetry. Crane's themes are abstractly, metaphysically conceived, but they are definitely confined to an experience of the American scene. In such poems as The Wine Menagerie, For the Marriage of Faustus and Helen, Recitative, he is the poet of the complex urban civilization of his age: precision, abstraction, power. There is no *pastiche;* when he employs symbols from traditional literature, the intention is personally symbolic; it is never falsely pretentious with the common baggage of poetical speech, the properties coveted by the vulgar as inherently poetic.

Hart Crane's first experiments in verse are not, of course, collected in this volume, which contains with one or two exceptions only those poems exhibiting the qualities likely to be permanent in his work. Of these exceptions there is the perfectly written piece of Imagism, Garden Abstract. This poem evinces several properties of the "new poetry" of a decade ago, the merits and the limitations of the Imagists. To the Imagists Crane doubtless went to school in poetry. He learned their structural economy; he followed their rejection of the worn-out poetic phrase; he must have studied the experiments in rhythm of Pound, Aldington, Fletcher. From Pound and Eliot he got his first conception of what it is, in the complete sense, to be contemporary.

But Crane suddenly and profoundly broke with the methods of Imagism, with its decorative and fragmentary world. To the conceptual mind a world set up not by inclusive assertion but by exclusive attention to the objects of sense lacks imaginative coordination; a method which refuses to exceed the dry presentation of *petites sensations* confines the creative vision to suggestions, to implicit indications, but it cannot arrive at the direct affirmation, of a complete world. A series of Imagistic poems is a series of worlds. The poems of Hart Crane are facets of a single vision; they refer to a central imagination, a single evaluating power, which is at once the motive of the poetry and the form of its realization.

The poet who tries to release the imagination as an integer of perception attempts the solution of the leading contemporary problem of his art. It would be impertinent to enumerate here the underlying causes of the dissociation of the modern consciousness: the poet no longer apprehends his world as a Whole. The dissociation appears decisively for the first time in Baudelaire. It is the separation of vision and subject; since Baudelaire's time poets have in some sense been deficient in the one or the other. For the revolt of Rimbaud, in this distinction, was a repudiation of the commonly available themes of poetry, followed by a steady attenuation of vision in the absence of thematic control. Exactly to the extent to which the ready-made theme controls the vision, the vision is restricted by tradition and may, to that extent, be defined by tradition. In The Waste Land, which revives the essence of the problem, Mr. Eliot displays vision and subject once more in traditional schemes; the vision for some reason is dissipated, and the subject dead. For while Mr. Eliot might have written a more ambitiously unified poem, the unity would have been false; tradition as unity is not contemporary. The important contemporary poet has the rapidly diminishing privilege of reorganizing the subjects of the past. He must construct and assimilate his own subjects. Dante had only to assimilate his.

If the energy of Crane's vision never quite reaches a sustained maximum, it is because he has not found a suitable theme. To realize even partially, at the present time, the maximum of poetic energy demonstrates an important intention. Crane's poems are a fresh vision of the world, so intensely personalized in a new creative language that only the strictest and most unprepossessed effort of attention can take it in. Until vision and subject completely fuse, the poems will be difficult. The comprehensiveness and lucidity of any poetry, the capacity for poetry being assumed as proved, are in direct proportion to the availability of a comprehensive and perfectly articulated given theme.

Crane wields a sonorous rhetoric that takes the reader to Marlowe and the Elizabethans. His blank verse, the most sustained medium he controls, is pre-Websterian; it is measured, richly textured, rhetorical. But his spiritual allegiances are outside the English tradition. Melville and Whitman are his avowed masters. In his sea poems, Voyages, in Emblems of Conduct, in allusions to the sea throughout his work, there is something of Melville's intense, transcendental brooding on the mystery of the "high interiors of the sea." I do not know whether he has mastered Poe's criticism, yet some of his conviction that the poet should be intensely local must stem from Poe. Most of it, however, he undoubtedly gets from Whitman. Whitman's range was possible in an America of prophecy; Crane's America is materially the same, but it approaches a balance of forces; it is a realization; and the poet, confronted with a complex present experience, gains in intensity what he loses in range. The great proportions of the myth have collapsed in its reality. Crane's poetry is a concentration of certain phases of the Whitman substance, the fragments of the myth.

The great difficulty which his poetry presents the reader is the style. It is possible that his style may check the immediate currency of the most distinguished American poetry of the age, for there has been very little preparation in America for a difficult poetry; the Imagistic impressionism of the last ten years has not supplied it. Although Crane is probably not a critical and systematic reader of foreign literatures, his French is better than Whitman's; he may have learned something from Laforgue and, particularly, Rimbaud; or something of these poets from Miss Sitwell, Mr. Wallace Stevens, or Mr. T. S. Eliot.

He shares with Rimbaud the device of oblique presentation of theme. The theme never appears in explicit statement. It is formulated through a series of complex metaphors which defy a paraphrasing of the sense into an equivalent prose. The reader is plunged into a strangely unfamiliar *milieu* of sensation, and the principle of its organization is not immediately grasped. The *logical* meaning can never be derived (see Passage, Lachrymae Christi); but the *poetical* meaning is a direct intuition, realized prior to an explicit knowledge of the subject-matter of the poem. The poem does not *convey;* it *presents;* it is not topical, but expressive.

There is the opinion abroad that Crane's poetry is, in some indefinite sense, "new." It is likely to be appropriated by one of the several esoteric cults of the American soul. It tends toward the formation of a state of mind, the critical equivalent of which would be in effect an exposure of the confusion and irrelevance of the current journalism of poetry, and of how far behind the creative impulse the critical intelligence, at the moment, lags. It is to be hoped, therefore, that this state of mind, where it may be registered at all, will not at its outset be shunted into a false context of obscure religious values, that a barrier will not be erected between it and the rational order of criticism. For, unless the present critic is deceived as to the structure of his tradition, the well-meaning criticism since Poe has supported a vicious confusion: it has transferred the states of mind of poetry from their proper contexts to the alien contexts of moral and social aspiration. The moral emphasis is valid; but its focus on the consequences of the state of mind, instead of on its properties as art, has throttled a tradition in poetry. The moral values of literature should derive from literature, not from the personal values of the critic; their public circulation in criticism, if they are not ultimately to be rendered inimical to literature, should be controlled by the literary intention. There have been poetries of "genius" in America, but each of these as poetry has been scattered, and converted into an *impasse* to further extensions of the same order of imagination.

A living art is new; it is old. The formula which I have contrived in elucidation of Crane's difficulty for the reader (a thankless task, since the difficulty inheres equally in him) is a formula for most romantic poetry. Shelley could not have been influenced by Rimbaud, but he wrote this "difficult" verse:

> Pinnacled dim in the intense inane.

The present faults of Crane's poetry (it has its faults: it is not the purpose of this Foreword to disguise them) cannot be isolated in a line-by-line recognition of his difficulty. If the poems are sometimes obscure, the obscurity is structural and deeper. His faults, as I have indicated, lie in the occasional failure of meeting between vision and subject. The vision often strains and overreaches the theme. This fault, common among ambitious poets since Baudelaire, is not unique with them. It appears whenever the existing poetic order no longer supports the imagination. It appeared in the eighteenth century with the poetry of William Blake.

The Progress of Hart Crane

by Yvor Winters

It is necessary, before attempting to criticize Mr. Crane's new book [*The Bridge*], to place it in the proper genre and to give as accurate an account as one is able of its theme. The book cannot be called an epic, in spite of its endeavor to create and embody a national myth, because it has no narrative framework and so lacks the formal unity of an epic. It is not didactic, because there is no logical exposition of ideas; neither Homer nor Dante will supply a standard of comparison. The structure we shall find is lyrical; but the poem is not a single lyric, it is rather a collection of lyrics on themes more or less related and loosely following out of each other. The model, in so far as there is one, is obviously Whitman, whom the author proclaims in this book as his master.

The book is composed of eight parts, of which two contain more than one lyric. There is a *Proem: To Brooklyn Bridge,* in which the initial inspiration of the book is suggested. Part I, *Ave Maria,* is a monologue spoken by Columbus on his first return to Spain; one receives the impression that Columbus is not only the herald of the new world to the old, but that he is in some way the herald of life to the unborn. Part II, *Powhatan's Daughter,* deals with the soil, the flesh of the continent (Pocahontas), and is composed of five lyrics: the first, *Harbor Dawn,* shows a protagonist, perhaps the author, or better simply man, awakening not only to day but to life after "400 years and more...or is it from the soundless shore of sleep?"; the second, *Van Winkle,* gives a kind of fragmentary glimpse of American boyhood (the boy is Van Winkle, one gathers, because he is exploring the new world in a somewhat dazed condition after "400 years and more"); the third, *The River,* shows the adolescent joining

"The Progress of Hart Crane," by Yvor Winters. From *Poetry* XXXVI, (June 1930), 153-65.

the vagrants and coming to his first realization of the soil, the body
of Pocahontas; the fourth, *The Dance,* projects the personality of
the author into an imagined Indian brave, Maquokeeta, whose
apotheosis at the stake and amid a war dance effects a permanent and
spiritual union with Pocahontas; fifth, *Indiana,* depicts an old
pioneer bidding goodbye to her adopted son, who is setting out in
search of adventure. Part III, *Cutty Sark,* is a kind of ghost-dance of
the old clippers, the early days of American navigation. Part IV,
Cape Hatteras, is a long prayer to Walt Whitman, into the midst of
which is inserted a brief history of aviation, beginning with the first
flight of the Wrights and ending with a contemporary crash; the
exact relationship of this section to the book as a whole remains
obscure to me, as does the formal intention of the lyric itself. Part V
is composed of *Three Songs,* which provide an interlude and which
deal in a purer and more condensed form with themes treated elsewhere. The intention of the sixth section, *Quaker Hill,* remains as
obscure to me as that of the fourth; the poem is prefaced by selections from Isadora Duncan and Emily Dickinson, both of whom are
mentioned in the poem as symbols, one would guess, of the Quaker,
Puritan, and other "ideals" of the past, the decay of which the poem
indicates; these constituting a combination that is almost enough to
freeze the blood of one with my own prejudices and inhibitions.
Part VII, *The Tunnel,* deals with the subway, the modern metropolitan Purgatory, the trial and purification by fire and hallucination, in which the ghost of Poe appears to be rather incidentally
entangled. Part VIII, *Atlantis,* is the apotheosis of the bridge
addressed in the proem, in the form of the new Atlantis, the future
America. It ends with Mr. Crane's version of Whitman's "Look for
me under your bootsoles":

> O Answerer of All,—Anemone,—
> Now while thy petals spend the suns about us, hold—
> (O Thou whose radiance doth inherit me)
> Atlantis,—hold thy floating singer late!

I do not offer this analysis as complete or final, but as the best I
have been able to devise so far; I have discovered in the past that
Mr. Crane's work is likely to clear up in a measure with familiarity.
Nevertheless, it should be apparent from the looseness of the progression—and it will be more apparent after an inspection of the

variety of meters—that the book as a whole has no more unity than the *Song of Myself;* it must be treated, as I have said, as a series of lyrics on a theme that is basically Whitmanian, but that, under the influence of Blake and Mr. Crane's own inclinations, is extended into regions with which Whitman did not concern himself.

Now Whitman doubtless regarded himself as something of an epic writer, and it is possible that Mr. Crane feels that he is one; the difference between Whitman (who is his own epic hero) and *pius Aeneas* is that the latter is not only obeying destiny, he is obeying his mother. That is, destiny, for Aeneas, is not a vague surge toward an infinite future, it is a deliberate effort to achieve a definite aim, and the effort is composed of specific moral duties; it is the serious attitude toward those duties that made him *pius* to the Augustan Roman. It is the same attitude that gives to every one of his acts a definite and absolutely individual value, as well as a definite bearing on the theme of the book as a whole. That is, destiny for Vergil was a clear and comprehensible thing and had a clear relationship to a complete scale of human values. Whitman found all human values about equal and could envisage good only as an enthusiastic acceptance of everything at hand; but if nothing is bad it follows equally that nothing is good—that is, everything is equivalent to everything else and there are no values at all; unless one can envisage as good a kind of meaningless and inexhaustible energy, or unless one can face about with Mr. Jeffers and regard annihilation, complete negation, as the only good. It is therefore natural that Whitman's poems, like Mr. Jeffers', should be little save boundless catalogues. Both of these poets, and Mr. Crane as well, are headed precisely for nowhere, in spite of all the shouting. All three are occasionally betrayed by their talents into producing a passage better than their usual run, but this only goes to prove the fallacy of their initial assumptions. Mr. Crane, since he possesses the greatest genius in the Whitmanian tradition, and since, strangely enough, he grafts onto the Whitmanian tradition something of the stylistic discipline of the Symbolists, most often exceeds himself in this manner. The Whitmanian basis of Mr. Crane's book makes a hero, as I have said, impossible. And the "destiny" of a nation is hard to get at in the abstract, since it is a vague generality, like "the French temperament" or "the average American." It reduces itself, when one comes to describe it—without a hero—to the most elementary and the least interesting aspects of the general landscape, aspects which cannot possibly be imbued with any definite significance, no matter how excited one may get, for the simple reason that no definite significance is available. It is on this rock that *Atlantis* shatters; and on a similar rock, we shall presently see, occurs the wreck of *The Dance,* the other climax of the volume.

There is only one poem in the volume that endeavors to treat clearly of an individual human relationship; the poem is *Indiana,* and it fails miserably—it could scarcely be more mawkish and helpless. The fact is unimportant except that it strengthens one's suspicion that Mr. Crane is temperamentally unable to understand a very wide range of experience, and one's feeling that even his best poems—which, in spite of this limitation, are very fine—have about them something of the fragility of innocence. The two most powerful poems in the book, though they are not the most perfect, are *The River* and *The Dance.*

The River falls into three distinct and unsynthesized parts. The first is a catalogue of the "din and slogans of the year"—prefatory information thrown at one in the raw and absolutely unmastered. The second part, which deals with the hoboes, the intercessors with Pocahontas "who have touched her knowing her without name," is better organized but is still turgid and confused; it has magnificent moments. The third part—each of the three parts is metrically distinct from the rest—though not quite as clean as Mr. Crane's finest writing, carries the epic quality of the Whitmanian vision (the vision of humanity *en masse,* or undifferentiated) to the greatest dignity and power of which it is, probably, capable; the stream of humanity becomes fused, poetically, with the stream of the Mississippi, and the result is a passage of extraordinary poetry:

> Down, down—born pioneers in time's despite,
> Grimed tributaries to an ancient flow—
> They win no frontier by their wayward plight,
> But drift in stillness, as from Jordan's brow.
>
> You will not hear it as the sea; even stone
> Is not more hushed by gravity. ...But slow,
> As loth to take more tribute—sliding prone
> Like one whose eyes were buried long ago
>
> The River, spreading, flows—and spends your dream.
> What are you, lost within this tideless spell?

> You are your father's father, and the stream—
> A liquid theme that floating niggers swell.

The complete passage contains eight stanzas of mounting intensity; it has a few faults of detail, but I cannot read it—much less read it aloud—without being profoundly moved.

The Dance is more even, but chiefly because it is more evenly impure. I have already indicated briefly the theme of *The Dance*. It is in the following stanza that the apotheosis of Maquokeeta begins:

> O, like the lizard in the furious noon,
> That drops his legs and colors in the sun,
> —And laughs, pure serpent, Time itself, and moon
> Of his own fate, I saw thy change begun!

It is obvious from such a stanza that we are analyzing the flaws in a genius of a high order—none of the famous purple patches in Shelley, for example, surpasses this stanza, and probably none equals it; so be it. But the flaws in Mr. Crane's genius are, I believe, so great as to partake, if they persist, almost of the nature of a public catastrophe. The most that we can learn about the nature of the apotheosis follows a few lines further on:

> Thy freedom is her largesse, Prince, and hid
> On paths thou knewest best to claim her by.

> High unto Labrador the sun strikes free
> Her speechless dream of snow, and stirred again,
> She is the torrent and the singing tree;
> And she is virgin to the last of men. ...

> And when the caribou slant down for salt
> Do arrows thirst and leap? Do antlers shine
> Alert, star-triggered in the listening vault
> Of dusk?—And are her perfect brows to thine?

These lines are in themselves, for the most part, very good; placed in the proper poetic setting and with an adequate ideational background, they might contribute to a wholly sound poem. Here, however, they represent the climax of that poem which would appear to be intended as one of the two climactic points of the sequence. They constitute an assertion of the faith on which the sequence is built; there is no evidence here or elsewhere in the poem or the book that they are merely a poetic and incomplete hint of a more definite belief; and there is a great deal of evidence that Mr. Crane suspects continually the inadequacy of his belief, or at any rate is continually hampered and frustrated by that inadequacy. Mr. Crane demands of his medicine-man to "lie to us—dance us back the tribal morn." Let us examine another passage:

> Spears and assemblies: black drums thrusting on—
> O yelling battlements,—I, too, was liege
> To rainbows currying each pulsant bone:
> Surpassed the circumstance, danced out the siege!
>
> And buzzard-circleted, screamed from the stake;
> I could not pick the arrows from my side.
> Wrapped in that fire, I saw more escorts wake—
> Flickering, sprint up the hill groins like a tide.

Any one of these lines is a brilliant performance; but only two of them, I believe, at the most, are brilliant on a poetic level—the fourth (possibly) and the sixth. The sixth is worthy of Racine. The others are brilliant on what I should call a descriptive level. To make this clear, I offer several others taken nearly at random from the same poem:

> A cyclone threshes in the turbine crest,
> Swooping in eagle feathers down your back.
>
> I left my sleek boat nibbling margin grass.
>
> I learned to catch the trout's moon-whisper.

These lines, though they are perceived with great precision, have no evident connection with the theme except as they are a part of the natural landscape, and that connection is inadequate for art. One feels no fluid experience bathing the perceptions and giving them a significant relation; one feels rather fact after fact, each, or nearly each, admirably presented but only very casually relevant, being hurled at one by the author in a fine frenzy as if he were trying to convince one, to hypnotize one, that he might in turn be convinced himself.

There are moments throughout the poem when the hypnosis is achieved, and lines of pure electricity occur; but the lapse to the descriptive is sudden and immediate. The poem is composed mainly of unfused details, and is excited rather than rhythmic. The quality which we call restraint; and which is here lacking, is the result of a feeling on the part of a poet that the motivation of his emotion is sound and needs no justification, that the emotion is inevitable; his problem, then, is only to give order to his emotion. In Mr. Crane we see an attempt to emotionalize a theme to the point where both he and the reader will forget to question its justification. It is, whatever fragmentary success may result from it, a form of hysteria. In this case, the author is endeavoring to evoke a plane of experience higher than that of this world, about which he knows nothing and is able to imagine little or nothing, by the use of details taken from the plane of experience (this world) from which he is trying to escape. The details, as I have said, are good, but they almost never have meaning, for the simple reason that the meaning is not available. I do not wish to imply that a wholly concrete statement may not have poetic value—it may, as in some of the best work of the Imagists and the Imagist fringe (Dr. Williams, Miss Moore, and so on), if the author is clearly aware of the value when he writes it; if, in other words, the feeling is definitely implicated in the perception. *Atlantis,* as I have already said, is an attempt to embody another non-existent "destiny" in miscellaneous concrete details. It contains, like *The Dance,* superb poetry; unlike *The Dance,* its low spots are imprecise—in place of exact description we get vague thunder.

The same faults of rhetoric are to be found in *National Winter Garden,* one of the *Three Songs,* but are almost absent from the first of its companion pieces, *Southern Cross,* a poem which very nearly, though not quite, equals the two most perfect poems, to my mind, that Mr. Crane has written, *Repose of Rivers* and *Voyages II,* from his former volume. *The Harbor Dawn, Van Winkle, The Tunnel, Cape Hatteras,* and *Quaker Hill* are too vague in detail and chaotic in form to be worth much; *Cape Hatteras,* indeed, in its attitude toward Whitman, strikes me as desperately sentimental. Mr. Crane's estimate of Whitman and his complete failure to understand Emily Dickinson (for which see his charming but uncomprehending poem addressed to her and published several years ago in *The Nation)* are of a piece not only with each other but with his own failures and limitations as a poet.

Cutty Sark is a frail but exquisite and almost incomparably skillful dance of shadows. Its conclusion is a perpetual delight. It is a kind of radio question sent into the past to locate certain lost clippers, clippers the names of which, though apparently made for Mr. Crane's purpose, are historical:

> Buntlines tusseling (91 days, 20 hours and anchored!)
> *Rainbow, Leander*
> (last trip a tragedy) where can you be
> *Nimbus?* and you rivals two—
> a long tack keeping—
>
> *Taeping?*
> *Ariel?*

The remaining poems—the *Proem* and *Ave Maria*—are, so far as I can see, basically sound; that is, I am aware of no earthly reason why Mr. Crane should not write a poem expressing his admiration of the Brooklyn Bridge, or an imaginary monologue spoken by Columbus. Both poems contain fine things; both, unfortunately, contain a great deal that is empty. As in *Atlantis,* the weak portions are composed of inexact poetic verbiage. These poems illustrate the danger inherent in Mr. Crane's almost blind faith in his moment-to-moment inspiration, the danger that the author may turn himself into a kind of stylistic automaton, the danger that he may develop a sentimental leniency toward his vices and become wholly their victim, instead of understanding them and eliminating them.

Mr. Crane is not alone in this danger; it is one of the greatest dangers of the entire body of anti-intellectualist literature of our time. It can be seen in Miss Roberts' latest novel, *The Great Meadow,* a book in which the dangers potential in the style of her first two novels have become actual and almost smother a good plot. It can be seen in a good deal of the latest work of Mr. Joyce, who, while revolutionizing the word, spends an appalling lot of detailed revolution telling us how little clouds commit suicide and the like. It can be seen, I regret above all to add, in the last three or four years' work of Dr. Williams, whose experiments in perpetual motion are becoming so repetitious as to appear very nearly mechanical or even static. Dr. Williams, though a writer of greater range and mastery, in all likelihood, than any of these others, is a bigot and is bound to be the victim of his own bigotry just as are the intellectual bigots whom he damns. Mr. Frost, at the age of fifty-odd, can continue to grow amazingly. Mr. Joyce and Dr. Williams appear to be disintegrating in their forties, Miss Roberts and Mr. Crane in their thirties. Thomas Hardy could grow in his eighties. Two things would appear certain about the situation: it is profoundly alarming, and it is not inevitable.

It is possible that Mr. Crane may recover himself. In any event, he has given us, in his first book, several lyrics that one is tempted to call great, and in both books several charming minor lyrics and many magnificent fragments. And one thing he has demonstrated, the impossibility of getting anywhere with the Whitmanian inspiration. No writer of comparable ability has struggled with it before, and, with Mr. Crane's wreckage in view, it seems highly unlikely that any writer of comparable genius will struggle with it again.

Hart Crane [1899-1932]

by *William Carlos Williams*

"WHITE BUILDINGS" (1926)

It is startling to come upon lines with such a sound of continual surf in them as these:

> *...within your breast is gathering*
> *All bright insinuations that my years have caught*
> *For islands where must lead inviolably*
> *Blue latitudes and levels of your eyes,*

The alternate peak and back rush of waves is clearly audible—
It begins again in the next movement:

> *Meticulous, past midnight in clear rime,*
> *Infrangible and lonely, smooth as though cast*
> *Together in one merciless white blade—*
> *The bay estuaries fleck the hard sky limits.*

This is music which an attentive and willing ear will be sure to recommend without quibble to the intelligence. And the music alone will carry all that need be said—

Then there are the words: he wrote sometimes, really, as though he were seeking to please (perhaps he was just indifferent, in view of the music) someone who had charge of a New York Sunday Book Supplement. That is to say he could be at times as bad as that—the gently bubbling putridity of the saleable—

> *Creation's blithe and petalled word etc, etc.*

and much more of that "profound" sort in rhymed quatraines for which I can find no excuse whatever—

"Hart Crane [1899-1932]" by William Carlos Williams. From *Contempo*, Vol. II, No. 4 (July 5, 1932). Reprinted by permission of *New Directions*, agents for the estate of Florence H. Williams. All rights reserved.

Worse than that, Crane wanted to be cosmic, I think. This is the reason he often took his eye from the word—and the word slipped away from him. It amounts to a sentimentality, a sentimentality that verges upon the pulpit, when the pulpit is very bad and embracing instead of tending to business—which is its business. When the church goes "good" it is lost.

But in his music Crane was often superb; that is thought enough. When he let the damned words go to the intelligence which was in them, occasionally, the music forced them to distinction—to clarity, as in *The Wine Menagerie:*

> *The glozening decanters that reflect the street*
> *Wear me in crescents on their bellies—*

with accuracy—

"THE BRIDGE" (1930)

—is a more advanced realization on Crane's part of this interplay of words and music—and a further demonstration of its dangers: Go with the music—and bash your brains out on the stones. But while it lasts it is lovely, austere (I don't mean actually to bash your brains out, I speak of the verse)—satisfying, correct, enviable.

One should be as savage as he is able to be toward the dead—since they have such an advantage over us. Only stupidity spares them in order to go on flattering itself.

Crane quotes (*The Bridge,* VIII, Atlantis) from Plato—

> *Music is then the knowledge of that which relates*
> *to love in harmony and system.*

But I cannot grow rhapsodic with him, the Evangel of the post-war, the replier to the romantic apostle of *The Waste Land*—when he musics:

> *Onward and up the crystal-flooded aisle*
> *White tempest nets file upward, upward ring*
> *With silver terraces the humming spars,*
> *The loft of vision, palladium of stars.*

I do not accept the metaphors, "tempest nets," etc., etc.

It seems to me that this use of words is a direct step backward to the bad poetry of any age but especially to that triumphant re-gression which followed Whitman and imitated—whatever his name was—the Frenchman—and came to a head in T. S. Eliot—excellently.

Sweetness there is and great charm in *Indiana*—but not to the enhancement of Crane's genius—

It is not possible to praise anyone after his own work, it is impossible to find faults in his work without encouraging blackguards and the incompetent—

Crane didn't write as low as he knew, or should have known, his life to be. Instead he continually reached "up," out of what he *knew,* to that which he didn't know. He was fascinated by a long, billowy music which deceived him very often. He grew vague instead of setting himself to describe in detail—Achilles greave and shield. His eyes seem to me often to have been blurred by "vision" when they should have been held hard, as hard as he could hold them, on the object—

His agony, which was real and which raised him to distinction above danger from attack, throws a white glare over his best work— in the manner of the light in Van Gogh's painting. But the sheer objectivity of the pigment kept the latter anchored whereas Crane appears to me often to have neglected the equal objectivity of words in making up his compositions. Edges, facets often escape him—to his undoing.

An Introduction to Hart Crane

by Waldo Frank

Harold Hart Crane was born in Garrettsville, Ohio, July 21, 1899. His parents, Clarence Arthur Crane and Grace Hart, were of the pioneer stock that trekked in covered wagons from New England to the Western Reserve. But his grandparents, on both sides, had already shifted from the farm to small-town business, and Clarence Crane, who had inherited his father's general store in Garrettsville, became a wealthy candy manufacturer in Cleveland. Here, the poet, an only child, lived from his tenth year. At thirteen, he was composing verse; at sixteen, in the words of Gorham Munson, "he was writing on a level that Amy Lowell never rose from." In the winter of 1916, he went with his mother, who was separated from her husband, to the Isle of Pines, south of Cuba, where his grandfather Hart had a fruit ranch; and this journey, which gave him his first experience of the sea, was cardinal in his growth. The following year, he was in New York, in contact with Margaret Anderson and Jane Heap, editors of The Little Review; tutoring for college; writing; already passionately and rather wildly living.

At this time, two almost mutually exclusive tendencies divided the American literary scene. One was centered in Ezra Pound, Alfred Kreymborg, the imagists, Harriet Monroe's Poetry and The Little Review: the other was grouped about The Seven Arts. Young Crane was in vital touch with both. He was reading Marlowe, Donne, Laforgue, Rimbaud; but he was also finding inspiration in Whitman, Sherwood Anderson and Melville. His action, when the United States lurched into war, reveals the complexity of his interests. He decided not to go to college and by his own choice returned to Cleveland, to work as a common laborer in a munition plant and a shipyard on the lake. He loved machines, the earth-

"An Introduction to Hart Crane", by Waldo Frank. From *The New Republic*, Vol. 74 (Feb. 15, 1933), 11-15.

tang of the workers. He was no poet in an ivory tower. But he also loved music; he wanted time to write, to meditate, to read. The conflict of desires led him, perhaps, to accept what seemed a comfortable compromise: a job in the candy business of his father.

The elder Crane seems to have been a man of turbulent and twisted power, wholly loyal to the gods of Commerce. He was sincerely outraged by the jest of fortune which had given him a poet for a son. Doubtless, he was bitter at his one child's siding with the mother in the family conflict. But under all, there was a secret emotional bond between the two, making for the ricochet of antagonism and attraction that lasted between them until the father's death, a year before the poet's. The candy magnate set laboriously to work to drive the "poetry nonsense" out of his boy. Hart became a candy salesman behind a counter, a soda-jerker, a shipping clerk. He received a minimum wage. Trusted employees were detailed to spy on him, lest he read "poetry books" during work hours. Hart Crane escaped several times from the paternal yoke, usually to advertising jobs near home or in New York. And at last, in 1920, he decided to break with both Cleveland and his father.

His exquisite balance of nerves was already permanently impaired. The youthful poet, who had left a comfortable household to live with machines and rough men, who had shouldered "the curse of sundered parentage," who had tasted the strong drink of literature and war, carried within him a burden intricate and heavy — a burden hard to hold in equilibrium. Doubtless the chaos of his personal life led him to rationalize the accessible tangent ease from the strain of balance which excess use of alcohol invited. Yet there was a deeper cause for the disequilibrium which, when Crane was thirty-two, was finally to break him from his love of life and to destroy him. Hart Crane was a mystic. The mystic is a man who *knows*, by immediate experience, the organic continuity of his self with the cosmos. This experience, which is the normal fruit of sensitivity, becomes intense in one whose native energy is great; and lest it turn into an overwhelming, shattering burden, it must be disciplined and ordered. A stable nucleus within the self must be achieved, to bear and finally transfigure the world's impinging chaos. Personally, Crane did not win this synthesis.

But the poet was clearer and shrewder than the man. His mind sought a poetic principle to integrate the exuberant flood of his impressions. The early poems, collected in "White Buildings" (1926), reveal the quest, not the finding. Allen Tate, in his Introduction to this volume, writes: "The poems...are facets of a single vision; they refer to a central imagination, a single evaluating power, which is at once the motive of the poetry and the form of its realization."[1] But the central imagination, wanting a unitary principle, wavers and breaks; turns back upon itself instead of mastering the envisaged substance of the poem. That is why, often, a fragmentary part of a poem is greater than the whole: and why it is, at times, impossible to transpose the series of images into the sense-and-thought sequence that originally moved the poet and that must be perceived, in order to move the reader. The mediate principle, coterminous with the image logic of the poem and the feeling logic of the poet, is imperfect. The first lines of the volume:

> As silent as a mirror is believed
> Realities plunge in silence by....

are a superb expression of chaos and of the poet's need to integrate this chaos in the active mirror of self. Page after page, "realities plunge by," only ephemerally framed in a mirroring mood which alas! melts, itself, into the turbulent procession. Objective reality exists in these poems only as an oblique moving-inward to the poet's mood. But the mood is never, as in imagist or romantic verse, given for and as itself. It is given only as an organic moving-outward toward the objective world. Each lyric is a diapason between two integers of a continuous whole. But the integers (subjective and objective) are almost never clear. This makes of the poem an abstract, wavering, esthetic body. There is not yet, as in the later work, a conscious substantiated theme or principle of vision to stratify the interracting parts of the poems into an immobile whole.

But in the final six lyrics of this volume ("Voyages") there is the beginning of a synthesis. Its symbolic theme is the Sea. The turbulent experience of Crane's childhood and youth is fused in a litany to the Sea.

---

[1]Reprinted from *White Buildings*, poems by Hart Crane, with the permission of Liveright Publishing Corporation. Copyright 1926 by Boni and Liveright, Inc. Copyright renewed 1954 by Liveright Publishing Corporation. Copyright ©1972 by Liveright Publishing Corporation.

> ...Sleep, death, desire,
> Close round one instant in one floating flower.

The sea, first source of life, first Mother, is death to man. To woo it
is to return to death's simple singleness. This solution from the
burden of chaos is like the erotic mysticism of D. H. Lawrence.
Immersion—hence loss—of the burdened mystic self in perfect
sexual union is a romantic myth, old as the myth of the Sea. It
satisfied Lawrence. But Crane was intellectually too strong, and too
robust an artist, to abide it. "White Buildings" closes on the unitary
theme of surrender. But the poet is ready to begin his quest again.

In 1924, the poems of "White Buildings" written but not yet
published, Crane was living in Brooklyn, in range of the Harbor,
the Bridge, the sea-sounds....

> Gongs in white surplices, beshrouded wails,
> Far strum of fog horns....

And now, the integrating theme came to him.

The will of Crane in "The Bridge" is deliberately myth-making.
But this will, as we have seen, is born of a desperate, personal need:
the mystic *must* create order from the chaos with which his associa-
tive genius overwhelms him. The poem retains this personal origin.
The revelation of "The Bridge," as principle and myth, comes to an
individual in the course of his day's business; and that individual is
the poet. In this sense, "The Bridge" is allied to the "Commedia"
of Dante, who also, in response to desperate need, takes a journey
in the course of which his need finds consummation.

Lest the analogy be misleading, I immediately amend it. Dante's
cosmos, imaged in an age of cultural maturity, when the life of man
was coterminous with his vision, contains Time and persons: only
in the ecstatic last scenes of the "Paradiso" are they momently merged
and lost. Therefore, the line of Dante's poem is clear, being forth
and back in Time: and the focus of the action is cogent, being the
person of the Poet with whom the reader can readily graph points
of reference. Crane's cosmos has no Time and his person-sense is
vacillant and evanescent Crane's journey is that of an individual
unsure of his own form and lost to Time. This difference at once
clarifies the disadvantageous esthetic of "The Bridge" as compared with that of broadly analogous poems of cosmic search, like

the "Commedia" or "Don Quixote." It exemplifies the role played by the cultural epoch in the creation of even the most personal work of genius.

In "Proem," the poet exhorts the object of his choice—the Bridge. It shall synthesize the world of chaos. It joined city, river and sea; man made it with his new hand, the machine. And parabola-wise, it shall now vault the continent, and, transmuted, reach that inward heaven which is the fulfilment of man's need of order. Part One, "Ave Maria," is the vision of Columbus, mystic navigator who mapped his voyage in Isaiah, seeking to weld the world's riven halves into one. But this Columbus is scarcely a person; he is suffused in his history and his ocean; his will is more substantial than his eye. Nor does he live in Time. Part Two, "Powhatan's Daughter" (the Indian Princess is the flesh of America, the American earth, and mother of our dream), begins the recital of the poet's journey which traces in extension (as Columbus in essence) the myth's trajectory. The poet awakes in his room above the Harbor, beside his lover. Risen (taking the harbor and the sea-sounds with him), he walks through the lowly Brooklyn streets: but walks with his cultural past: Pizarro, Cortés, Priscilla, and now Rip Van Winkle whose eyes, fresh from sleep, will abide the poet's as they approach the transfigured world of today. The poet descends the subway that tunnels the East River (the Bridge is above); and now the subway is a river "leaping" from Far Rockaway to Golden Gate. A river of steel rails at first, bearing westward America's urban civilization ("Stick your patent name on a signboard") and waking as it runs the burdened trudge of pioneers and all their worlds of factory and song. The patterning march of the American settlers traces the body, gradually, of Pocahontas; the flow of continent and man becomes the Great River; the huge travail of continental life, after the white man and before him, is borne southward, "meeting the Gulf." Powhatan's daughter, America's flesh, dances and the flesh becomes spirit. Dances the poet's boyhood memories of star and lake, of "sleek boat nibbling margin grass"; dances at last into the life of an Indiana mother home from a frustrate trek to California for gold, who is bidding her son farewell; he is going east again to follow the sea. ("Write me from Rio.")

There are no persons in the universe, barely emergent from chaos, of Hart Crane; and this first crystallization—the prairie mother—is the first weak block in the Poem's structure. Now, with Part Three, "Cutty Sark," the physical course of the poet (the subway ride has exploded into the cosmic implication of the River) returns to view, but blurred. The poet is in South Street, Manhattan, near midnight: he is carousing with a sailor who brings him in snatches of song Leviathan, Plato, Stamboul—and a dim harbinger of Atlantis. "I started walking home across the Bridge": there, in the hallucinatory parade of clippers who once winked around the Horn "bright skysails ticketing the Line," the poet is out again, now seaward.

Part Four, "Cape Hatteras," is the turning point of the Poem. Thus far, we have seen the individual forms of the poet's crowded day melt into widening, deepening cycles of association. Columbus into the destiny and will of the Atlantic: two lovers into the harbor, the harbor into the sea: subway into a transcontinental railroad, into a continent, into a River; the River into the Gulf; the Indian princess into the Earth Mother, and the dance into the tumult and traffic of the nation; ribald South Street into a vision—while the Bridge brings the clippers that bring China—of Atlantis. Now, the movement turns back toward crystallization. "Cape Hatteras" at first invokes the geologic age that lifted the Appalachians above the sea; the cosmic struggle sharpens into the birth of the airplane—industrial America; the "red, eternal flesh of Pocahontas" gives us, finally, Walt Whitman. "Years of the Modern! Propulsions toward what capes?" The Saunterer on the Open Road takes the hand of the poet. Parts Five and Six are interludes. Part Seven, "The Tunnel," carries the poem to its climax. The poet, in midair and at midnight, leaves the Bridge; he "comes down to earth" and returns home as he had left, by subway. This unreal collapse of bridge into subway has meaning. The subway is the tunnel. The tunnel is America, and is a kind of hell. But it has dynamic direction. In this plunging subway darkness, appears Poe:

> And why do I often meet your visage here,
> Your eyes like agate lanterns...?

If the reader understands Poe, he will understand the apparition. Of all the classic poets of the great tradition in America, Poe—perhaps the least as artist—was the most advanced, the most prophetic, as thinker. All, as we have noted, were content more or less with the merely transplanted terms of an agrarian culture. Only Poe guessed the transfiguring effect of the Machine upon the forms of human life, upon the very concept of the person. The Tunnel gives us man in his industrial hell which the machine—his hand and heart—has made; now let the machine be his godlike hand to uplift him! The plunging subway shall merge with the vaulting bridge. Whitman gives the vision, Poe—however vaguely—the method. The final part, "Atlantis," is a transposed return to the beginning. The Bridge, in Time, has linked Atlantis with Cathay. Now it becomes an absolute experience. Like any human event, *fully known,* it links man instantaneously, "beyond time," with the Truth.

The principle that Crane sought to make him master of his sense of immediate continuity with a world overwhelmingly chaotic gave him "The Bridge"; but in actual life it did not sustain him. The later poems, despite their technical perfection (and with the exception of "The Broken Tower"), mark a retreat to the mood of the last pages of "White Buildings." The Sea, symbol of the return to a unity of personal abolition, had ebbed while the poet stood upon his mythic bridge; now again it was rising. The periodicity of his excesses grew swifter; the lucid intervening times when he could write were crowded out. Crane went to Mexico, where personal extinction has for a thousand years inspired a cult and a culture. On his return to New York, symbol of the chaos in his life, there was the Sea; and he could not resist it. As his boat was bearing him from the warm waters which fifteen years before had given him a symbol, he took off his coat, quietly, and joined the Sea forever.

The Americanism of Hart Crane

by Derek Savage

It is strange that the peculiar significance of Hart Crane in the light of the modern poet's relationship to an industrial society has not been more generally recognized than it has. Crane is the unofficial laureate of modern America—although perhaps an America that is passing away. With important differences, he bore to the hustling, industrially expanding America of the 'twenties a relationship in some ways very similar to that of Mayakovsky towards revolutionary Russia of the same period. Like the Russian, Crane embraced his life and time feverishly and with open arms; he, also, was homosexual and suffered from a deep disharmony of his personal life, lived wildly and wretchedly, and died eventually by his own hand.

When his *Collected Poems* were belatedly published in London for the first time a few years ago they fell curiously flat, considering his reputation on the other side of the Atlantic. Yet Crane is an impressive poet, and his work bears the unmistakable stamp of genius. It possesses a largeness of theme together with a depth of feeling and delicacy of verbal manipulation and a confident power of execution which cannot be waved aside. He is, however, exceedingly "obscure" in a very real sense. And, with all its magnificence of rhetoric and subtlety of suggestion, his collected work appears fragmentary, the spars and wreckage of what we feel was intended to be a much larger design, an integrated whole. Towards the end he tended to write more and more wildly, and the overloading of his language resulted sometimes in a merely muddled clogging and inflation of the verse. Poetically he must, judged by his own aspirations, be written down as a failure—if a glorious one—as he must, too, I suppose, in his life. But why, and how, was Hart Crane a

"The Americanism of Hart Crane." From *The Personal Principle* by Derek Savage (London: Routledge, Kegan Paul, 1944). Reprinted by permission of Derek Savage.

failure? What was he trying to do, and what can we learn from his aspirations and achievements?

Crane's family background was that of prosperous middle-class American industrialism. His father was a factory-owner, and on both sides his family traditions were those of successful commercialism. He was a man of the cities, without palpable roots in any particular region of locality — and America is a vast country. In his adult life he moved aimlessly from place to place — New York, Cleveland, the Caribbean Isles, London, Paris, Mexico. His middle-class social background providing little opportunity or encouragement for the cultivation of artistic propensities, Crane early rejected it for the social vacuum, the underworld, inhabited by the writers and artists of the time. Both socially and regionally, therefore, Crane was rootless. He was particularly vulnerable to the impact of the impersonal world of modern experience. He worked in the dockyards as a riveter, he wrote advertising copy, he filled various petty positions in the literary-commercial hinterland, and finally, in the economic sense, he became frankly parasitic. It is because he was so completely at the mercy of his time that Crane is so interesting.

The accusation of "Americanism" implied by the quotation from Georges Duhamel above would of course not be adequate or just in the case of Crane, and needs some qualification. Crane was a poet, necessarily concerned with the interior values. His peculiarity was, however, that parallel with this concern there ran an uncritical, open-armed acceptance of the outward technical achievements of American civilization. While detesting the uncouth *commercial* spirit that animated the American scene, and while feeling intensely his own isolation, as an artist, from the whole life of his time, its spirit of *industrialism* he accepted unquestioningly. "The modern artist," he once wrote, "needs *gigantic assimilative capacities,*[1] emotion, — and the greatest of *all* — vision. Potentially I feel myself quite fit to become a suitable Pindar for the dawn of the machine age, so-called." These words are important. It was upon this cross that Crane allowed himself to be crucified.

In his attitude towards the variegated phenomena of the contemporary scene, Crane provides an illuminating contrast as man and poet to his contemporary, T. S. Eliot. Eliot had published *The Waste Land* just as Crane was nearing the completion of one of his most

[1]My italics.

important poems, *For the Marriage of Faustus and Helen,* a poem
which attempted a poetic reconciliation of Helen as the "symbol of
the abstract sense of beauty" and the scientific temper of the modern
world in the person of the poet, Faustus. But whereas Eliot turned,
pessimistically or nostalgically, to the past, emphasizing the importance of tradition and of the historical sense, Crane looked opti-
mistically forward, although not in a naively materialistic manner
only, to a new Utopian integration of life and culture.

When *The Waste Land* appeared, Crane wrote to a friend:

> "There is no one writing in English who can command so much
> respect, to my mind, as Eliot. However, I take Eliot as a point of de-
> parture towards an almost complete reverse of direction. His pessi-
> mism is amply justified, in his own case. But I would apply as much of
> his erudition and technique as I can absorb towards a more positive,
> or (if I must put it so in a sceptical age) ecstatic goal."

As Mr. Philip Horton himself says in his biography, *Hart Crane:
The Life of an American Poet* [published in New York by W.W. Norton
in 1937]:

> "The difference in temper between the two men was clearly indicated
> by the nature of their leading symbols: for Eliot the wasteland with its
> rubble of disintegrated values and desiccated spirits; for Crane the
> bridge with its hope of spiritual harmony and order above and beyond
> the acceptance of contemporary chaos."

That difference is illuminating in many respects—Crane, warring
with an inward chaos, with a powerful but uneducated mind, projecting upon the world his need for an external order; and Eliot,
precise and intelligent, with an extremely orderly and disciplined
mind, looking outward and seeing disharmony and disintegration.
Here, however, I want to single out only the main point of diver-
gence between these so strongly contrasted poets of the post-Great-
War years—their attitudes towards the framework of technical
civilization in which they found themselves.

For Crane, modern progress was a reality. Seeing the modern
world, as it were, moving ahead without a corresponding spiritual
or artistic advance, he regarded it as his poetic responsibility to
catch up, to infuse external society, in the consciousness of man,
with "positive poetic content." Eliot saw only an increased inward
anarchy, a loosening of standards and decay of real values, accom-
panying the increased, hallucinatory, unreality of metropolitan life.
Crane accepted the urban cyclorama joyously, ecstatically:

O harp and altar, of the fury fused,
(How could mere toil align thy choiring strings!)
Terrific threshold of the prophet's pledge,
Prayer of pariah, and the lover's cry,—

Against the traffic lights that skim thy swift
Unfractioned idiom, immaculate sigh of stars,
Beading thy path—condense eternity:
And we have seen night lifted in thine arms.

It is Brooklyn Bridge he is addressing in such terms. Contrast it with the familiar lines from *The Waste Land:*

Unreal City,
Under the brown fog of a winter dawn,
A crowd flowed over London Bridge, so many,
I had not thought death had undone so many.
Sighs, short and infrequent, were exhaled,
And each man fixed his eyes before his feet. ....[2]

The differences apparent from these two fragments in the entire style and approach of the two poets are sufficiently outstanding to need no comment.

Crane's attitude towards modern civilization and its dynamic factor, the machine, was not solely one of simple-minded adoration. It is best expressed, perhaps, in the words of Mr. Horton describing the philosophical opinions held by the small group of younger *avant-garde* writers of the 'twenties with which Crane was associated:

"Munson's own contribution seems to have been the insistence upon a positive creative attitude towards the machine, rather than the negative one held by the older group, which rejected or evaded it. Briefly, he held that the spiritual life of man and his culture had now become dependent on three factors: man, nature, and the machine; that this had brought about an art of maladjustment rooted in a dangerous dualism; and that, finally, the only means of regaining an organic vital art lay in accepting the machine on the same level as nature, or, as he wrote, 'to put positive and glowing spiritual content into Machinery.' This was the dogma he had evolved and brought back with him from Dadaist Europe, and it was the section of his study suggesting ways and means of assimilating such new material as subject matter for poetry that Crane found so stimulating."

[2]T.S. Eliot, "The Waste Land" in *Collected Poems 1909-1962.* Reprinted by permission of Harcourt Brace Jovanovich, Inc. and Faber and Faber, Ltd.

It was under the stimulus of such conceptions that Crane began to write his *Faustus and Helen,* and indeed his whole work is conditioned by them. In Mr. Horton's words:

> "Carried away by...the sweeping conception of a spiritual union between man, nature and machine, both he and Munson seem to have had a utopian vision of a new order of humanity about to arise."

What Crane was really trying to do, as a poet, was to give an inward, spiritual significance to the material, outward conditions of twentieth-century industrial civilization. He wanted to take the whole complex structure of American mechanized society into his soul and to give it back again endowed with the spiritual significance and meaning of his own personality. Also, no doubt, he desired to escape from the burden of his personal existence by a process of objectification. The attempt was heroic—and pathetic. When the prevailing American optimism received a serious set-back in the financial crisis of Crane's latter years, and most of Crane's literary associates turned for their salvation to some form of social criticism, Crane rejected them and pursued his path in isolation. His tenacious fidelity to the aesthetic path he had chosen seems to suggest that his choice of it was rooted deeply in the division of his own nature. With that it is not necessary to deal now. It is enough to say that we should be grateful that one poet undertook such a task as this, if only for the lesson he leaves for others, but mostly for his charting of a realm which might otherwise have remained unexplored.

Crane regarded it as the main task of modern poetry to "absorb the machine, i.e. acclimatize it as naturally and casually as trees, cattle, galleons..." and most of his verse was written with this precept well to the foreground. However, his poems are never *about* machines and machinery. They are *about* (if the word may be used at all) Crane's own experience. But into his own experience he tried to incorporate the whole of urban society and, in *The Bridge,* the history of the American nation. This last poem, his most ambitious effort, which in his own mind he seems to have associated with the *Paradiso* of Dante, he described while writing it as "A mystical synthesis of America" and "Symbol of our constructive future, our unique identity, in which is also included our scientific hopes and achievements of the future." I have said that Crane's poetry is obscure. It is as obscure as the poetry of the intensely isolated modern poet forced by his dislocation from society to cultivate deeply into his own private experience can well be. Yet the poetry he wanted to write, as the potentially great poet he knew himself to be, was public poetry. But the time of great public poetry is past. Crane was faced with two worlds, the inward private world of his own experience and the outward highly centralized world of mechanical civilization, and he wanted to reconcile the two. The bridge that he took as a symbol, symbolized just that reconciliation. It was that attempt to reconcile the irreconcilable that set up such a terrific tension in Crane's mind and drove him to stimulants and debaucheries, the need for which became more and more violent as his life went on, culminating in his nightmarish last days and that final leap from the stern of the *s.s. Orizaba.*

The evidence of that strain is to be found internally in his poems, and in the story of his life as told by Mr. Horton. In its efforts to achieve a union between those two worlds Crane's mind thrust itself out beyond the limits of human possibility. The mind recoils—just as Crane's own mind recoiled after each intoxicating spell of inspiration. The ecstasy he achieved was very nearly a delirium:

> Let the same nameless gulf beleaguer us—
> Alike suspended from atrocious sums
> Built floor by floor on shafts of steel that grant
> The plummet heart, like Absalom, no stream.

At times, as in certain of the *Voyages,* his poetry achieves a sickening vertiginous quality—a real biliousness. And that, indeed, is a measure of his success.

The question of "obscurity" is a delicate one. Nearly all good modern poets are, or have been, accused of "obscurity," "unintelligibility" and the like by those who like their verse to be genteel and slightly sedative. In Crane's case there is generally some basis for this charge. When critics speak of "obscurity," however, they usually mean that the poem in question fails in its presumed task of intellectual communication. Most poetry is in the nature of a comment upon experience. Crane's, by this test, fails completely. His poems are entities in which is caught and transfused a vast complexity of experience: they hang, as it were, plummet-wise over the abyss between the inner world of the poet or reader and the outer world of extra-personal actuality which the poet strove so tenaciously to bring into poetic focus.

Crane wanted to be, felt himself potentially to be, a great poet—

"the greatest singer of my generation." What are the distinguishing features of the "greatness" which we recognize in certain "great" poets of the past? In the first place, it is a social quality. It is a capacity, belonging to a certain "time" and place, to dominate, *as a poet,* the society of that period. The "great" poet emerges as a social force, a focus of his society's strivings, yearnings, achievements and confusions. For the production of a great poet in this sense there must be an integration of personality and society, of the inner and outer worlds, which modern society, with its top-heavy mechanical superstructure and its network of extra-human relationships, cannot afford.

Crane and Munson were wrong in their attempt to "accept the machine in the same level as nature...to put positive and glowing spiritual content into Machinery." Their response to "the firm entrenchment of machinery into our lives," which, said Crane, had produced "a series of challenging new responsibilities for the poet," should have operated, not on the aesthetic but on the social level. Crane accepted without question the centralized, top-heavy industrial environment, tagging along behind the racketeers and financiers whose creation it all was. We cannot say he was "wrong" to do so in any condemnatory sense. But it seems unlikely that any poet writing since his death will follow, in this respect, where Crane led. In choosing Faustus for a symbol in his first lengthy poem he was, perhaps, writing more profoundly than he knew.

Acknowledgement is made to Messrs. John Lane The Bodley Head in respect of the above quotations from *The Collected Poems of Hart Crane.*

New Thresholds, New Anatomies:
Notes on a Text of Hart Crane

by R. P. Blackmur

It is a striking and disheartening fact that the three most ambitious poems of our time should all have failed in similar ways: in composition, in independent objective existence, and in intelligibility of language. *The Waste Land,* the *Cantos,* and *The Bridge* all fail to hang together structurally in the sense that "Prufrock," "Envoi," and "Praise for an Urn"—lesser works in every other respect—do hang together. Each of the three poems requires of the reader that he supply from outside the poem, and with the help of clues only, the important *controlling* part of what we may loosely call the meaning. And each again deliberately presents passages, lines, phrases, and single words which no amount of outside work can illumine. The fact is striking because, aside from other considerations of magnitude, relevance, and scope, these are not the faults we lay up typically against the great dead. The typical great poet is profoundly rational, integrating, and, excepting minor accidents of incapacity, a master of ultimate verbal clarity. Light, radiance, and wholeness remain the attributes of serious art. And the fact is disheartening because no time could have greater need than our own for rational art. No time certainly could surrender more than ours does daily, with drums beating, to fanatic politics and despotically construed emotions.

But let us desert the disheartening for the merely striking aspect, and handle the matter, as we can, within the realm of poetry, taking up other matters only tacitly and by implication. Let us say provisionally that in their more important works Eliot, Pound, and Crane lack the ultimate, if mythical, quality of aseity, that quality of completeness, of independence, so great that it seems underived and an effect of pure creation. The absence of aseity may be approached variously in a given poet; but every approach to be instructive, even to find the target at all, must employ a rational mode and the right weapon. These notes intend to examine certain characteristic passages of Hart Crane's poems as modes of language and to determine how and to what degree the effects intended were attained. The rationale is that of poetic language; the weapons are analysis and comparison. But there are other matters which must be taken up first before the language itself can be approached at all familiarly.

Almost everyone who has written on Crane has found in him a central defect, either of imagination or execution, or both. Long ago, in his Preface to *White Buildings,* Allen Tate complained that for all his talent Crane had not found a suitable theme. Later, in his admirable review of *The Bridge,* Yvor Winters brought and substantiated the charge (by demonstrating the exceptions) that even when he had found a theme Crane could not entirely digest it and at crucial points simply was unable to express it in objective form. These charges hold; and all that is here said is only in explication of them from a third point of view.

Waldo Frank, in his Introduction to the *Collected Poems,* acting more as an apologist than a critic, proffers two explanations of Crane's incompleteness as a poet, to neither of which can I assent, but of which I think both should be borne in mind. Mr. Frank believes that Crane will be understood and found whole when our culture has been restored from revolutionary collectivism to a predominant interest in the person; when the value of expressing the personal in the terms of the cosmic shall again seem supreme. This hypothesis would seem untenable unless it is construed as relevant to the present examination; when it runs immediately into the hands of the obvious but useful statement that Crane was interested in persons rather than the class struggle. Mr. Frank's other explanation is that Crane's poetry was based upon the mystical perception of the "organic continuity between the self and a seemingly chaotic world." Crane "was too virile to deny the experience of continuity; he let the world pour in; and since his nuclear self was not disciplined to detachment from his nerves and passions, he lived exacerbated in a constant swing between ecstasy and exhaustion." I confess I do not understand "organic continuity" in this context, and all my efforts to do so are defeated by the subsequent word "detachment." Nor can I see how this particular concept of continuity can be very useful without the addition and control of a thorough supernaturalism. The control for mystic psychology is theology, and what is thereby controlled is the idiosyncrasy of insight, not the technique of poetry.

What Mr. Frank says not-rationally can be usefully re-translated to that plane on which skilled readers ordinarily read good poetry; which is a rational plane; which is, on analysis, the plane of competent technical appreciation. Such a translation, while committing grave injustice on Mr. Frank, comes nearer doing justice to Crane. It restores and brings home the strictures of Tate and Winters, and it brings judgment comparatively back to the minute particulars (Blake's phrase) which are alone apprehensible. To compose the nuclear self and the seemingly chaotic world is to find a suitable theme, and the inability so to compose rises as much from immaturity and indiscipline of the major poetic uses of language as from personal immaturity and indiscipline. Baudelaire only rarely reached the point of self-discipline and Whitman never; but Baudelaire's language is both disciplined and mature, and Whitman's sometimes so. *Les Fleurs du Mal* are a profound poetic ordering of a life disorderly, distraught, and deracinated, a life excruciated, in the semantic sense of that word, to the extreme. And Whitman, on his side, by a very different use of language, gave torrential expression to the romantic disorder of life in flux, whereas his private sensibility seems either to have been suitably well-ordered or to have felt no need of order.

Whitman and Baudelaire are not chosen with reference to Crane by accident but because they are suggestively apposite. The suggestion may be made, not as blank truth but for the light there is in it, that Crane had the sensibility typical of Baudelaire and so misunderstood himself that he attempted to write *The Bridge* as if he had the sensibility typical of Whitman. Whitman characteristically let himself go in words, in any words and by all means the handiest, until his impulse was used up. Baudelaire no less characteristically caught himself up in his words, recording, ordering, and binding together the implications and tacit meanings of his impulse until in his best poems the words he used are, as I. A. Richards would say, inexhaustible objects of meditation. Baudelaire aimed at control, Whitman at release. It is for these reasons that the influence of Whitman is an impediment to the *practice* (to be distinguished from the reading) of poetry, and that the influence of Baudelaire is re-animation itself. (It may be noted that Baudelaire had at his back a well-articulated version of the Catholic Church to control the moral aspect of his meanings, where Whitman had merely an inarticulate pantheism.)

To apply this dichotomy to Crane is not difficult if it is done tentatively, without requiring that it be too fruitful, and without requiring that it be final at all. The clue or nexus is found, aside from the poems themselves, in certain prose statements. Letters are suspect and especially letters addressed to a patron, since the aim is less conviction by argument than the persuasive dramatization of an attitude. It is therefore necessary in the following extract from a letter to Otto Kahn that the reader accomplish a reduction in the magnitude of terms. Of the section of *The Bridge* called "The Dance" Crane wrote:

> "Here one is on the pure mythical and smoky soil at last! Not only do I describe the conflict between the two races in this dance—I also became identified with the Indian and his world before it is over, which is the only method possible of ever really possessing the Indian and his world as a cultural factor."

Etc. I suggest that, confronted with the tight, tense, intensely personal lyric quatrains of the verse itself, verse compact with the deliberately inarticulate interfusion of the senses, Crane's statement of intention has only an *ipse dixit* pertinence; that taken otherwise, taken as a living index of substance, it only multiplies the actual confusion of the verse and impoverishes its achieved scope. Taken seriously, it puts an impossible burden on the reader: the burden of reading two poems at once, the one that appears and the "real" poem which does not appear except by an act of faith. This would be reading by legerdemain, which at the moment of achievement must always collapse, self-obfuscated.

Again, in the same letter, Crane wrote that,

> "The range of *The Bridge* has been called colossal by more than one critic who has seen the ms., and though I have found the subject to be vaster than I had at first realized, I am still highly confident of its final articulation into a continuous and eloquent span.... *The Aeneid* was not written in two years—nor in four, and in more than one sense I

feel justified in comparing the historical and cultural scope of *The
Bridge* to that great work. It is at least a symphony with an epic
theme, and a work of considerable profundity and inspiration."

The question is whether this was wishful thinking of the vague
order commonest in revery, convinced and sincere statement of
intention, or an effect of the profound duplicity—a deception in the
very will of things—in Crane's fundamental attitudes toward his
work; or whether Crane merely misunderstood the logical import
of the words he used. I incline to the notion of duplicity, since it
is beneath and sanctions the other notions as well; the very duplicity
by which the talents of a Baudelaire appear to their possessor disguised and disfigured in the themes of a Whitman, the same fundamental duplicity of human knowledge whereby an accustomed disorder seems the order most to be cherished, or whereby a religion
which at its heart denies life enriches living. In the particular reference, if I am right, it is possible to believe that Crane labored to
perfect both the strategy and the tactics of language so as to animate
and maneuver his perceptions—and then fought the wrong war
and against an enemy that displayed, to his weapons, no vulnerable
target. He wrote in a language of which it was the virtue to accrete,
modify and interrelate moments of emotional vision—moments at
which the sense of being gains its greatest access—moments at which,
by the felt nature of knowledge, the revealed thing is its own meanings; and he attempted to apply his language, in his major effort,
to a theme that required a sweeping, discrete, indicative, anecdotal
language, a language in which, by force of movement, mere cataloguing can replace and often surpass representation. He used
the private lyric to write the cultural epic; used the mode of
intensive contemplation, which secures ends, to present the mind's
actions, which have no ends. The confusion of tool and purpose
not only led him astray in conceiving his themes; it obscured at
crucial moments the exact character of the work he was actually
doing. At any rate we find most impenetrable and ineluctable,
in certain places, the very matters he had the genius to see and
the technique to clarify: the matters which are the substance of
rare and valid emotion. The confusion, that is, led him to content
himself at times with the mere cataloguing statement, enough for
him because he knew the rest, of what required completely objective embodiment.

Another, if ancillary, method of enforcing the same suggestion (of radical confusion) is to observe the disparity between Crane's announced purpose and the masters he studied. Poets commonly profit most where they can borrow most, from the poets with whom by instinct, education, and accident of contact, they are most nearly unanimous. Thus poetic character is early predicted. In Crane's case, the nature of the influences to which he submitted himself remained similar from the beginning to the end and were the dominant ones of his generation. It was the influence of what we may call, with little exaggeration, the school of tortured sensibility—a school of which we perhaps first became aware in Baudelaire's misapprehension of Poe, and later, in the hardly less misapprehending resurrection of Donne. Crane benefited, and was deformed by, this influence both directly and by an assortment of indirection; but he never surmounted it. He read the modern French poets who are the result of Baudelaire, but he did not read Racine of whom Baudelaire was himself a product. He read Wallace Stevens, whose strength and serenity may in some sense be assigned to the combined influence of the French moderns and, say, Plato; but he did not, at least affectively, read Plato. He read Eliot, and through and in terms of him, the chosen Elizabethans—though more in Donne and Webster than in Jonson and Middleton; but he did not, so to speak, read the Christianity from which Eliot derives his ultimate strength, and by which he is presently transforming himself. I use the word *read* in a strong sense; there is textual evidence of reading throughout the poems. The last influence Crane exhibited is no different in character and in the use to which he put it than the earliest: the poem called "The Hurricane" derives immediately from the metric of Hopkins but not ultimately from Hopkins' integrating sensibility. Thus Crane fitted himself for the exploitation of the peculiar, the unique, the agonized and the tortured perception, and he developed language-patterns for the essentially incoherent aspects of experience: the aspects in which experience assaults rather than informs the sensibility. Yet, granting his sensibility, with his avowed epic purpose he had done better had he gone to school to Milton and Racine, and, in modern times, to Hardy and Bridges—or even Masefield— for narrative sweep.

Crane had, in short, the wrong masters for his chosen fulfillment, or he used some of the right masters in the wrong way: leeching upon them, as a poet must, but taking the wrong nourishment, taking from them not what was hardest and most substantial— what made them great poets—but taking rather what was easiest, taking what was peculiar and idiosyncratic. That is what kills so many of Crane's poems, what must have made them impervious, once they were discharged, even to himself. It is perhaps, too, what killed Crane the man—because in a profound sense, to those who use it, poetry is the only means of putting a tolerable order upon the emotions. Crane's predicament—that his means defeated his ends—was not unusual, but his case was extreme. In more normal form it is the predicament of immaturity. Crane's mind was slow and massive, a cumulus of substance; it had, to use a word of his own, the synergical quality, and with time it might have worked together, clarified, and become its own meaning. But he hastened the process and did not survive to maturity.

Certainly there is a hasty immaturity in the short essay on Modern Poetry, reprinted as an appendix to the *Collected Poems,* an immaturity both in the intellectual terms employed and in the stress with which the attitude they rehearse is held. Most of the paper tilts at windmills, and the lance is too heavy for the wielding hand. In less than five pages there is deployed more confused thinking than is to be found in all his poems put together. Poetry is not, as Crane says it is, an architectural art—or not without a good deal of qualification; it is a linear art, an art of succession, and the only art it resembles formally is plain song. Nor can Stravinsky and the cubists be compared, as Crane compares them, in the quality of their abstractions with the abstractions of mathematical physics: the aims are disparate; expression and theoretic manipulation can never exist on the same plane. Nor can psychological analyses, in literature, be distinguished in motive and quality from dramatic analyses. Again, and finally, the use of the term *psychosis* as a laudatory epithet for the substance of Whitman, represents to me the uttermost misconstruction of the nature of poetry: a psychosis is a mental derangement not due to an organic lesion or neurosis. A theory of neurosis (as, say, Aiken has held it in *Blue Voyage*) is more tenable scientifically; but neither it seems to me has other than a stultifying critical use. Yet, despite the confusion and positive irrationality of Crane's language the general tendency is sound, the aspiration sane. He wanted to write good poetry and his archetype was Dante; that is enough. But in his prose thinking he had the wrong words for his thoughts, as in his poetry he had often the wrong themes for his words.

II

So far, if the points have been maintained at all, what I have written adds up to the suggestion that in reading Hart Crane we must make allowances for him—not historical allowances as we do for Shakespeare, religious allowances as for Dante and Milton, or philosophical as for Goethe and Lucretius—but fundamental allowances whereby we agree to supply or overlook what does not appear in the poems, and whereby we agree to forgive or guess blindly at those parts of the poems which are unintelligible. In this Crane is not an uncommon case, though the particular allowances may perhaps be unique. There are some poets where everything is allowed for the sake of isolated effects. Sedley is perhaps the supreme example in English; there is nothing in him but two lines, but these are famous and will always be worth saving. Waller is the more normal example, or King, where two or three poems are the whole gist. Crane has both poems and passages; and in fact there is hardly a poem of his which has not something in it, and a very definite something, worth saving.

The nature of that saving quality, for it saves him no less than ourselves, Crane has himself most clearly expressed in a stanza from the poem called "Wine Menagerie."

> New thresholds, new anatomies! Wine talons
> Build freedom up about me and distill
> This competence—to travel in a tear
> Sparkling alone, within another's will.

I hope to show that this stanza illustrates almost inexhaustibly, to minds at all aware, both the substance and the aspiration of Crane's poetry, the character and value of his perceptions, and his method of handling words to control them. If we accept the stanza as a sort of declaration of policy and apply it as our own provisional policy to the sum of his work, although we limit its scope we shall deepen and articulate our appreciation—a process, that of appreciation, which amounts not to wringing a few figs from thistles but to expressing the wine itself.

Paraphrase does not greatly help. We can, for the meat of it, no more be concerned with the prose sense of the words than Crane evidently was. Crane habitually re-created his words from within, developing meaning to the point of idiom; and that habit is the constant and indubitable sign of talent. The meanings themselves are the idioms and have a twist and life of their own. It is only by ourselves meditating on and *using* these idioms—it is only by emulation—that we can master them and accede to their life.

Analysis, however, does help, and in two directions. It will by itself increase our intimacy with the words as they appear; and it will as the nexus among comparisons disclose that standard of achievement, inherent in this special use of poetic language, by which alone the value of the work may be judged. (Analysis, in these uses, does not cut deep, it does not cut at all: it merely distinguishes particulars; and the particulars must be re-seen in their proper focus before the labor benefits.)

Moving in the first direction, toward intimacy, we can say that Crane employed an extreme mode of free association; that operation among words where it is the product rather than the addition that counts. There was, for example, no logical or emotional connection between thresholds and anatomies until Crane verbally juxtaposed them and tied them together with the cohesive of his meter. Yet, so associated, they modify and act upon each other mutually and produce a fresh meaning of which the parts cannot be segregated. Some latent, unsuspected part of the cumulus of meaning in each word has excited, so to speak, and affected a corresponding part in the others. It is the juxtaposition which is the agent of selection, and it is a combination of meter and the carried-over influence of the rest of the poem, plus the as yet undetermined expectations aroused, which is the agent of emphasis and identification. It should be noted that, so far as the poem is concerned, the words themselves contain and do not merely indicate the feelings which compose the meaning; the poet's job was to put the words together like bricks in a wall. In a lesser poetry of the same order, and in poetry of different orders, words may only indicate or refer to or substitute for the feelings; then we have the poetry of vicarious statement, which takes the place of, often to the highest purpose, the actual complete presentation, such as we have here. Here there is nothing for the words to take the place of; they are their own life, and have an organic continuity, not with the poet's mind nor with the experience they represent, but with themselves. We see that thresholds open upon anatomies: upon things to be explored and understood and felt freshly as an adventure; and we see that the anatomies, what is to be explored, are known from a new vantage, and that the vantage is part of the anatomy. The separate meanings of the words fairly rush at each other; the right ones join and those irrelevant to the juncture are for the moment—the whole time of the poem—lost in limbo. Thus the association "New thresholds, new anatomies!" which at first inspection might seem specious or arbitrary (were we not used to reading poetry) not only does not produce a distortion but, the stress and strain being equal, turns out wholly natural and independently alive.

In the next phrase the association of the word "talons" with the context seems less significantly performed. So far as it refers back and expresses a seizing together, a clutching by a bird of prey, it is an excellent word well-chosen and spliced in. The further notion, suggested by the word "wine," of release, would also seem relevant. There is, too, an unidentifiable possibility—for Crane used words in very special senses indeed—of "talons" in the sense of cards left after the deal; and there is even, to push matters to the limit, a bare chance that some element of the etymon—ankle, heel—has been pressed into service. But the possibilities have among them none specially discriminated, and whichever you choose for use, the dead weight of the others must be provisionally carried along, which is what makes the phrase slightly fuzzy. And however you construe "wine talons" you cannot, without distorting what you have and allowing for the gap or lacuna of what you have not, make your construction fit either or both of the verbs which it governs. Talons neither build nor distill even when salvation by rhyme is in question. If Crane meant—as indeed he may have—that wines are distilled and become brandies of spirits, then he showed a poverty of technique in using the transitive instead of the intransitive form. Objection can be carried too far, when it renders itself nugatory. These remarks are meant as a kind of exploration; and if we now make the allowance for the unidentified distortion and supply with good will the lacuna in the very heart of the middle phrases, the rest of the stanza becomes as plain and vivid as poetry of this order need ever be. To complete the whole association, the reader need only remember that Crane probably had in mind, and made new use of Blake's lines:

> For a Tear is an Intellectual Thing,
> And a Sign is the Sword of an Angel King.

It is interesting to observe that Blake was talking against war and that his primary meaning was much the same as that expressed negatively in "Auguries of Innocence" by the following couplet:

> He who shall train the Horse to War
> Shall never pass the Polar Bar.

Crane ignored the primary meaning, and extracted and emphasized what was in Blake's image a latent or secondary meaning. Or possibly he combined—made a free association of—the intellectual tear with

> Every Tear from Every Eye
> Becomes a Babe in Eternity;

only substituting the more dramatic notion of will for intellect. What is important to note is that, whatever its origin, the meaning as Crane presents it is completely transformed and subjugated to the control of the "new thresholds, new anatomies!"

The stanza we have been considering is only arbitrarily separated from the whole poem—just as the poem itself ought to be read in the context of the whole *White Buildings* section. The point is, that for appreciation—and for denigration—all of Crane should be read thoroughly, at least once, with similar attention to detail. That is the way in which Crane worked. Later readings may be more liberated and more irresponsible—as some people read the Bible for what they call its poetry or a case history for its thrill; but they never get either the poetry or the thrill without a preliminary fundamental intimacy with the rational technique involved. Here it is a question of achieving some notion of a special poetic process. The principle of association which controls this stanza resembles the notion of wine as escape, release, father of insight and seed of metamorphosis, which controls the poem; and, in its turn, the

notion of extra-logical, intoxicated metamorphosis of the senses
controls and innervates Crane's whole sensibility.

To illustrate the uniformity of approach, a few examples are presented, some that succeed and some that fail. In "Lachrymae Christi"
consider the line

> Thy Nazarene and tinder eyes.

(Note, from the title, that we are here again concerned with tears
as the vehicle-image of insight, and that, in the end, Christ is
identified with Dionysus.) Nazarene, the epithet for Christ, is here
used as an adjective of quality in conjunction with the noun tinder
also used as an adjective; an arrangement which will seem baffling
only to those who underestimate the seriousness with which Crane
remodeled words. The first three lines of the poem read:

> Whitely, while benzine
> Rinsings from the moon
> Dissolve all but the windows of the mills.

Benzine is a fluid, cleansing and solvent, has a characteristic tang
and smart to it, and is here associated with the light of the moon,
which, through the word "rinsings," is itself modified by it. It is,
I think, the carried-over influence of benzine which gives startling
aptness to Nazarene. It is, if I am correct for any reader but myself,
an example of suspended association, or telekinesis; and it is, too,
an example of syllabic interpenetration or internal punning as
habitually practiced in the later prose of Joyce. The influence of
one word on the other reminds us that Christ the Saviour cleanses
and solves and has, too, the quality of light. "Tinder" is a simpler
instance of how Crane could at once isolate a word and bind it in,
impregnating it with new meaning. Tinder is used to kindle fire,
powder, and light; a word incipient and bristling with the action
proper to its being. The association is completed when it is remembered that tinder is very nearly a homonym for tender and, *in this
setting,* puns upon it.

Immediately following, in the same poem, there is a parenthesis
which I have not been able to penetrate with any certainty, though
the possibilities are both fascinating and exciting. The important
words in it do not possess the excluding, limiting power over themselves and their relations by which alone the precise, vital element

in an ambiguity is secured. What Crane may have meant privately cannot be in question—his words may have represented for him a perfect tautology; we are concerned only with how the words act upon each other—or fail to act—so as to commit an appreciable meaning. I quote the first clause of the parenthesis.

> Let sphinxes from the ripe
> Borage of death have cleared my tongue
> Once and again..

It is syntax rather than grammar that is obscure. I take it that "let" is here a somewhat homemade adjective and that Crane is making a direct statement, so that the problem is to construe the right meanings of the right words in the right references; which will be an admirable exercise in exegesis, but an exercise only. The applicable senses of "let" are these: neglected or weary, permitted or prevented, hired, and let in the sense that blood is let. Sphinxes are inscrutable, have secrets, propound riddles to travelers and strangle those who cannot answer. "Borage" has at least three senses: something rough (sonantly suggestive of barrage and barrier), a blue-flowered, hairy-leaved plant, and a cordial made from the plant. The Shorter Oxford Dictionary quotes this jingle from Hooker: "I Borage always bring courage." One guess is that Crane meant something to the effect that if you meditate enough on death it has the same bracing and warming effect as drinking a cordial, so that the riddles of life (or death) are answered. But something very near the contrary may have been intended; or both. In any case a guess is ultimately worthless because, with the defective syntax, the words do not verify it. Crane had a profound feeling for the hearts of words, and how they beat and cohabited, but here they overtopped him; the meanings in the words themselves are superior to the use to which he put them. The operation of selective cross-pollination not only failed but was not even rightly attempted. The language remains in the condition of that which it was intended to express: in the flux of intoxicated sense; whereas the language of the other lines of this poem here examined—the language, not the sense—is disintoxicated and candid. The point is that the quality of Crane's success is also the quality of his failure, and the distinction is perhaps by the hair of accident.

In the part of *The Bridge* called "Virginia," and in scores of places

elsewhere, there is a single vivid image, of no structural importance, but of great delight as ornament: it both fits the poem and
has a startling separate beauty of its own, the phrase: "Peonies with
pony manes."[1] The freshness has nothing to do with accurate observation, of which it is devoid, but has its source in the arbitrary
character of the association: it is created observation. Another example is contained in

> Down Wall, from girder into street noon leaks,
> A rip-tooth of the sky's acetylene;

which is no more forced than many of Crashaw's best images. It
is, of course, the pyramiding associations of the word acetylene
that create the observation: representing as it does an intolerable
quality of light and a torch for cutting metal, and so on.

Similarly, again and again, both in important and in ornamental
phrases, there are effects only half secured, words which are not the
right words but only the nearest words. E.g.: "What eats the pattern with *ubiquity*.... Take this *sheaf* of dust upon your tongue...
Preparing *penguin* flexions of the arms...[A tugboat] with one
galvanic blare...I heard the *hush of lava wrestling* your arms."
Etc. Not that the italicized words are wrong but that they fall short
of the control and precision of impact necessary to vitalize them
permanently.

There remains to consider the second help of analysis (the first
was to promote intimacy with particulars), namely, to disclose the
standard of Crane's achievement in terms of what he actually accomplished; an effort which at once involves comparison of Crane
with rendered possibilities in the same realm of language taken
from other poets. For Crane was not alone; style, like knowledge,
of which it is the expressive grace, is a product of collaboration;
and his standard, whether consciously or not, was outside himself,
in verse written in accord with his own bent: which the following,
if looked at with the right eye, will exemplify.

> Sunt lacrimae rerum et mentem mortalia tangunt.—Vergil.
>
> Lo giorno se n'andava, e l'aer bruno
>   toglieva gli animai, che sono in terra,
>   dalle fatiche loro.—Dante.

[1]Compare Marianne Moore's "the lion's ferocious chrysanthemum head."

A brittle glory shineth in his face;
As brittle as the glory is the face.—Shakespeare.

Adieu donc, chants du cuivre et soupirs de la flûte!
Plaisirs, ne tentez plus un coeur sombre et boudeur!
Le Printemps adorable a perdu son odeur!—Baudelaire.

But Love has pitched his mansion in
The place of excrement;
For nothing can be sole or whole
That has not been rent.[2]—Yeats.

She dreams a little, and she feels the dark
Encroachment of that old catastrophe,
As a clam darkens among water-lights[3]—Stevens.

The relevant context is assumed to be present, as we have been assuming it all along with Crane. Every quotation, except that from Yeats which is recent, should be well known. They bring to mind at once, on one side, the sustaining, glory-breeding power of magnificent form joined to great intellect. Before that impact Crane's magnitude shrinks. On the other side, the side of the particulars, he shrinks no less. The significant words in each selection, and so in the lines themselves, will bear and require understanding to the limit of analysis and limitless meditation. Here, as in Crane, words are associated by the poetic process so as to produce a new and living, an idiomatic, meaning, differing from and surpassing the separate factors involved. The difference—which is where Crane falls short of his standard—is this. Crane's effects remain tricks which can only be resorted to arbitrarily. The effects in the other poets—secured by more craft rather than less—become, immediately they are understood, permanent idioms which enrich the resources of language for all who have the talent to use them. It is perhaps the difference between the immediate unbalance of the assaulted, intoxicated sensibility and the final, no less exciting, clarity of the sane, mirroring sensibility.

It is said that Crane's inchoate heart and distorted intellect only witness the disease of his generation; but I have cited two poets, if not of his generation still his contemporaries, who escaped the contagion. It is the stigma of the first order of poets (a class which includes many minor names and deletes some of the best known) that they master so much of life as they represent. In Crane the poet succumbed with the man.

What judgment flows from these strictures need not impede the appreciation of Crane's insight, observation, and intense, if confused, vision, but ought rather to help determine it. Merely because Crane is imperfect in his kind is no reason to give him up; there is no plethora of perfection, and the imperfect beauty, like life, retains its fascination. And there is about him, too—such were his gifts for the hearts of words, such the vitality of his intelligence— the distraught but exciting splendor of a great failure.

Hart Crane and Moby Dick

by Joseph Warren Beach

Hart Crane's series of mystical love-poems, "Voyages," would be better known if they were better understood. They have the double interest of reflecting the same general religious philosophy as *The Bridge* at the same time that they are an intimate confession of Crane's private experience as a lover. Their imaginative quality is so fine that Yvor Winters can say of the second of these lyrics, "it seems to me, as it has seemed to others, one of the most powerful and one of the most perfect poems of the past hundred years." But Mr. Winters must have been thinking in terms of poetry pure and simple; for he has been very hard on Crane for what he considers the unsoundness of his philosophy of pantheistic optimism, and he is certainly not the critic to condone what he must consider the perverseness of Crane's life and character. These poems are certainly "difficult" and in need of "explication" if they are to be widely appreciated even by discriminating readers of poetry. It seems never to have been noted, for example, how much they owe, in imagery and phrasing, to Melville's *Moby Dick*. The affiliation between these two distinguished American writers makes a curious story in itself. And the poetic genius of Crane is brought into higher relief by noting how his imagination transformed and glorified the hints taken from Melville's brilliant but often meretricious prose.

In the second of Crane's lyrics, what first reminds one of Melville is a curious phrase in the second line, "unfettered leewardings." The word *leewardings* is obviously derived from the nautical adjective leeward, "being in the direction toward which the wind is blowing." One is familiar with several derivative expressions, "leeward tide," "to leeward," etc. But the dictionaries list no *verb* leeward, still less any participal or participial noun *leewarding*. And one begins to wonder whether the word as used by Crane had an actual existence

Joseph Warren Beach, "Hart Crane and Moby Dick," *Western Review,* 20, no. 3 (Spring 1956), 183-96.

in nautical literature other than what it has in *Moby Dick*. There it
occurs in one of Captain Ahab's lyrical monologues when, in the
135th chapter, he is surveying the sea from the masthead while keen
in his pursuit of the White Whale.

> An old, old sight, and yet somehow so young; aye, and not changed
> a wink since first I saw it, a boy, from the sandhills of Nantucket!...
> There's a soft shower to leeward. *Such lovely leewardings!*[1] They must
> lead somewhere—to something else than common land, more palmy
> than the palms.

Thus Captain Ahab, on a fair morning in the Pacific, looking to
leeward, observes a soft shower and is reminded of palmy isles and
peaceful vistas quite out of key with the stern business of killing
on which he is bent. He allows his mind to relax an instant at the
thought of lovely scenery in the direction the wind blows, and with
the Elizabethan daring that characterizes his speech, he (apparently)
invents a word for these attractive operations of nature on the surface of the sea. *Such lovely leewardings!*

And then comes Crane, visioning the sea as "this great wink of
eternity,/ Of rimless floods, *unfettered leewardings.*" His phrase is
much more evocative than Melville's, since eternity calls up for him
an infinity of rimless floods and of winds blowing without check
far as imagination will carry. Since he is also writing a love poem,
pondering on uninhibited movements of the blood, and upon love
that transcends time and death, the adjective *unfettered* bears a
double charge of feeling.

Crane was, we know, an assiduous reader of Melville, and the
most natural supposition is that his imagination had been impressed
in *Moby Dick* with this rare and precious word, especially when we
consider that Captain Ahab is explicitly reflecting on the change-
lessness of the ocean, and that this is a direction that brings Crane
naturally to his view of the sea as "this great wink of eternity." I
will not insist on the presence in Melville of the word *wink* ("not
changed a wink since first I saw it"), though who knows what stray
flotsam will be taken up by a poet's imagination and transmuted
into precious metal? Perhaps more emphasis should be laid on the
fact that his "lovely leewardings" remind Ahab of palmy isles, as
Crane's "unfettered leewardings" carry him on to his "adagios of

[1]In quotations from Melville and Crane the italics are mine.

islands" and to his quite different "penniless rich palms," where only the word remains.

And then there is a second, less peculiar phrase in Crane which has its antecedent and its probable inspiration in Melville. Crane says of his sea that "its diapason knells/ On scrolls of silver snowy sentences." In the 51st chapter of *Moby Dick* the Pequod is cruising

> one serene and moonlight night, when all the waves rolled by like *scrolls of silver;* and by their soft, suffering seethings, made what seemed like a silvery silence, not a solitude; on such a silent night a silvery jet was seen far in advance of the white bubbles at the bow. Lit up by the moon, it looked celestial; seemed like some plumed and glittering god uprising from the sea.

This is a rather extreme example of the showy style in which Melville was all too prone to indulge, under the lure of the iambic pentameter and the odious lure of alliteration. And taken by itself, "scrolls of silver" is not particularly arresting or original. But in Crane these silver scrolls are inscribed with snowy sentences, or judgments, upon the subjects of the sea. These sentences are pronounced in judicial sessions by the "sceptred terror." And the only persons not subject to them are lovers. For they rend (or destroy) "all but the pieties of lovers' hands." And thus the scrolls of silver have their immediate relevance to the central theme of this poem, which is the way love is exempt from, though deeply involved with, the sea and the several metaphysical entities symbolized by the sea.

As for the "sceptred terror," Philip Horton has shown how the sceptre image, taken from a poem of Samuel Greenberg's, passed through six successive variant forms until, in Crane's seventh revision, it appeared in the present form:

> The sceptred terror of whose sessions rends
> As her demeanors motion well or ill
> All but the pieties of lovers' hands.

But Greenberg's "sceptres roving" had no association either with scrolls of silver or with terror. For these we have to return to *Moby Dick* and the "plumed and glittering god" suggested to Melville by the spouting whale. Greenberg's sceptres were simply moving sky shadows; whereas Crane's sceptres (in the original version "roving wide from isle to isle") from their first appearance perfectly fitted Melville's description of spouting whales. And then there was but one step from scrolls of silver and sceptred terror to judicial "sessions."

Of course there is throughout Melville's story plentiful suggestion of images that might culminate in Crane's sceptred terror. The white whale itself is a sceptred terror. And Melville's dealing with the color white might have disposed Crane's imagination to the emphasis upon that color noted by Leonard Unger and William O'Connor in their suggestive treatment of this lyric in *Poems for Study*. It is in the final paragraphs of Chapter 42|that Ishmael particularly dwells on "the demonism of the world" that is figured for him in the color white, in speculations that culminate in these far-reaching questions:

> Is it that by its indefiniteness it shadows forth the heartless voids and immensities of the universe, and thus stabs us from behind with the thought of annihilation, when beholding the white depths of the milky way? or is it that as in essence whiteness is not so much a color as the visible absence of color; and at the same time the concrete of all colors; is it for these reasons that there is such a dumb blankness, full of meaning; in a wide landscape of snows, —*a colorless, all-color of atheism from which we shrink?*

Of all these things, he concluded, "the Albino Whale was a symbol."

We know that it was the effort of Crane's life in all his work to deny this "demonism of the world," this dualistic opposition of Atheism and Christian Theism. With all his admiration for the poetic power of Eliot, for example, he was strongly in reaction against what he considered his pessimism. His aim in *The Bridge,* according to Brom Weber, was to make a "mystical synthesis" of all aspects of American life, and not merely that, but to establish the harmony, or identity, of the visible and the invisible, the finite and the infinite. He would not, in his periods of perfect sanity, have agreed to the superstitious demonism of Ishmael. But Crane was first of all a poet, and he was also a man tragically acquainted with sorrow, with frustration, and with what an Eliot, a Melville, would call Evil. He was certainly capable of conceiving the sea as a malign power, a "sceptred terror," and of whiteness in the sea as a color symbolizing annihilation and doom. He could conceive of the sea as knelling on scrolls of silver snowy, lethal sentences.

II

And here is the place to note that the second of the "Voyages" is closely, and even syntactically, linked to the first of the series. They form together statement and counterstatement about the sea, and, even, one may guess, about the passion of love, perhaps in its forbidden or "inverted" forms. And here again it is not too fanciful to suppose that Melville counts for something in the direction taken by Crane's imagination. The first lyric describes boys playing innocently and fearlessly on the margin of the sea; and the poet is moved to warn them of the dangers of their situation. Let them play freely on the beach with their dog, their shells and sticks.

> ...but there is a line
> You must not cross nor even trust beyond it
> Spry cordage of your bodies to caresses
> Too lichen-faithful from too wide a breast.
> *The bottom of the sea is cruel.*

There are in *Moby Dick* many references to the destructiveness of the sea, and especially to the monsters that lurk beneath the surface. In the 58th chapter Melville draws a contrast between the safety of the familiar land and the perils of the unknown sea, and makes application of this to the spiritual life of man. In the soul of man as in the physical world there are peaceful islands surrounded by spiritual horrors.

> For as this appalling ocean surrounds the verdant land, so in the soul of man there lies one insular Tahiti, full of peace and joy, but encompassed by all the horrors of the half known life. God keep thee! Push not off from that isle, thou canst never return!

The parallelism here does not lie on the surface in specific imagery and verbal likeness. It consists mainly in the warning to men (or boys) not to trust themselves to the watery element, not to cross a certain line on the shore, not to "push off from that isle." In Melville it is an explicitly moral warning. And knowing all that we do about Crane's dealings with love in its tabu form, knowing also that in the later poems it was homosexual love that was being celebrated, though without specific reference to that deviationist aspect, one may well suppose that, in this early poem, Crane had in mind, if only half-consciously, the perils of sex to which young boys are particularly subject. Crane wrote to Munson that this poem amounted to a "stop, look and listen" sign.

Such is, in the first lyric, the statement, and the second follows as

specific counter-statement. "—And yet this great wink of eternity...."
The first is a warning against the sea, and implicitly a warning
against "love." The second is an ecstatic celebration of both love
and sea.

But still in his treatment of the sea there is considerable ambiva-
lence or ambiguity. And the ambiguity appears in the imagery of
whiteness. The sea is

> Samite sheeted and processioned where
> Her undinal vast belly moonward bends,
> Laughing the wrapt inflections of our love.

Samite, is, as the dictionary tells us, "a heavy silk fabric, generally
interwoven with gold and silver, and used in the Middle Ages for
luxurious cushions, ecclesiastical garments, etc." But surely more
helpful than the dictionary here are Tennyson's lines, infallibly
encountered by Crane in his impressionable high school years,
describing the Lady of the Lake's arm, rising from out the bosom
of the lake, "clothed in white samite, mystic, wonderful," to hand
King Arthur the sword Excalibur. The Lady of the Lake was of
course a dubious, an ambiguous character. The "samite sheeted"
here is the ocean, and very white, even if streaked with gold and
silver. It is she who in the next stanza "knells/ On scrolls of silver
snowy sentences." She can spell doom to "all but the pieties of lovers'
hands." But here she is the very incarnation of love, where

> Her undinal vast belly moonward bends,
> Laughing the wrapt inflections of our love.

I will not dwell on the linguistic atrocities of the last line, nor on
the great imaginative power of the Undine figure, but go on at once
to the third stanza, where we have a further development of the sea
as a fosterer and interpreter of love. This brings in new aspects of
marine scenery for which hints might perhaps have been taken
from Melville.

> And onward, as bells off San Salvador
> Salute the crocus lustres of the stars.
> In these poinsettia meadows of her tides,—
> Adagios of islands, O my Prodigal,
> Complete the dark confessions her veins spell.

The open sea has been shown as sympathetic to lovers. And now island archipelagoes strewn through the meadows of the sea make their further contribution to the lore of love. Here the connection of the sea with love grows more intimate. Dark confessions are secret confessions; they are a part of the mystery or ritual of love. Perhaps they are dark as having to do with forbidden love, and so refer back, but now without shame, to the love against which, in the earlier poem, the playing boys were warned. Perhaps they are dark because of the final association of love with death.

There is nothing of Melville in all this. What might suggest *Moby Dick* is "the meadows of her tides," taken together with the islands. In Chapter 58 we have "vast meadows of brit, the minute, yellow substance, upon which the Right Whale largely feeds"; and in Chapter 114, sea pastures, wide rolling watery plains, milky-ways of islands, archipelagoes, and even lovers walking in the sweet island woods. No "poinsettia meadows" nor "adagios of islands"! The items are much the same, and their collocation, but the quality of imagination is very different. Melville is a prose writer of genius, too often betrayed by the rhetoric of a bad period, writing here well enough, indifferently well, in his discursive essay manner. Crane is a genius in poetry, himself too often betrayed by the rhetoric of a period of new creation and confusion of styles, often extravagant and outrageous in his disregard for idiom, for the conventions of English speech, and for the traditional associations of words, but always concerned—indeed too much concerned—to "load every rift with ore"; and here, by some miracle of imagination controlled by feeling, writing darkly, to be sure, but with true ore gleaming in every crevice.

III

There is one all-essential item in the thought-complex that has not yet been noted. Crane's poem declares in essence the triumph of love over death, and it is the thought of death that comes into the first two lines of the third stanza:

> And onward, as bells off San Salvador
> Salute the crocus lustres of the stars...

Philip Horton in his life of Crane has explained this allusion. Crane was at this period having his desperately serious love-affair with a young seaman, and from him he heard "such legends as that of the sunken city off the island of San Salvador" and of bells pealing in towers undersea. Thus with the tolling of ghostly bells from buried cities, death comes into the poem, and the thought of hours that measure the lives even of lovers. It is the turning shoulders of the sea that wind the hours, and convey to the lovers their admonition of *Carpe Diem, Gather ye rosebuds.*

> Mark how her turning shoulders wind the hours,
> And hasten while her penniless rich palms
> Pass superscription of bent foam and wave,—
> Hasten while they are true,—sleep, death, desire
>   Close round one instant in one floating flower.

The hands of the sea are penniless palms, but still rich to the lovers so long as they pass on, or admit and validate (?), the precious coinage of foam and wave. Perhaps the suggestion for this image came from a familiar passage in the Gospels, where Christ is being questioned as to the propriety of giving tribute to Caesar.

> But he perceived their craftiness, and said unto them, Why tempt ye me? Show me a *penny.* Whose *image and superscription* hath it? They answered and said, Caesar's. And he said unto them, Render therefore unto Caesar the things which be Caesar's, and unto God the things which be God's.

This use of the *superscription* for Caesar's stamp on the imperial coinage is the one most likely to have been familiar to the boy Crane from his days at church and Sunday School. And it is that connection with the word *penny* that might have suggested to him the "penniless rich palms" of the sea. The bent foam and wave were the riches of the sea granted to the lovers while she was still winding the hours with her shoulders. But time is limited. Let them hasten while she still passes these cheques—while sleep, death and desire are realities for men still living. If time for them is short, let them roll all their strength and all their sweetness into one ball. ...

This mood deepens and broadens, this way of circumventing time and death is more boldly declared, in the following stanza.

> Bind us in time, O seasons clear, and awe,
> O minstrel galleons of Carib fire,
> Bequeath us to no earthly shore until
> Is answered in *the vortex of our grave*
> The seal's wide spindrift gaze toward paradise.

The poet here declares his contentment with the temporal conditions and limitations of life for the lover. He bids the halcyon seasons (of sea and love) bind him and his lover in time and give them an awesome realization of the grandeur of their state. He bids the galleons of Carib fire still give them passage among the islands of the sea, and not return them to land till their vision of paradise is "answered in the vortex of our grave." This may be taken literally in the sense that he wishes the lovers not to return to land before they have found their grave in the sea. Or, equating the experience of the sea with the experience of love, and contrasting this with the earthly shore as a state of lovelessness, we may take it as a prayer that they may never return to the loveless but remain till death in the marine embrace of love. In the one case it would be the sort of death-wish that was later realized by Crane's suicide. In the other it would be simply a prayer for the persistence of the state of love—a prayer that was so often offered vainly by Hart Crane, owing to frequent "betrayals." And in any case it does not rule out the further notion of realizing through death the condition of "eternity."

What has not, I think, been pointed out, is that "the vortex of our grave" was probably suggested by the vivid and detailed descriptions of the sinking of the Pequod in the final chapter and the Epilogue of *Moby Dick*. There was first the sinking of the ship, and this was followed by the sucking down of the whaleboat.

> And now, concentric circles seized the long-boat itself, and all its crew, and each floating oar, and every lancepole, and spinning, animate and inanimate, all *round and round in one vortex,* carried the smallest chip of the Pequod out of sight.

There follows the last minute salvation of Ishmael, who had been tossed out of the whale-boat, and "drawn towards *the closing vortex* ...till the coffin life-buoy shot lengthwise from the sea, fell over, and floated by my side."

As it happens, there is more positive evidence that Crane had already associated the word "vortex" with Melville and *Moby Dick*. In *Poetry* of October, 1926, was printed Crane's "At Melville's Tomb," and in the appendix "A Discussion with Hart Crane," consisting of two letters from Harriet Monroe, and one from Crane explaining the meaning of certain obscure phrases in the poem. In this remarkable letter Crane had some very good things to say about the special dynamics of metaphor in poetry, and of the distinction between this and the logic of prose or scientific writing. It is true that he did not fully realize the risk a poet runs through excessive reliance on purely individual, accidental and private associations with given words and images. But he did acknowledge that he might be subject to this danger, and he proceeded to make for Miss Monroe an "explication" of certain different images in his poem, and above all, and most "dark" of all, that of "the calyx of death's bounty" in the following stanza:

> And wrecks passed without sound of bells,
> The calyx of death's bounty giving back
> A scattered chapter, livid hieroglyph,
> The portent wound in corridors of shells.

In this poem Crane is saying that Melville had often looked out upon the sea from some ledge and noted the message (embassy) delivered by the dice of drowned men's bones (their bones ground up and cast upon the shore as sand), or the wreckage of ships still floating but without their crews ("without sound of bells"). Of the "calyx of death's bounty" he writes Miss Monroe:

> This calyx refers in a double ironic sense both to a cornucopia and the *vortex made by a sinking vessel.* As soon as the water has closed over a ship this whirlpool sends up broken spars, wreckage, etc., which can be alluded to as a livid hieroglyph, making a scattered chapter so far as any complete record of the recent ship and her crew is concerned.

This of a calyx, implying a vortex, is a peculiarly telling instance of a fault to which Crane was often liable, and of which he confesses that he may be guilty,—the failure "to supply the necessary emotional connectives to the content featured," Miss Monroe may indeed have shown a lack of imagination when she asked him "how a *portent* can possibly be wound in a shell." But no one could accuse her of denseness in not discovering the vortex hidden in the "calyx of death's bounty."

A little less blind are the images in the following stanza, in which the figure of the vortex is further developed, and the eyes of the drowned sailors are conceived as "frosted eyes" that "lifted altars."

> Then in the circuit calm of one vast coil,
> Its lashings charmed and malice reconciled,
> Frosted eyes there were that lifted altars;
> And silent answers crept across the stars.

Crane briefly draws out for Miss Monroe the implications of the third line. "Refers simply to a conviction that a man, not knowing perhaps a definite god yet being endowed with reverence for deity —such a man naturally postulates a deity somehow, and the altar of that deity by the very *action* of the eyes *lifted* in searching."

Thus, at Melville's tomb, Crane is reflecting on the message—the many messages—sent to the living by drowned sailors, as interpreted by Melville in *Moby Dick*. *Moby Dick* was certainly crowded with philosophical messages, or at any rate with searching and Melville was himself a man "not knowing perhaps a definite god yet... endowed with a reverence for deity."

Everything about "At Melville's Tomb" indicates that Crane there had in mind the closing scenes of *Moby Dick*. He describes the vortex when it had entered its final quiet phase, "the circuit calm of one vast coil," etc., in terms suggestive of Ishmael's notations about the creamy pool and slowly wheeling circle. Even the "scattered chapter" of the wreckage corresponds to Melville's account of the sinking ship. It was doubtless this same incident that inspired the image, in "Voyages II," of a gaze toward paradise "answered in the vortex of our grave." And it may be noted in passing that "the seal's wide spindrift gaze toward paradise" is a sort of alternative version of "frosted eyes" that "lifted altars."

IV

There is one further, and major, theme in "Voyages II" yet to be noted; and in the treatment of this theme there is possibly a further trace of Melville and *Moby Dick*. This theme is religious and metaphysical. The poem culminates in the suggestion that "the seal's wide spindrift gaze toward paradise" will be "answered in the vortex of our grave." In "At Melville's Tomb" the eyes of the drowned men lifted altars to an unknown god, and their reverential inspiring gaze was rewarded by "silent answers that crept across the stars." Again, in the last one of the "Voyages" (VI), we have the figure of a blind swimmer gazing at a rainbow-wreathed isle and being enlightened by an "image Word" or "name unspoke." In this final poem, which has been plausibly interpreted in detail by Charles C. Walcutt in *The Explicator* for May, 1946, the theme of love has been virtually dropped, and what remains is a search for light, for some Word that will be the answer to all betrayal and separation.

> The imaged Word, it is, that holds
> Hushed willows anchored in its glow.
> It is the unbetrayable reply
> Whose accents no farewell can know.

This is a later stage in the experience of love of which the second lyric is the triumphant affirmation, and it follows directly upon the fifth poem, in which we have intimations of growing alienation between the lovers.

In the final poem the Imaged Word is a consolation prize for love betrayed or lost. In the triumphant second poem paradise is the natural condition and end of lovers united in life and in death. And we know that here too the conception is religious. For it is notorious that Crane—like Whitman—insisted on including every aspect of human experience in his vision of the divine. And above all love. So that he could write to a friend in 1920, a propos of an ecstatic love-affair, that through this, "I believe in, or have found God again." (Brom Weber, ed., *Letters of Hart Crane,* p. 49.) And four years later he wrote to Waldo Frank, referring to the very love celebrated in "Voyages," "I have seen the Word made Flesh." As for the answer to the paradise gaze, he writes:

> I think the sea has been thrown upon me and been answered, at least in part, and I believe I am a little changed—not essentially, but changed and transubstantiated as anyone is *who has asked a question and been answered.* (p. 182)

And again, in the same letter, "I know that there is such a thing as indestructibility."

The *indestructibility* which Crane felt in himself, or in his love, was, I suppose, an aspect, or an evidence, of that all-embracing *eternity* of being which he held to be the answer to all the indignities

of time. In "Atlantis," the concluding poem of *The Bridge,* he has
the most elaborate and involved set of symbols for embodying the
poetic vision of eternity. In the bridge itself, symbol of what unites
and harmonizes all things, and in its superstructure of piers and
cables, he saw a great loom weaving the hymn of eternity, a Jason's
voyage leading to Atlantis and Cathay—Atlantis, symbol of eternity,
Cathay, of "consciousness, knowledge, spiritual unity." The bridge
is for him the psalm of Cathay—it is a

> ....choir, translating time
> Into what multitudinous Verb the suns
> And synergy of waters ever fuse.

Here again is the "imaged Word" of the "Voyages."

In "Atlantis," while the bridge is *Love's* "white, pervasive Paradigm," there is relatively little reference to love with a small l.
Still it is "through smoking pyres of love and death" that the true
traveler "searches the timeless laugh of mythic spears." In his personal life Crane was more deeply involved with *love* than with *Love.*
But, as we have seen, he strove earnestly to identify the two, conceiving of his love-affair as a means of insight into religious "truths."
Crane tried to make himself a philosophy that would take into
account the methods and findings of science and yet pass beyond
scientific positivism through spiritual insight. As a very young
man he shared his mother's faith in Christian Science. Later, his
biographers agree that, among many writers of the past and of his
own time, he was particularly impressed with the thinking of
Ouspensky, whose *Tertium Organum* was in his day the bible of so
many "intellectuals" and, we might say, amateur mystics. According
to Ouspensky, "there are certain aspects" of our phenomenal
existence "in which we come into direct contact with eternity...
These are death and love." In our "Voyages" poem it is the two in
conjunction that bring the poet his assurance of eternity (or paradise).

V

And now at length for the image of the seal in the last line of the
poem. It has been suggested somewhere that the figure of the seal's
gaze toward paradise was inspired by a reading of Kipling's "The

White Seal" in *The Jungle Book*. There is in Kipling no gaze toward paradise, but there is the persistent search by Kotick, the anomalous young white seal, for a suitable nursery for seals, to take the place of other resorts where they are liable to be killed for their skins, and where they are so crowded together that the life of the older males is one long fight for position. The secluded beaches that Kotick finds at last after years of searching make an ideal place for seals—one might almost say a paradise—and Kotick has something of the quality of a "seeker" and crusader. He might well have impressed the imagination of Crane as a boy and have suggested to him as a man "the seal's wide spindrift gaze toward paradise."

I will not attempt to set it up as a rival theory that Crane's seal comes from *Moby Dick*. But since we have found so much that might have come from there, it is at least worth noting that seals do make their appearance in *Moby Dick* in a not unimpressive manner. It is in Chapter 126 that the sailors hear wild and unearthly cries near some rocky islands they are passing, which some take for the utterance of mermaids and some for that of men newly drowned. They are at length identified as the cries of "some young seals that had lost their dams, or some dams that had lost their cubs." But what might have appealed most to the imagination of a young poet was the facial appearance of the seals when they rose near the ship. For, as Melville says:

> Most mariners cherish a very superstitious feeling about seals, arising not only from their peculiar tones when in distress, but also from *the human look of their round heads and semi-intelligent faces,* seen *peeringly uprising from the water* alongside. In the sea, under certain circumstances, seals have more than once been mistaken for men.

A seal's gaze toward paradise does strike one as a trifle odd in Crane's context. The seal is not a creature of especially august and spiritual associations. Perhaps between Kipling and Melville we have the combination of imaginative appeal that would explain the poet's going so far afield for an image to close his rather solemn hymn. Kotick's devoted search for an asylum and ideal summer resort for seals might account for the quest for paradise. For the seal's *gaze,* the suggestion might have come from human-looking faces, "peeringly uprising from the water," with cries that make the sailors think of mermaids and drowned men. It would be a follow-up to "frosted eyes" that "lifted altars," an anticipation of blind eyes looking out for sunrise, rainbow, and "some splintered garland for the seer."

In these "Voyages," then, Crane would seem to be interpreting the message—the "embassy"—bequeathed, as Melville saw from his ledge, by the "dice of drowned men's bones." He was suggesting the "silent answers" that, for Melville, "crept across the stars."

As for the title "Voyages," it is clear that Crane thought of these poems as not merely love-poems but also as journeys in search of supernal truth. His lovers were such travellers as "through smoking pyres of love and death/ Search(es) the timeless laugh of mythic spears." Their voyages were earlier versions of the Jason's-quest so elaborately figured in "Atlantis." But of all legendary voyages in search of truth it was perhaps that of the Pequod which had most impressed the poet's imagination.

The Architecture of *The Bridge*

by John Unterecker

Perhaps our principal difficulty in appreciating *The Bridge* as a work of art is that we read it too carefully. It is a long poem and, for most readers, a difficult one. Somewhere along the way, most of us, I suspect, get bogged down in a passage that seems to demand concentrated work. Good explicators that we are, we stop to work on it.

Such explication is, needless to say, ultimately necessary. And in the course of these remarks I want to suggest certain kinds of explicatory approaches which seem to me most fruitful. The poem is a good one and it can stand all the careful readings we can bring to it. Yet if we start with explication, we may never get around to reading the poem straight through—end to end—without interruption.

I am convinced, however, that if we do read it straight through, a good many of our difficulties will disappear. What looks like fragmentation and downright disorganization is likely in an uninterrupted reading to fall together into coherence. Because they will pass by rapidly enough for us to remember them, we will either notice or at least properly be affected by the dozens and dozens of linking devices that Crane carefully put into his work to hold the individual and very different sections together.

The sections do, of course, appear disorganized. Yet precisely in the appearance of disorganization—the seeming unrelatedness of section to section—may be something very close to the basic form of the work. I am not trying here to be ingenious. I am simply trying

"The Architecture of *The Bridge*," by John Unterecker. From *Wisconsin Studies in Contemporary Literature*, Vol. III, No. 2, 5-20. Copyright © 1962 by the Regents of the University of Wisconsin. Reprinted by permission of *Wisconsin Studies in Contemporary Literature*.

to describe what I think Crane himself regarded as an important form in the tradition in which he was working.

Perhaps if I name a few works in that tradition, I can suggest a little more accurately what I think Crane was doing in organizing *The Bridge* as he did.

Some writers of his tradition are, in fact, referred to in *The Bridge:* particularly Blake, Melville, and Whitman. To these, I think, we should add T. S. Eliot, Ezra Pound, and James Joyce. There are others, but these at least suggest a pattern that Crane fits into.

Blake, Melville, Whitman, Eliot, Pound, and Joyce. At first they look like strange bedfellows; but if one lines up Blake's prophetic books, *Moby Dick,* Whitman's "Passage to India," *Ulysses,* the Mauberley poems, and "The Waste Land," certain structural similarities all but leap at one. For one thing, each of these works has a mosaic structure. Each is compounded from a number of what at first look like almost completely independent sections. And in most of these works, the authors have gone to some trouble to make the sections as different as possible.

One has only to recollect the jolting experience of a first reading of *Moby Dick* to see what I mean: the shock of bouncing from that enormous collection of epigraphs, the "extracts," to the simple narrative of the opening chapters, to the considerably more complex narrative that follows—a narrative broken by direct address to the reader, reported dreams, and intrusive low-level symbolic imagery—to annotated catalogues of whales, to such set pieces of dense symbolism as the chapter on "The Whiteness of the Whale," and finally to "The Chase" itself which, if one's reading has been lucky, pulls the whole work together.

Similarly, the "form" of *Ulysses* involves as many different forms as there are chapters. And the sections of the Mauberley poems and those of "The Waste Land," are radically different one from the other. Even in Blake and in Whitman, where there seems to be a little more continuity of technique, one's first reaction is an awareness of the disjointedness of things.

The reader always, of course, in any successful work puts the pieces together; but in works of the sort I have listed, he knows that he is doing it. He is constantly being reminded—by the form itself—that the whole work is made up of a series of parts. And he is also constantly being reminded that the structure the author is working on is not going to be finished until the reader has finished the last page. When he gets to that last page, the reader, if the work is successful, ought to have a feeling of congruence. The large sections that have seemed independent will be discovered to be bolted together into a substantial unit that will be remembered as *Ulysses* or *Moby Dick* or even as *The Bridge.*

We are, I think, best adjusted to forms of this sort in the other arts—particularly in music and in painting, where the element of "composition" is accepted to be at the heart of the work. One has only to think, for instance, of the water colors of such a painter as William Sommer or John Marin, both of whom Crane greatly admired, to find analogous structures—great blocks of color held together by the echoing pattern of a superimposed linking design.

What the writer gains from a structure of this sort is, of course, the advantage of shifted ground. All of the sections point in toward one center and are, needless to say, linked by it; but as we move from section to section in reading the work, perspectives change and we see the subject the writer is working on from new and illuminating angles. (Some readers, who like always to see things only from one point of view, find such shifts disconcerting. Disliking catalogues, they object to catalogues in Whitman—who sometimes uses them very deftly indeed. Bored by catechisms, they find dull the questions and answers of the Ithaca section of *Ulysses.* Or, able to use information only if it is pleasantly disguised in plot, they criticize Melville for his spectacularly intrusive sections of whaling facts. Readers of this kind, needless to say, find the superficial fragmentation of such a work as *The Bridge* upsetting. Incapable of liking all of its parts, they label it a failure—sometimes a brilliant one.)

Crane certainly exploits all of the possibilities of superficial fragmentation. He moves backwards and forwards in time, he shifts suddenly from third person, to first, to second, and back again to third; he examines the bridge he is constructing from above and below, from north, south, east, and west; he employs diction that ranges from advertising jargon and slang on the one hand to lyrical elegance on the other; he shifts tone rapidly, drawing, among a good many others, on elegiac, satirical, and even sentimental attitudes.

Gradually, as he circles his subject, letting us see it from as many angles as we can, his bridge emerges. Hinting his technique in the epigraph from *The Book of Job*—"From going to and fro in the earth, and from walking up and down in it"—he leads us up and down, in and out, to and fro until we have built, as he intended, his bridge in ourselves. Like the motion picture audience of the "Proem"—"multitudes bent toward some flashing scene"—we construct from the flashed separate frames of the sections something "never disclosed" in any one of them.

I labor this point about the total organization of the poem because all too often *The Bridge* is criticized as if it were a volume of unrelated or at best loosely related lyrics. The "Indiana" subsection is a favorite target of such criticism. By itself, of course, "Indiana" is as sentimental as it is accused of being. And if it were an independent personal lyric, which it is not, it would certainly merit the attack. Yet in context, it very neatly opposes the whirlwind of "The Dance" and both anticipates the subject matter of "Cutty Sark" and acts as a foil to its jazz rhythms.

In spite of its radically different sections, the poem is remarkably coherent, the sections being locked together in all sorts of ways; and some, at least, of its integrating devices have clear associations with other works in the tradition that I have been discussing.

The "plot" of the poem, for example, sounds almost like a digest of Joyce's *Ulysses*. A young man awakens in the early dawn, gazes out over harbor and city, spends a day wandering through the streets of his metropolis, gradually becoming involved in its corruption, and, after agonizing disillusionment and drunkenness—a kind of spiritual descent to Hades—comes, at the very end of the poem, in the pre-dawn hours of the next morning, to an illuminating vision of order in which he can accept himself and his world.

During his wanderings in his city, its sights and sounds trigger memories both of his own youth and of the youth of his country, its history and its mythology.

Like Joyce's young man, Crane's young man is also concerned with the writers and artists who have significantly shaped his world. Americans—Whitman, Poe, Melville, Emily Dickinson, and Isadora Duncan—rub shoulders with Plato, Seneca, Marlowe, Shakespeare, Milton, and Hopkins.

If plot and a good deal of the organization seem to hint of a careful reading of Joyce—and we know, of course, that Crane not only read *Ulysses* but that he even went so far as to prepare a gloss of parts of it, a gloss which he copied out with passages from the text for a friend who had not yet seen a copy—both the notion of an American myth and much of its machinery come from Whitman, particularly Whitman's "Passage to India" and "Crossing Brooklyn Ferry," though Crane also paraphrases or quotes very, very widely from other works by Whitman in the course of his poem.

But the Whitman influence, though real, works most directly into the poem by way of contemporary admirers of Whitman, particularly Waldo Frank and William Carlos Williams. Frank, in letters to and in conversations with Crane, insisted on the primacy of Whitman's view of American life. It was Williams, however, who in poetry that could accurately be described as Whitmanesque and in his prose study *In the American Grain,* gave Crane material that was immediately useful. For not only did Crane take the epigraph to "Powhatan's Daughter" from *In the American Grain,* he also, as he acknowledged in a now-lost letter to Williams, drew on the thesis of *American Grain* for much of the "argument" of *The Bridge* and on Williams' early poem "The Wanderer" for a good deal of the imagistic structure. Even without that letter (it was destroyed by Dr. Williams' overly zealous, neat maid), the reader of "The Wanderer" should have no difficulty in identifying material that Crane adapted to his own needs.

Published in 1917 as the final poem in Williams' *A Book of Poems, Al Que Quiere!,* "The Wanderer" developed in seven sections an account of the still-vital power of a symbolic feminine force. In "Advent," the opening section, she puts to a young poet "crossing the ferry/ With the great towers of Manhattan" before him, a question that anticipates neatly the crucial question that runs not only beneath *The Bridge* but as well beneath all of Crane's work: "How shall I be a mirror to this modernity?" The young poet sees her much as Crane sees his Pocahontas figure: "She sprang from the nest, a young crow,/ Whose first flight circled the forest." Later she reappears to him as a swimmer in the Manhattan-enclosing river and at the end of the first section as a sea gull rising above it, "vanishing with a wild cry." She becomes for Williams' young poet a figure representing the total past of the country "In whom age in age is united—/ Indifferent, out of sequence, marvelously!" He sees her "attiring herself" before him, "Taking shape before me for worship,/ A red leaf that falls upon a stone!" And though in modern times she may possess no longer her one-time forest grace, she is still remarkably potent: "At her throat is loose gold, a single chain/ From among many." Like the figures of Crane's poem, she is to be found where river and land meet: "Toward the river! Is it she there?" And like Crane's spirit-of-the-land-fallen-on-evil-days, the corrupt women of "Southern Cross" and "National Winter Garden," Williams' woman in the "Broadway" section is reduced to a harlot, "After the youth of all cities" but from whom still can come release as the poet calls for "A new grip upon those garments that brushed me/ In days gone by on beach, lawn, and in forest!/ May I be lifted still, up and out of terror,/ Up from before the death living around me—."

If, like Crane later, Williams associated his female spirit of the land with water, he also associated his male figure with wind. Like Crane's Maquokeeta, Williams' masculine figure is revealed toward the end of "The Wanderer" in the "Soothsay" section to be "the wind coming that stills birds," and is addressed directly in a prophetic apostrophe almost precisely parallel to Crane's vision of the whirlwind:

> The din and bellow of the male wind
> Leap then from forest into foam!
> Lash about from low into high flames...

Finally the poet is led to the river itself, where the ancient female, now both mother and mistress, insists on his identification with it also: "Enter, youth, into this bulk!/ Enter, river, into this young man!" He experiences it completely—both "the crystal beginning of its days" and the "utter depth of its rottenness."

Crane's reliance on Williams' poem is, I think, obvious, just as is his reliance on Joyce's novel. I do not, however, mean to suggest that he imitated either. As every writer borrows, he borrowed; but his borrowings are inevitably woven into a poem uniquely his own. Second-hand themes and images are nothing new in literature. What Crane found in these writers and in a good many others was material that could be adapted to the mythic structure that he was creating. *The Bridge* as a mythic structure has, however, been very fully and very recently discussed by L. S. Dembo in his book *Hart Crane's Sanskrit Charge* and, except for these observations on Joyce and Williams, all I could say on that subject would be no more than marginalia to Mr. Dembo's very thorough study.

Not quite so much attention, however, has been paid to the very careful way in which section of *The Bridge* is linked to section and the equally ingenious way in which the temporal and spatial schemes of the poem are integrated.[1]

One of Crane's favorite devices is simple verbal repetition. A phrase or word will be picked up in one section and reworked in the next, almost always in a completely different context. It is exactly this sort of repetition which binds the lyrical "Proem" entitled "To Brooklyn Bridge" to the following "Ave Maria" section, a dramatic monologue by Columbus as he approaches Europe on his return voyage from America.

Crane set up in his "Proem" a great deal of the imagery he will draw on throughout his poem—the Brooklyn Bridge itself (his core image), the air over it patterned by a circling gull and above that gull a blazing sun, the river which flows under the bridge, the two shores, and the underworld counterpart of the bridge, the subway which cuts below the river.

The particular link, however, that most firmly joins "Proem" to "Ave Maria" comes in the last stanza of the "Proem," a direct address to the bridge:

> O Sleepless as the river under thee,
> Vaulting the sea, the prairies' dreaming sod,
> Unto us lowliest sometime sweep, descend
> And of the curveship lend a myth to God.

The bridge, as Crane has indicated earlier in the "Proem," is sleepless because always simultaneously active and passive. Though fixed, it is an image of freedom. The "traffic lights," for instance, that "skim" its surface in constant motion, like the stars moving across the fixed bridge of the sky, "condense eternity" by giving us a way of apprehending a still form filled with motion. The bridge itself, as he says, is an unmoving "stride" across the river, yet an unmoving stride which contains "some motion ever unspent."

This paradox of the still form compounded from motion pro-

[1]Perhaps the strongest discussion of the imagistic structure of *The Bridge* is in Sister M. Bernetta Quinn's *The Metamorphic Tradition in Modern Poetry* (New Brunswick, N. J., 1955).

duces the bridge, held in place by the active conflict between its lifting cables and its dragging span, "stayed" by its freedom, and imitated by the seagull above it which moves in an "inviolate curve" and which builds above the bridge, "over the *chained* bay waters," "Liberty."[2]

The sleepless bridge is linked therefore to river and sea—also sleepless (always in motion and always contained by shores) and like the bridge both *free* and *chained*—and is opposed to the "dreaming sod" of land. And Crane's plea at the end of the "Proem" is that, unlike the gull above it which curves out of sight, the sleepless bridge will descend "and of the curveship lend a myth to God"—give God a shape contemporary humans can deal with—for God is also ideally both bridge and perfect curve, the chastiser and protector who once had made a covenant with man in the shape of a rainbow.

All of this material and a good deal more finds an echo in the first main division of the poem, Columbus' "Ave Maria" as he "gazes toward Spain." The bridge itself is echoed, as Columbus' invoked God is praised for his omnipresence, his "teeming span" which bridges the distance between Ganges and Spain. The form of the double uprights of the suspension bridge is echoed in the "poles" of the ship and even in the waves themselves—"the sea's green crying towers"—the trough of the waves forming one more of those curves which from this point on dominate the poem. The circling seagull that had made an "inviolate curve" above the curve of the bridge is echoed as Columbus recollects the natives who "came out to us crying/ 'The Great White Birds'"; and the "white rings of tumult" that the gull had made in the "Proem" are echoed in Columbus' vision of a round earth—his sailing eyes finally having "accreted," "enclosed,"

> This turning rondure whole, this crescent ring
> Sun-cusped and zoned with modulated fire
> Like pearls that whisper through the Doge's hands.

Similarly, above the round earth that Columbus thought he had circled lies the circle of the heavens and the stars, the "sapphire wheel" of the night, where, again circling, God's "once whirling feet" had one-time raced. God himself is seen here as circle within

[2]Unless otherwise noted, all italics in passages quoted from Crane are mine.

circle, the "white toil of heaven's cordons" who musters "in holy
rings" all sails on earth—those of gull and those of ship. And on
God's brows is set—one last circle—a crown, "the kindled Crown"
beneath the cruel, loving flames of which "meridians reel" God's
purpose.

But unlike the bridge Crane had evoked in the "Proem"—"O
Sleepless as the river under thee," the sleepless bridge which was
of its curveship to "lend a myth to God"—Columbus' God is "apart"
and is invoked in terms of a *sleeping* consciousness, both distant
from yet acting on man. "O Thou who *sleepest* on Thyself," he is
addressed. And the passage goes on to recapitulate by-now-familiar
imagery:

> O Thou who sleepest on Thyself, apart
> Like ocean athwart lanes of death and birth,
> And all the eddying breath between dost search
> Cruelly with love thy parable of man,—
> Inquisitor! incognizable Word
> Of Eden and the enchained Sepulchre,
> Into thy steep savannahs, burning blue,
> Utter to loneliness the sail is true.

The sleepless bridge is therefore a myth for God, and man is
sleeping God's parable. Like the bridge, God is himself both free
and bound—the abstract free Word but as well the enchained mun-
dane Sepulchre.

The joints between the first and second large sections—the watery
"Ave Maria" and the continental "Powhatan's Daughter"—are
if possible even more numerous, largely because "Powhatan's
Daughter" is so very long and is broken into subsections. But the
joints which please me most come precisely at the end of "Ave
Maria" and at the very beginning of "Powhatan's Daughter"—in
fact, within the epigraph; and they are, in a way, almost outlandishly
unlikely, for they connect the awful fiery God of Columbus' vision
with the twelve-year-old girl who was the flesh, not the myth, of
Pocahontas. (It is worth observing in passing, incidentally, that it is
Crane's habit always to begin with the simplest level of any image
that is going eventually to be destined for symbolic extension.
Though before he is finished, almost everything in his poem will
be bridge or bridging, all of the bridges are keyed closely to the real
Brooklyn Bridge with which the poem begins. Similarly, though

Pocahontas is to become symbolic of the red clay of the American soil, she appears in Crane's first reference to her as an altogether physical "wanton" child.)

The God Columbus invoked in his section had been seen in terms of the "once whirling feet" that had swept through the heavens and that were associated with the "sapphire wheel" of stars. He had been an unforgettable God of thunder and lightning (Columbus insists: "Elohim, still I hear thy sounding heel"), and his manifestations continue to strike terror "naked in the/ trembling heart" through the power of his still potent "Hand of Fire."

All of this imagery—wheel, whirling feet, heel, and naked illumination—is reduced in the epigraph of "Powhatan's Daughter" to entirely human terms:

> "—Pocahuntus, a well-featured but wanton yong girle...of the age of eleven or twelve years, get the boyes forth with her into the market place, and make them *wheele*, falling on their *hands*, turning their *heels* upwards, whom she would followe, and *wheele* so herself, *naked* as she was, all the fort over."

The sapphire wheel becomes here the wheeling children, the whirling feet and Hand of Fire of God becomes the hands and feet of cartwheeling seventeenth-century juvenile delinquents and the naked terror that God inspires becomes a naked "wanton yong girle."

Within "Powhatan's Daughter" unobtrusive joints of the same kind hold subsection to subsection—unobtrusive because the second appearance is almost always in a context completely different from the first. One really has to do a little looking to see such links. It is easy enough, for example, to notice *dream* [editor's italics] in "Harbor Dawn," the first subsection of "Powhatan's Daughter," because the subject matter is itself an awakening from sleep. With dawn comes "a tide of voices" "midway in your dream." But only the perceptive reader notes consciously that all the subsequent material in the remaining parts of "Powhatan's Daughter" is dream material—a dream of the continental past that gives us a history and a myth to balance Columbus' seagoing freight from Europe. Yet Crane almost leans over backwards to insist on the dream-center of this very large division of his poem. Dreams interweave all through "Van Winkle" and into "The River," which explicitly "spends your dream," a dream that earlier in that section had been assembled by the "keen instruments" of telegraph and telephone which, "strung to a vast precision/ Bind town to town and dream to ticking dream." The whirlwind manifestation of Maquokeeta in "The Dance" is really nothing more nor less than dream-vision. And, again explicitly, in "Indiana," Crane tells us in no uncertain terms that the Indian dream is very much ending ("Bison thunder rends my *dreams* no more"), that it is ending—as it should—with the last subsection of the dream-oriented "Powhatan's Daughter" section:

> The morning-glory, climbing the morning long
>   Over the lintel on its wiry vine,
> Closes before the dusk, furls in its song
>   As I close mine...

If the dream of the Indian past binds together all five subsections of "Powhatan's Daughter," other links tie individual subsections one to the other. The last word of "Harbor Dawn," for example, *sleep,* is echoed almost immediately in the opening of the "Van Winkle" section: "'Is this *Sleepy* Hollow, friend?'" And the last three lines of the "Van Winkle" section

> Keep hold of that nickel for car-change, Rip,—
> Have you got your *"Times"*—?
> And hurry along, Van Winkle—it's getting late![3]

anticipate the rush of the express train that opens "The River" section, Rip's nickel subway ride expanding to a trip on "The EXpress," the 20th Century Limited which hurtles across the continent; the plea that he "hurry along...it's getting late" expanding to a whole crescendo of motion: "whistling down the tracks/a headlight rushing," "windows flashing roar," "Breath-taking," "so/ whizzed the Limited—roared by"; and that New York *Times* that Rip clutches expanding into modern event-making journalism: "an EXpress makes time," the capitalized EX of *EXpress* emphasizing the newspaper pun, the ex-press which in the modern world not only records but actually "makes" time.

All of the examples of linking material that I have been so far concerned with are simple enough for quite casual explication. Much more complicated—so complicated that I can only hint at

[3]Crane's italics.

some of their relationships—are the sorts of links which bind the two principal subsections of "Powhatan's Daughter," "The River" and "The Dance," for within these sections is the first full development of a pair of symbols Crane has from the beginning of the poem been preparing us for. I mean, of course, the serpent of time and the eagle of space.

Crane reaches his first explicit reference to these symbols in a very witty passage which immediately follows his reconstruction of the whizzing express and those hoboes who, "dotting immensity," experience America along the express tracks. Suddenly confessional in the midst of a very elegant rhetorical passage—a literary device he almost certainly adapted from Whitman—Crane insists:

> ...I have trod the rumorous midnights, too,
> And past the circuit of the lamp's thin flame
> (O Nights that brought me to her body bare!)
> Have dreamed beyond the print that bound her name.
> Trains sounding the long blizzards out—I heard
> Wail into distances I knew were hers.
> Papooses crying on the wind's long mane
> Screamed redskin dynasties that fled the brain,
> —Dead echoes! But I knew her body there,
> Time like a serpent down her shoulder, dark,
> And space, an eaglet's wing, laid on her hair.

Perhaps that thinly veiled attack on the newspapers—"the print that bound her name"—is close enough to Rip's *"Times"* and the "EXpress" pun to be obvious to most readers, but it takes a real railroad buff to realize that the "papooses crying on the wind's long mane" who "screamed redskin dynasties that fled the brain" and who are now nothing more than "dead echoes" are in fact pullman cars whipping along after the express and named after Indian tribes— our last "literary" link with the Indian.

Both funny and serious, the crying papooses are most valuable in letting Crane introduce his image of serpent time and eagle space.

The timely serpent itself is, needless to say, involved in all of the river references of the poem—the river that flows under the Brooklyn Bridge, the Mississippi which is the explicit subject of this "river" section, and all the "streams" and "RUNning brooks" with which the section abounds. (Those "RUNning brooks," more ingen-

ious even than the crying papooses of the Pullman, are perhaps
worth a digression. Like the papooses, they are also part of the
modern streamliner, cropping up at the end of its violent passage
across the landscape. Crane works into them in a whirlwind of
capital letters:

> ...WE HAVE THE NORTHPOLE
> WALLSTREET AND VIRGINBIRTH WITHOUT STONES OR
> WIRES OR EVEN RUNning brooks connecting ears
> and no more sermons windows flashing roar
> breathtaking—as you like it...eh?

"Connecting," as Crane tells us to, we join sermons to stones and
stones to running brooks to come up with the crucial images from
Duke Senior's speech on the sweet uses of adversity:

> ...this our life exempt from public haunt
> Finds tongues in trees, books in the running brooks,
> Sermons in stones and good in everything.

Crane, needless to say, has identified it: "as you like it...eh?"
But running brooks are one aspect only of the serpent of time.)

Just as all of the river and stream imagery is associated with time
and with the serpent, so too is all of the other winding imagery of
the poem: the trains, the subways, the telegraph wires, the sea-
lanes, the gold trail, the canyons and labyrinths and burrows, the
Open Road. Eve's serpent is explicitly associated with it, as are the
"stinging coils" of Medusa-Eve's hair, and the "silly snake rings"
that mount the strip-tease Magdalene of "National Winter Garden."
It is part of the "worm's eye" view that Crane warns us in "Quaker
Hill" we shall have to take before we are to find salvation. And
finally it comes most fully into its own in "The Tunnel," the serpent's own territory. Only at the very end of the poem, in "Atlantis,"
do we escape its "labyrinthine mouths of history" and ascend from
"Time's realm" upward out of time.

One could, similarly, locate all of the strategically placed bird
associations of eagle-space—from circling gulls that begin the
poem to "seagulls stung with rime" that end it, from the whirlwind "Dance" subsection in which the imagery is given its first
really extensive development to the "Cape Hatteras" section (the
aboveground counterpart of "The Tunnel") which is built around a

central imagery of airplanes and open air. Suffice to say, almost every serpent figure is balanced somewhere by a bird.

But time and space, as Crane recognized, though antithetical are interdependent. And it is appropriate therefore that he joins them always following each separate treatment. "The River" glides serpent-like down the length of the continent and its section gives way to "The Dance," a cyclone "swooping in eagle feathers" through the sky. But the more the cyclonic Maquokeeta dances, the more he acquires snake-like characteristics until finally he is recognized in transformation: "Dance, Maquokeeta! snake that lives before,/ That casts his pelt and lives beyond!" The narrator both recognizes the transformation—"I saw thy change begun"—and participates in it in something approaching total identification, finding within himself as within Maquokeeta "pure serpent, Time itself." However, even this sort of imagery—one of transformation—is not adequate for the design Crane planned, and in the end of the paired "River"-"Dance" subsections, serpent and eagle, time and space, are interwoven: "The serpent with the eagle in the boughs."

Imagistic links of this sort bind section to section and can be found functioning brilliantly in even the most minor divisions of the poem.

Other devices, however, are quite as important in giving *The Bridge* an extraordinary coherence.

I have already mentioned the temporal scheme—the twenty-four-hour action of the plot. This same chronological pattern recurs in each of the major divisions, though it is not always stressed. The "Proem," for example, opens with a reference to dawn ("How many dawns, chill from his rippling rest"), at dead center ticks off noon ("Down Wall, from girder into street noon leaks"), goes on through the afternoon ("All afternoon the cloud-flown derricks turn") and ends in deep night after the "traffic lights" that "skim" the surface of the bridge in early evening have been stilled ("Under thy shadow by the piers I waited;/ Only in darkness is thy shadow clear").

This is only one, however, of a number of temporal patterns that can be recognized in the poem. Crane insists that "some men... count.../ The river's minute by the far brook's year." And his poem is organized as carefully along a January to January scheme as it is along a dawn to dawn one.

The "Proem" opens almost precisely on January 1: "Already snow submerges an iron year," Crane tells us; and if that doesn't give us the date, he lets us know far more than Christmas is over—for "the City's fiery parcels" are "all undone." We are still in cold weather through the snow storm of "Harbor Dawn"; but by the time we reach "Van Winkle," springtime imagery—like Crane's mother's smile—begins to flicker "through the snow screen." "Cape Hatteras," the center of the poem and a section which in itself contains reference to all four seasons, is dominated by Walt Whitman, the Open Road, and a riotous, airy summer. But it is not until we reach "Quaker Hill," the sixth section of the eight which constitute *The Bridge,* the three-quarter mark, that autumn imagery can come into its own. In "Quaker Hill," however, it runs rampant—from the second eipgraph, Emily Dickinson's lines on the autumn, "The gentian weaves her fringes,/ The maple's loom is red," to the last lines of the section, "Leaf after autumnal leaf/ break off,/ descend—/." And when we do descend and enter the seventh section and "The Tunnel," we have already returned to winter, "preparing penguin flexions of the arms" to ward off the "brisk" chill of an early December night which finally drives us into that subway which "yawns the quickest promise home." "Atlantis," the last section, brings us completely round again to our frosty beginning, its imagery all whiteness, its bridge rising in cold shining elegance from black night into the faint azure of a frozen dawn.

Larger still than this temporal division is one in which America's varied pasts are recapitulated, each of the first four major sections investigating one of them: the European heritage in "Ave Maria," the primitive past of the continent in "Powhatan's Daughters," the past of whaling days and exploration in "Cutty Sark," and the nineteenth-century democratic past of Whitman's Open Road in "Cape Hatteras." Splitting past from present, the middle of the poem brings us to those years of the modern celebrated by Whitman; and the last four sections—"Three Songs," "Quaker Hill," "The Tunnel," and "Atlantis"—are devoted to our own time, its corruption of love the subject of "Three Songs," its corruption of friendship and commerce the subject of "Quaker Hill," and its corruption of art a principal subject of "The Tunnel." "Atlantis," unique, differs from the three other modern sections in founding itself on the healthiest aspects of the past and so rising to a vision of future possibilities.

Just as time is expanded in the poem, so too is space. The bridge moves from the East River first to span the ocean, then the continent, and finally to span the universe. This expanding bridge is in Crane's scheme always firmly assembled. And to emphasize his point makes all of his bridges elemental ones—structures that spring from earth, that bridge water, that are suspended in air, and that are fused into form through the agency of fire. Within the poem, consequently, space is compartmentalized in very much the way time is compartmentalized; and though each section of the poem incorporates all four of the traditional elements of space, each section also stresses most strongly its own logically dominant element —water in "Ave Maria," for instance, or earth in "Powhatan's Daughter."

Finally, *The Bridge* is organized in terms of psychological and spiritual and aesthetic patterns. For just as man is compounded from the tensions of time and space—the oppositions of day and night, winter and summer, past and present; the opposition of water and shore, of earth and air, of fire and frost—so too he is compounded from Dionysian and Appollonian forces: freedom and restraint; a love that perpetually shuttles between passion and friendship; a God who sleeps in the earth and who awakens in vegetation ceremonies to ride the whirlwind and another God, apart, who searches cruelly with love his parable of man. For each of these oppositions, Crane also finds a voice. And since he is an artist, Crane fits into his poem, too, the oppositions which almost every artist is conscious of: the vision of art that is democratic, open, and objective and which Crane identifies with Whitman; and its counterpart and opposite, an art that is intensely personal, secret, subjective—the art of the symbolist tradition which Crane associates with Poe.

But though Crane assigns Whitman in "Cape Hatteras" to the Open Road and to the open air and links his name to summer and to comradeship and to joy—though Whitman becomes for him a symbol of life and though Poe, Whitman's opposite, is found trapped in the underground subjective subway on a very cold, drunken, dark December night, his eyes brim-full of death, we should not—

indeed we must not—be led into the illusion that Crane finds one side of his design to be more praiseworthy than the other, or indeed that he fails to recognize that Whitman contains Poe and Poe, Whitman. Whitman and Poe, light and dark, joy and pain, life and death must—in Crane's scheme of things—finally both coexist and interpenetrate. For his bridge has two towers, each necessary for the support of the other. Only through the interaction of those opposed towers, as he points out at the end of "Atlantis," can the suspension —"One Song, one Bridge of Fire"—be achieved.

Unity seems finally to triumph; and as Crane brings his poem to an end, opposites harmoniously merge: "rainbows ring/ The serpent with the eagle in the leaves." But neither life nor death, neither land nor sea, neither present nor past can long remain fixed in such beautiful, hideous stasis, and in the last line of the poem Crane reminds us of that which we already know. Whispers hover through the cables of his bridge, warning us that already new appositions are forming in the midst of momentary order: From the two blazing towers of Crane's emerged white structure "Whispers *antiphonal* in azure *swing.*"

Hart Crane and the Clown Tradition

by R. W. B. Lewis

About no poem before "Faustus and Helen" did Hart Crane have so much to say in his letters as about "Chaplinesque"—written over a relatively few days in early October, 1921—and no work satisfied him more. It is the most finished of the early poems that, like "Black Tambourine" and "Porphyro in Akron," depict the posture or status of the poet in modern America. But it is much more than that.

The central image in "Chaplinesque" is that of the clown, of the poet as clown, or of the poet, perhaps of Everyman, as Fool. This figure has a long and shifting European history, some of which is profitable to sketch while discussing "Chaplinesque," though only a portion of it was in fact known to Crane. At the same time, it has a continuing American history, and one to which Crane gave fresh life. By presenting the poetic self as a clown of sorts "Chaplinesque" not only voiced part of the essential mood of its epoch, it did as much as any short poem can to establish a mood; the subsequent projections of the artist as comedian—by Wallace Stevens, by E. E. Cummings, later yet by Nathaniel West and Henry Miller—tend to thicken an image and an atmosphere introduced in their generation by Hart Crane.

To writers like these, the figure of the poet, and of the human being, as clown has seemed singularly approprate in a world where the environment—materialistic, industrial, scientific, militant—turns the human being into a grotesque. Crane's "Chaplinesque" thus participates in a comic tradition at once ancient and specifically American—and which, indeed, has reached the point where it is probably the most vital aspect in American writing today. Crane's place in this whole complex development illustrates as well as anything can his great talent for deploying images not only forceful but

Reprinted from the Massachusetts Review, ©1963 The Massachusetts Review, Inc.

roundly representative: a talent that makes him perhaps the most immediately communicative of twentieth-century American poets.

"Chaplinesque" was written soon after Crane had seen and been enthralled by Charlie Chaplin's film, *The Kid*. He announced at once to Gorham Munson that "comedy has never reached a higher level in this country before," and that Chaplin was "a dramatic genius" of "the fabulous sort." Despite such stated enthusiasm and despite the poem's title (Crane's titles were not always so helpful or so cogent), the first readers quite failed, as Crane said, to "get" his "idiom" in it. This must have cost him a grimace or two: he was sure that in "Chaplinesque" he had hit closer to his own idiom than ever before; while the necessary elusiveness of the poet in the contemporary world was the poem's very subject—that, and the hidden, tenuous rewards of the poetic life.

> We make our meek adjustments,
> Contented with such random consolations
> As the wind deposits
> In slithered and too ample pockets.

To one correspondent, who was apparently unable to identify the voice speaking in those lines, Crane explained carefully that he had been "moved to put Chaplin with the poets [of today]; hence the 'we' "; in *The Kid,* he added, Chaplin had "made me feel myself, as a poet...'in the same boat' with him." The comedian's film-gesture thus becomes a metaphor of the poet's shy strategy:

> For we can still love the world, who find
> A famished kitten on the step, and know
> Recesses for it from the fury of the street,
> Or warm torn elbow coverts.

The passage and the one that immediately followed were paraphrased by Crane in a dogged but noteworthy account to his friend William Wright: "Poetry, the human feelings, 'the kitten,' is so crowded out of the humdrum, rushing, mechanical scramble of today that the man who would preserve them must duck and camouflage for dear life to keep them or keep himself from annihilation." The very poetry ducks and camouflages, hugging its vulnerable tenderness to itself:

> We will sidestep and to the final smirk
> Dally the doom of that inevitable thumb
> That slowly chafes its puckered index toward us,
> Facing the dull squint with innocence
> And what surprise!

With almost any of Charlie Chaplin's films in mind, we can assign the "inevitable thumb," first off, to the city cop who looms up so persistently, hand upraised, to block the little tramp, even as Charlie manages for a while and with an ingratiating smirk to skip or sidestep past him. But when the digital allusion leads on from "thumb" to "index," another kind of prohibition enters the poem: the kind a poet has to dally or sidestep; the prohibition, or turning thumbs down upon, the publication and the reading of certain books, as in the Catholic Index.[1] The figure of the poet, the would-be producer of books in modern America, is the alter ego of the slippery, impoverished and obscurely outlaw tramp; for the poet, too, has to seek refuge for his insufficiently nourished sensibility from the fury of contemporary life. He must protect his small creations from the "dull squint" of a suspicious and forbidding public; and to that end, must invent poetic ways to sneak and slide around the obstacles to creative activity. He may, for instance, wear in his verses a disarming smirk and air of innocence, as though to assure the philistine reader that he (the poet) is neither serious nor dangerous. "Chaplinesque" is wreathed in just such a smirk; for it is not only an example of ironic self-deprecation, it is a defense of it, and of the poet's need to have recourse to it.

"And yet," Crane insists,

> And yet these fine collapses are not lies
> More than the pirouettes of any pliant cane;
> Our obsequies are, in a way, no enterprise.

If, like many of his literary ancestors and especially like Herman Melville, Crane was aware of the falsehoods into which cultural circumstance, as well as the very nature of poetic discourse, might

---

[1]Censorship was on Crane's mind—he was outraged at the reported censorship of *The Kid*. "What they could possibly have objected to, I cannot imagine. It must have been some superstition aroused by good acting."

seem to force a poet, he nonetheless affirms that the tactic of verbal trickery and the pose of self-abasement ("these fine collapses") only conceal, they do not violate, the truth perceived. This, on Crane's part, is a characteristic effort to evade even the image of ironic evasion; and the subsequent word "obsequies" represents that same effort in its most compressed form.

Over this word, we may instructively linger. Out of any context, "obsequies" has come to mean funeral rites; and given Crane's reference to "annihilation" in the letter quoted above, one might easily suppose that "Chaplinesque" is ultimately a poem about death: that the doom the poet-clown seeks to postpone is death itself; and that the inevitable thumb, the puckered index and the dull squint add up to a grim portrait of death personified. On the other hand, one might no less easily suppose that what Crane really meant was "obsequiousness," and that "obsequies" is simply an example of a muddled use of language. But it is safer with Crane to assume that he knew what he was doing in his selection of words. In the present case, such muddle as there is comes from medieval Latin—a little of which Crane knew—and he has cunningly exploited it. The original Latin word *obsequium* meant servile compliance; but that meaning eventually got confused with the word *exsequiae*, which does refer to funeral ceremonies. Out of these two initially quite unrelated Latin sources, Crane drew a word with a packed and paradoxical significance. Part of the poem's context—from "meek adjustments" through "smirk" to "fine collapses"—serve to reinvest "obsequies" with its etymological meaning of obsequiousness; another part— "the doom" and "the inevitable thumb"—gives it its familiar contemporary sense of death-and-burial. Under intense contextual pressure, Crane thus suggests that the self-demeaning compliance which the contemporary word demands of the poet or of any sensitive being would, if submitted to, lead only to utter spiritual death.

But this is not the poet's enterprise, neither compliance nor death. His true enterprise is revealed in the final passage of "Chaplinesque," when the enforced smirk of daytime experience becomes moon-changed into a kind of holy laughter:

> The game enforces smirks; but we have seen
> The moon in lonely alleys make
> A grail of laughter of an empty ash-can,
> And through all sounds of gaiety and quest
> Have heard a kitten in the wilderness.

Again, a physical image inspired by Chaplin symbolizes a poetic experience: an experience of beauty that is implicitly religious—or, at least, chivalric—in nature. Crane knew that both Chaplin and his poem about Chaplin might appear to some to be sentimental: "Chaplin may be a sentimentalist, after all," he agreed; "but he carries the theme with such power and universal portent that sentimentality is made to transcend itself into a new kind of tragedy, eccentric, homely and yet brilliant." This was the mode of transcendence Crane aimed at in his closing lines, and that, in my view, he achieved; in a hauntingly melodic vision of the moon transforming a slum-alley ash-can into a silver chalice—of the visionary imagination seeing in the jungle of the actual a vessel of supernal beauty.

But such a moment is as rare as it is precious; the main burden of "Chaplinesque" is still the image of the poet as a shabby and antic tramp, a meekfaced comedian on the run. This was the culmination, poetically speaking it was the perfection, of a series of prior images by which Crane had advanced towards artistic maturity (in a familiar way) by assessing the value of art itself, in the face of a derisive, indifferent or bluntly hostile world; and by appraising his own performance of it. In the interesting mish-mash, "Porphyro in Akron" (winter, 1920), he had made his point in a flagrantly Eliotic manner, by juxtaposing present ugliness with past beauty—the actualities of Akron ("a shift of rubber workers" pressing down South Main Street at dawn, townspeople "using the latest ice-box and buying Fords") and the story of Porphyro, who steals in "with heart on fire" to awaken and escape with the maid Madeline in Keats' "The Eve of St. Agnes." The original Porphyro succeeded valiantly, despite a horde of "hyena foemen and hot-blooded lords"; but the contemporary Porphyro—who is reading "The Eve of St. Agnes" nostalgically in his hotel room—is ignominiously defeated by a noisy, materialistic, utterly uninterested citizenry. In Akron, Porphyro-Crane reads aloud Keats' image of the moon and its magical effects:

> Full on this casement shone the wintry moon,
> And threw warm gules on Madeline's fair breast,
> As down she knelt for heaven's grace and boon...

But he is denied the moon; and his longing to awaken his own fair Madeline—the spirit of poetry itself—seems, under the circumstances, merely ludicrous:

> But look up, Porphyro—your toes
> Are ridiculously tapping
> The spindles at the foot of the bed.
>
> The stars are drowned in slow rain,
> And a hash of noises is slung up from the street.
> You ought, really, to try to sleep,
>
> Even though, in this town, poetry's a
> Bedroom occupation.

Thus, Crane felt, was the contemporary poet made to look absurd by a hash-slinging environment. In "My Grandmother's Love Letters" too, we remember, his best creative efforts were attended by slow rain—the rain that does not so much echo an oppressive world as comment upon his own creative inadequacy, with its "sound of gently pitying laughter." It is the kind of wordlessly sardonic comment the crematory clock would offer, in "Praise for an Urn"; "touching," as it does, "upon our praise of glories proper to the time." The image in "Black Tambourine" had been a good deal more brutal; there, the poet had been associated with the Negro, and, like the Negro, treated alternately as a subservient, tambourine-playing entertainer and as a sort of animal. But probably the most succinct and probing identification of his poetic self before "Chaplinesque" was contained in the lines from "Praise for an Urn":

> The everlasting eyes of Pierrot
> And of Gargantua—the laughter.

The face so composed out of contrasting comic traditions was of course a mask of sorts, a protection against further indignities; and "Chaplinesque" gives final articulation to the poet's felt need to adopt just that face of comedy. Crane's comic sense was natural enough, and it constituted a sizable portion of his temper. His efforts to be explicitly funny in verse were usually almost embarrassingly bad; but he possessed another quality of humor, a tough and toughening amusement which did not spare the so-called dilemma of the modern writer. He was fully aware that there was something preposterous as well as painful in the situation; and something preposterous, too, in the general condition of man amid "the rushing, mechanical scramble of today." He had a ready perception of the lunatic aspect of human conduct, and sometimes gave voice to it in the most athletic of obscenities. At moments like that, he saw himself as belonging in good part to the comic tradition of bawdiness and gusto—of writers like Petronius, Rabelais, Cervantes and Mark Twain, whom he had been reading with great relish (in 1919, especially) and whom he named in a letter telling Gorham Munson that the latter was "too damned serious."

> Humor is the artist's only weapon against the proletariat. Mark Twain knew this, and used it effectively enough, take *1601* for example. Mencken knows it too. And so did Rabelais. ...The modern artist has got to harden himself, and the walls of an ivory tower are too delicate and brittle a coat of mail for substitute. ...I pray for both of us,—let us be keen and humorous scientists. And I would rather act my little tragedy without tears, although I would insist upon a tortured countenance and all sleekness pared off the muscles.

Crane, it is not too much to say, passed his apprenticeship not only by writing poems about poetry, as young men have always done, but by refining on his own specific if complex feeling that the entire poetic enterprise was in one perspective ludicrous to the point of being clownish, and in another serious to the point of being sacred. He came into his own when he was able to see himself, and perhaps any other poet in modern times, as "a clown perhaps, but an aspiring clown"; an image registered in "Chaplinesque" a year before the poem in which those phrases actually occur, Wallace Stevens's "The Comedian as the Letter C." The nature of the achievement is indicated—more, it is explained—by some of the mingling contradictions just observed: The "fine collapses" and the "grail of laughter" in "Chaplinesque"; Pierrot's eyes and Gargantua's laughter; the "humorous scientist" (in the letter above) and the "tortured countenance"; clownishness and aspiration. The presence of these fertile contradictions in Crane's mind and imagination, in his letters and poetry, show how remarkably, though only half-knowingly, Crane from what he regarded as a provincial hinterland had come into tune with one of the major traditions of Europe.

II

The pirouetting clown in "Chaplinesque" is taken first, of course, from the little tramp invented by the Anglo-American comedian, Charlie Chaplin. But in the range of his wistful aspiration and in the mythic overtones of the final stanza (with its hint of the grail-quest), he is also the figure revered in France as Charlot—a personality saluted in French writing many times before "Chaplinesque," and twice by the surrealist poet Louis Aragon; a *persona,* a myth incarnate, a great illumination of the age and (as someone said) the creator of "a sublime beauty, a new laughter." This was not exactly Charlie Chaplin, it was a Gallic enlargement on him; the screen image of Chaplin underwent a great extension in the Parisian imagination. The French identified Charlot by grafting a native comic tradition onto the original character. Both Charlot and the native tradition were made known to Crane in letters from abroad, especially those from Matthew Josephson.

The tradition was that of the clown known most recently in France as Pierrot. Chief among the literary contributions to that tradition had been the twenty-three "Pierrot poems" in a volume of verse called *L'Imitation de Notre Dame La Lune,* published in 1886, the year before his death, by the then twenty-six-year-old poet Jules Laforgue. The lines converge. In the fall of 1920, Crane acquired from Paris volumes of the poetry of Laforgue, and of Arthur Rimbaud and Charles Vildrac. During the following summer and with help from more expert linguists, Crane translated three of Laforgue's sixteen "Locutions des Pierrots" ("Speeches"—perhaps "Soliloquies"—"of the Pierrots"; Laforgue sometimes spoke of Pierrots in the plural, as though they constituted a specific group, like the American Beatniks). A few months after that, when Crane came to write "Chaplinesque," he produced a remarkable fusion of images: his own image of the poet as tenderly comic and his own portrait of Chaplin; the Charlot of French commentary and the Pierrot of Laforgue; a portion of Whitman's comic hero; and something far older than any of these. The result is a figure of profoundly representative significance. [...]

The paradigm, however, came to Crane at first through the mediation of T. S. Eliot and (less so) of Ezra Pound. As an undergraduate at Harvard, Eliot had discovered Laforgue in Arthur Symons' book, *The Symbolist Movement in French Literature;* he went on to write a number of poems that he himself located "sous la ligne de Laforgue." Eliot was for some years intrigued to the point of obsession (as he much later acknowledged) by a number of elements in Laforgue's work, including Laforgue's ironical manipulation of older legends and stories like those of Parsifal and Hamlet; but he was perhaps especially drawn to the Pierrot poems, to their verbal and rhythmical innovations and to the rueful imagery he could find in them—imagery representing the modern sensibility hesitating and bemused among the perplexities, erotic and otherwise, of modern life. Something of this hovers in such Laforguian poems of Eliot's as "Conversation Galante," "Portrait of a Lady," and "La Figlia che Piange"; and it reaches full statement in "The Love Song of J. Alfred Prufrock"—"the great example of the Laforguian poem in English," according to Malcolm Cowley. Here the lover's wistfulness is less contaminated by self-defense and his gesture even more ineffectual than in Laforgue; Prufrock accepts his role not as Prince Hamlet but as a Polonius who is only a step away from being the court's comic relief—

> Full of high sentence, but a bit obtuse;
> At times, indeed, almost ridiculous—
> Almost, at times, the Fool.[2]

This is obviously a portrait of the artist as well as the confession of a lover; and if the capitalised word "Fool" suggests momentarily some paradoxical superiority in either role—as in the medieval Fool of Love—it is not, I think, a hint that long survives. [...]

Throughout his Laforguian phase, Crane had been a good deal more vulnerable than, say, Eliot had been to diametrically opposite poetic persuasions—including a diametrically opposite comic image. Eliot could beautifully absorb and be absorbed by Laforgue, because the latter's witty self-deprecation could add salt to Eliot's incipient and, as it would develop, profound strain of Christian humility. But while Hart Crane was congenitally modest, and although he too took on for a while the mask of self-derision, there was in him no great tendency towards Christian humility—not, anyhow, of that dark Jansenistic kind that Eliot stood for. Unlike Eliot, Crane was always responsive to the poetry of braggadocio. In his view, the doleful eyes of Pierrot were intended, not to replace but to blend with the laughter of Gargantua. In somewhat simplistic literary terms, the spirit of Jules Laforgue mingled in Crane's imagination with a

[2]T.S. Eliot, "The Love Song of J. Alfred Prufock" in *Collected Poems 1909-1962*. Reprinted by permission of Harcourt Brace Jovanovich, Inc. and Faber and Faber, Ltd.

spirit at once more robust and more American—to which we can give the name of Walt Whitman.

He was aided in this regard by his own ignorance. Certain educated friends, Crane wrote Tate in 1922, had lamented the fact that he (Crane) had been taken to Laforgue "without having placed [him] in relation to most of the older 'classics,' which I haven't read.... Nonetheless, my affection for Laforgue is none the less genuine for being led to him through Pound and Eliot than it would have been through Baudelaire." If he knew rather less than his educated friends about the French literary tradition, he knew or perhaps guessed rather more about the American; and "Chaplinesque," as I have said, participates in a specifically American comic tradition— one that takes its principal start with Whitman, and one that, given fresh impetus by Hart Crane, has continued after him to the point where it is a remarkably vital aspect of current American writing.

III

[...] It is Whitman's language that performs the function of clown, and no one put the case more precisely than Whitman himself. "Considering language, then, as some mighty potentate," he wrote in an early prose passage, "into the majestic audience-hall of the monarch ever enters a personage like one of Shakespeare's clowns, and takes possession there and plays a part even in the stateliest ceremonies. Such is Slang, or indirection...." Most of Whitman's long-debated verbal inventions belonged to his comic purpose; and his statement to Traubel in the late days at Camden that "I sometimes think the *Leaves* is only a language experiment" is almost exactly parallel to his statement during the same period that "I pride myself on being a real humorist underneath everything else." Nor was the allusion to Shakespeare's clowns merely vague, or grandiose; for Whitman's comedy of language proceeded in a manner very close to Shakespeare's comedy of action. In Shakespeare, the comic dimension provides an indispensable corrective by parodying the serious or tragic element so as to cast the latter in an ambiguous—hence a truer—light. In Whitman, it is not simply the slang, it is the audible slang in the midst of "the stateliest ceremonies" of speech that provides the comedy. We hear not only blab and chuff and drib and hap and lag and swash and yawp—we hear those blunt verbal bullets as they ricochet off the stately and pretentious sides of words like presidentiad and cartouche and ambulanza and imperturbe and lumine and sonambula. If we add to this the coiling unconventionality of Whitman's rhythm, with its capacity to leap or to relax, to startle or assuage at will, we are close to the heart of Whitman's comedy—perhaps to the heart of any authentic comic verse.

But there is another exceedingly significant aspect to Whitman's comedy, and one that comes into prominence in the late eighteen-fifties. In the poems of 1855 and 1856, both human nature and the creative enterprise were subjected to a sort of cheerful curative mockery only occasionally darkened by real doubt. In the 1860 edition, a new note appeared: new, that is, in Whitman and in American poetry, but remarkably similar to the note struck earlier in France. Whitman's comic sensibility, while not less prevalent than before, had deepened into a mysterious and melancholy sense of his own moral and artistic inadequacy. Some of the 1860 poems reflect a dolorousness like that of the French pantomimists; some a half-buried suicidal impulse like that of Jean-Gaspard Deburau; and some a sense of creative frustration that anticipates Laforgue. Pierrot joined Gargantua in these poems; and the junction is nowhere more impressive than in "As I Ebb'd with the Ocean of Life." Here, in a poem largely about psychic and artistic annihilation, Whitman introduced a supreme example of the poet's self-derision —an image of the poet and all his works mocked and derided by what Whitman called the Real Me:

> Withdrawn far, mocking me with mock-congratulatory signs and
> bows,
> With peals of distant ironical laughter at every word I have
> written,
> Pointing in silence to these songs, and then to the sand beneath.

The Real Me was Whitman's "Oversoul"—his divine muse. In the lines quoted, we have Whitman's version of the poet as fool: the poet as Everyman in the presence of his special God; of the way the most ambitious of human efforts looks in the mocking perspective of divinity.

Hart Crane presumably came to Whitman, as all too many readers have come to him, by an over-simplified route: via those prophetic or patriotic or "cosmic" chants behind which the best of Whitman lay hidden till recently, and on the basis of which Whitman earned a quite unjustified reputation for humorlessness. It is the cosmic Whitman whose hand Crane would clasp in the "Cape Hatteras" section of *The Bridge*. But Crane was always a tough-minded judge of poetry, and no less of Whitman's poetry. "You've heard me roar at too many of his lines," he reminded Tate in 1930, "to doubt that I can spot his worst, I'm sure." Something of Whitman's best—his verbal sporting, for example, and his sense of the irresistible flow of experience—is reflected elsewhere in *The Bridge*. Crane's imaginative association with Whitman appears to have grown abruptly with the first conception of *The Bridge*, in 1923. But it also appears that at some earlier stage Crane was infected, in the secretive manner of poetic influence, by Whitman's conception of the poet as something between a comedian and a divinity (a conception that expressed itself mainly in Whitman's writing up to 1860). Even in "Chaplinesque," there is a sort of implicit capering, almost a bumptiousness: a quality that, for lack of a better adjective and to distinguish it from the Gallic irony that it pushes against, we can only call American; which, for Crane at this time, is the same as to call it Whitmanian.

The matter is interestingly beclouded because of Whitman's diversity, including the diversity of his comic spirit. The force of Whitman's example is equally felt in another account of the poet as clown, much longer and more intricate than "Chaplinesque" and completed a year after Crane's poem: "The Comedian as the Letter C," by another of Whitman's literary grand-nephews, Wallace Stevens. But here the example works to a different effect. The effort of Steven's poet, whose failure is comically narrated, is an effort to do what Whitman has done: to render in poetry the hard, resistant and multiple reality of America. The surface of Stevens' poem is preternaturally alive with verbal comedy of a recognizably Whitman kind: an extraordinary interplay of the stately, the colloquial, the boldly invented, the bizarre, the imported. But the story told in that dazzling language belongs to comedy of a different but equally familiar order—the comedy of ruefully admitted defeat, the mask of witty self-deprecation. [...]

On a personal level, Crane adopted the mask of comedy in his poem to the same end that Stevens did in "The Comedian as the Letter C": simply as a device for poetic survival; in order to go on writing poetry in a society that despised it or a world (an America) not susceptible to it. But the comic role, for Crane in his career and within the poem, reaped unexpectedly large rewards. It was just because he accepted the role of comedian that the joint figure in "Chaplinesque" arrives at a sort of sacred vision:

> The game enforces smirks. But we have seen
> The moon in lonely alleys make
> A grail of laughter of an empty ash-can.

Crane's major development is here in small: from the game-enforcing smirk to the grail of laughter; from the comic spirit to the religious spirit; from clownish consent to overwhelming visionary affirmation. "Chaplinesque" is in this sense the touchstone of Crane's early career; and there is an organic continuity between it and the poem he began four months after its publication, "For the Marriage of Faustus and Helen"—in which the irony still present in "Chaplinesque" is altogether transcended. At the same time, on a level higher and broader than the personal, "Chaplinesque" contains insinuations—one dare not use a stronger word—vaster even than those claimed by Henry Miller.

They are insinuations about an epochal overturn in cultural and spiritual history; and their flickering presence in "Chaplinesque" is due to Crane's skill in fusing several different and even contradictory comic traditions. The nineteenth century French clown, mournful and agile, is re-animated in "Chaplinesque" through the immediate influence of Laforgue and Eliot; but he is re-animated in tonalities that at the same time recover a good deal of the medieval fool of which Pierrot had been a scrupulously truncated version. With some assistance from both the bumptious and the self-doubting Whitman, and with even more assistance from his own imagination, Crane at once Americanized and transvaluated the clown of Laforgue, and by a poetic method at once ironic and ritualistic. The resulting figure does participate in the long modern view of art as derided, and humanity as debased; but he also participates in a much more ancient view. In his very shabbiness and clownishness, as he submits to the transfiguring moon, he represents for a second that moment just prior to an immense inversion of values whereby the humble shall be exalted, the foolish become the source of wisdom, and the world renew itself by honoring the ridiculous, the disgraced, the outlaw.

If there is one moment above all others that is truly significant in European and American literature during the past few decades, it is a moment of just that sort—one marked by a continuing exploration of the lowest of the low to find and expose in it elements of the highest of the high, to dig in the human debris for intimations of mythic grandeur or of sanctity. This is what happens so fleetingly in "Chaplinesque," when the little tramp suddenly makes out by moonlight, in the actual and spiritual slums of the modern world, the holy grail in an empty ash-can; and it would happen again on an incomparably larger scale in *The Bridge*. It is a feat of the visionary imagination by a poet for whom *la lune* really was, once more, *Notre Dame*, an object to be imitated, revered and trusted in. But the grail is "a grail of laughter"; and it is by an extension of comedy that Crane's own bedraggled Harlequin becomes again the Fool of Love in the presence of grace. Just so, in medieval romance, it was the most clownish and uncouth of King Arthur's Knights, Sir Percival, who was elected to discover the sacred vessel and fulfill the aspiration of the age.

The Shadow of a Myth

by Alan Trachtenberg

Oh, grassy glades! oh, ever vernal endless landscapes in
the soul; in ye,—men yet may roll, like young horses in
new morning clover; and for some few fleeting moments,
feel the cool dew of the life immortal on them. Would to
God these blessed calms would last.

HERMAN MELVILLE, *Moby Dick* (1851)

In the winter of 1923, Hart Crane, a twenty-four-year-old poet
living in Cleveland, announced plans to write a long poem called
The Bridge. It was to be an epic, a "mystical synthesis of America."[1] Crane had just completed *For the Marriage of Faustus and
Helen,* a poem which sought to infuse modern Faustian culture (the
term was Spengler's, designating science and restless searching)
with love of beauty and religious devotion. Now, confirmed in his
commitment to visionary poetry and feeling "directly connected

[1] *The Bridge* was first published by The Black Sun Press, Paris, 1930; this edition
included three photographs by Walker Evans. The lines quoted throughout this
chapter are from *The Complete Poems of Hart Crane* (New York, 1933), ed., Waldo
Frank; references in the chapter are to *The Letters of Hart Crane* (New York, 1952),
ed., Brom Weber. The critical works I have profited from most in my reading of
The Bridge are, Allen Tate, "Hart Crane," *Reactionary Essays* (New York, 1936);
Yvor Winters, "The Significance of *The Bridge,*" *In Defense of Reason* (New York,
1947), 575-605; R. P. Blackmur, "New Thresholds, New Anatomies: Notes on a Text
of Hart Crane," *Language of Gesture* (New York, 1952) [See this book, p. 49].

with Whitman," Crane prepared for an even greater effort: to compose the myth of America. The poem would answer "the complete renunciation symbolized in *The Waste Land*," published the year before. Eliot had used London Bridge as a passageway for the dead, on which "each man fixed his eyes before his feet." Crane replied by projecting his myth of affirmation upon Brooklyn Bridge.

In the spring of 1923, Hart Crane left his father's home in Cleveland, and from then until his suicide in 1932, lived frequently in Brooklyn Heights, close to "the most beautiful Bridge of the world." He crossed the bridge often, alone and with friends, sometimes with lovers: "the cables enclosing us and pulling us upward in such a dance as I have never walked and never can walk with another." Part III of *Faustus and Helen* had been set in the shadow of the bridge, "where," Crane wrote, "the edge of the bridge leaps over the edge of the street." In the poem the bridge is the "Capped arbiter of beauty in this street," "the ominous lifted arm/ That lowers down the arc of Helen's brow." Its "curve" of "memory" transcends "all stubble streets."

Crane tried to keep Brooklyn Bridge always before him, in eye as well as in mind. In April 1924 he wrote: "I am now living in the shadow of the bridge." He had moved to 110 Columbia Heights, into the very house, and later, the very room occupied fifty years earlier by Roebling. Like the crippled engineer, the poet was to devote his most creative years to the vision across the harbor. In his imagination the shadow of the bridge deepened into the shadow of a myth.

I

The Bridge, Crane wrote, "carries further the tendencies manifest in 'F and H.'" These tendencies included a neo-Platonic conception of a "reality" beyond the evidence of the senses. The blind chaos of

Brom Weber, *Hart Crane: A Biographical and Critical Study* (New York, 1948); L. S. Dembo, *Hart Crane's Sanskrit Charge: A Study of The Bridge* (Ithaca, 1960); Sister M. Bernetta Quinn, *The Metamorphic Tradition in Modern Poetry* (New Brunswick, 1955), 130-68; Stanley K. Coffman, "Symbolism in *The Bridge*," *PMLA*, Vol. LXVI (March 1951), 65-77; John Unterecker, "The Architecture of The Bridge," *Wisconsin Studies in Contemporary Literature*, Vol. III (Spring-Summer 1962), 5-20 [See this book, p. 80].

sensation in the modern city apparently denies this transcendent reality, but a glimpse of it is available, through ecstasy, to the properly devout poet. Helen represents the eternal, the unchanging; Faustus, the poet's aspiration; and the "religious gunman" of Part III, spirit of the Dionysian surrender (sexual as well as aesthetic) necessary for a vision of the eternal. The threefold image constitutes what Kenneth Burke has called an "aesthetic myth"—a modern substitute for "religious myth."[2] The poet's impulse toward beauty is a mark of divinity. A part of the myth, and another "tendency" of the poem, is what Crane called its "fusion of our time with the past." The past is represented by the names Faustus and Helen; the present by the data of the poem: the "memoranda," the "baseball scores," and "stock quotations" of Part I; the jazz dance of Part II; the warplanes of Part III. The present fails to live up to the past. But the poet, a "bent axle of devotion," keeps his "lone eye" riveted upon Helen; he offers her "one inconspicuous, glowing orb of praise." At the end, in communion with the "religious gunman," he accepts and affirms past and present, the "years" whose "hands" are bloody; he has attained "the height/ The imagination spans beyond despair."

The idea of a bridge is explicit in the closing image; earlier, as I have indicated, it had appeared in fact, leaping over the street. In the projected poem, it will leap far beyond the street, but its function will be similar: an emblem of the eternal, providing a passage between the Ideal and the transitory sensations of history, a way to unify them.

In the earliest lines written for the new poem, the bridge was the location of an experience like that which ends *Faustus and Helen:* the imagination spanning beyond despair.

> And midway on that structure I would stand
> One moment, not as diver, but with arms
>
> That open to project a disk's resilience
> Winding the sun and planets in its face.
>
> * * *
>
> Expansive center, pure moment and electron
> That guards like eyes that must look always down
> In reconcilement of our chains and ecstasy

---

[2] *A Rhetoric of Motives* (New York, 1950), 203.

> Crashing manifoldly on us as we hear
> The looms, the wheels, the whistles in concord
> Tethered and welded as the hills of dawn...[3]

Somewhat like Wordsworth on Westminster Bridge, here the poet experiences harmony, his troubled self annihilated in a moment of worship. Subsequently Crane developed a narrative to precede this experience. In the narrative, or myth, the poet, like Faustus, was to be the hero, and his task a quest—not for Helen but her modern equivalent: Brooklyn Bridge.

Although the bridge lay at the end of quest, it was not, like the grail in *The Waste Land,* simply a magical object occupying a given location. It does not wait to be found, but to be created. That is, it represents not an external "thing," but an internal process, an act of consciousness. The bridge is not "found" in "Atlantis," the final section of the poem, but "made" throughout the poem. In "Atlantis" what has been "made" is at last recognized and named: "O Thou steeled Cognizance." Its properties are not magical but conceptual: it is a "Paradigm" of love and beauty, the eternal ideas which lie behind and inform human experience.

If we follow the poet's Platonic idea, to "think" the bridge is to perceive the unity and wholeness of history. In the poem, history is not chronological nor economic nor political. Crane wrote: "History and fact, location, etc., all have to be transfigured into abstract form that would almost function independently of its subject matter." Crane intended to re-create American history according to a pattern he derived from its facts. His version of American history has nothing in common with the ceremonial parade of Founding Fathers and bearded generals of popular culture. The poet's idea, and especially his distinction between history and "abstract form," is closer to what the anthropologist Mircea Eliade describes as the predominant ontology of archaic man—the myth of "eternal return." According to Eliade, the mind of archaic man sought to resist history—the line of "irreversible events"—by re-creating, in his rituals, the pre-temporal events of his mythology, such as the creation of the world. Unable to abide a feeling of uniqueness, early men identified, in their rituals, the present with the

[3]The first four lines are from "Lines sent to Wilbur Underwood, February, 1923," and the remainder from "Worksheets, Spring, 1923," in Brom Weber, *Hart Crane,* 425-6.

mythic past, thus abolishing the present as an autonomous moment of time. All events and actions "acquire a value," writes Eliade, "and in so doing become real, because they participate, after one fashion or another, in a reality that transcends them." The only "real" events are those recorded in mythology, which in turn become models for imitation, "paradigmatic gestures." All precious stones are precious because of thunder from heaven; all sacred buildings are sacred because they are built over the divine Center of the world; all sexual acts repeat the primordial act of creation. A non-precious stone, a non-sacred building, a non-sanctified act of sex—these are not real. History, as distinct from myth, consists of such random acts and events, underived from an archetype; therefore history is not real and must be periodically "annulled." By imitating the "paradigmatic gesture" in ritual, archaic men transported themselves out of the realm of the random, of "irreversible events," and "re-actualized" the mythic epoch in which the original archetypal act occurred. Hence for the primitive as for the mystic, time has no lasting influence: "events repeat themselves because they imitate an archetype." Like the mystic, the primitive lives in a "continual present."[4]

The Bridge is a sophisticated and well-wrought version of the archaic myth of return. The subject matter of the poem is drawn from legends about American history: Columbus, Pocahontas, Cortez, De Soto, Rip Van Winkel, the gold-rush, the whalers; and from contemporary reality: railroads, subways, warplanes, office buildings, cinemas, burlesque queens. Woven among these strands are allusions to world literature: the Bible, Plato, Marlowe, Shakespeare, Blake; and most important, to American artists: Whitman, Melville, Poe, Dickinson, Isadora Duncan. The action of the poem comprises through its fifteen sections, one waking day, from dawn in "Harbor Dawn," to midnight in "Atlantis." Through the device of dream, that single day includes vast stretches of time and space: a subway ride in the morning extends to a railroad journey to the Mississippi, then back in time, beyond De Soto, to the primeval world of the Indians,[5] then forward to the West of the pioneers. In

[4]*Cosmos and History: The Myth of the Eternal Return* ([New York,] 1959), 4, 90.

[5]Crane's conception of the Indian in "The Dance"—in the "Powhatan's Daughter" section of *The Bridge*—seems to owe something to Waldo Frank's *Our America* (1919). In his personal copy, Crane had underlined the following passage: "His

a sense, the entire day is a dream; the poet journeys through his own consciousness toward an awakening. He seeks to learn the meaning of American history which, in so far as the history is inseparable from his own memories, is the meaning of himself: Cathay, which designates the end of the journey, or the discovery of a new world, Crane wrote, is "an attitude of spirit," a self-discovery.

Thus in no sense of the word is *The Bridge* a historical poem. Its mode is myth. Its aim is to overcome history, to abolish time and the autonomy of events, and to show that all meaningful events partake of an archetype: the quest for a new world. In this regard the importance of Walt Whitman requires special notice. For among the many influences that worked upon Crane, few were as persuasive as Whitman's.[6]

In "Passage to India," we have seen, Whitman identified the quest for wholeness—the "rondure"—as the chief theme and motive of American life. In Whitman's version of history, man was expelled from Eden into time: "Wandering, yearning, curious, with restless explorations,/ With questions, baffled, formless, feverish." Divided into separate and warring nations, at odds with nature,

---

[the Indian's] magic is not, as in most religions, the tricky power of men over their gods. It lies in the power of Nature herself to yield corn from irrigation, to yield meat in game. The Indian therefore does not pray to his God for direct favors. He prays for harmony between himself and the mysterious forces that surround him: of which he is one. For he has learned that from this harmony comes health." Hart Crane Collection, Columbia University Library.

[6]A word should be said about the powerful influence upon Crane's sensibility— and his plans for *The Bridge*—of the Russian mystic, P. D. Ouspensky, and his work, *Tertium Organum: The Third Canon of Thought, A Key to the Enigmas of the World,* tr. Nicholas Bessaraboff and Claude Bragdon (New York, 1922). Crane read this book early in his creative life—possibly in 1920 (an earlier edition had been published that year). It seems very likely that he derived most of his philosophical idealism, and a good deal of his language and imagery, from Ouspensky. A case could be made for the fact that he interpreted Whitman in Ouspenskian terms—as a mystic who saw through the world to a higher reality. "Higher consciousness" was a typical Ouspenskian term. So was "vision," in its literal and metaphoric senses. Plato's parable of the cave, in which most men sit in darkness, hidden from the truth, is the unstated assumption of Ouspensky's book. The book attempts to place the mystical experience of light and oneness on accountable grounds; its method is to prove by analogies that the true or noumenal world lies beyond space and time, beyond the capacity of the normal mind to perceive. Limited to a three-dimensional view of the world (a consequence of education and bad science), the mind normally interprets what are really flashes from the true world as things moving in time. In truth, however, the "whole" is motionless and self-contained;

historical man was a sufferer. Now, however, in modern America, the end of suffering was in sight. The connecting works of engineers —the Suez Canal, the Atlantic Cable, the Union Pacific Railroad— had introduced a new stage; the separate geographical parts of the world were now linked into one system. The physical labors of engineers, moreover, were spiritual food for the poet; the "true son of God" recognized that by uniting East and West such works completed Columbus's voyage. Now it was clear: The "hidden" purpose of history was the brotherhood of races that would follow the bridges and canals of modern technology.

Crane was not interested principally in Whitman's social vision, but in his conception of poetry as the final step in the restoration of man's wholeness. Not the engineer nor the statesman nor the captain of industry, but the poet was the true civilizer. Translating engineering accomplishments into ideas, the poet completed the work of history, and prepared for the ultimate journey to "more than India," the journey to the Soul: "thou actual Me." Thus the poet recognized that all of history culminated in self-discovery; and he would lead the race out of its bondage in time and space to that moment of consciousness in which all would seem one. That moment of "return" would redeem history by abolishing it. In short, Crane inherited from Whitman the belief in the poet's function to judge history from the point of view of myth.

Whitman himself appears in "Cape Hatteras," which represents a critical phase of the action of *The Bridge*. In the preceding sections, the poet had set out to find Pocahontas, the spirit of the land. With Rip Van Winkle his Muse of Memory, and the Twentieth

---

time itself is man's illusion: "The idea of time recedes with the expansion of consciousness." The true world being "invisible" to normal sight, it is necessary to cultivate the inner eye. This can be accomplished only by exercising the outer eye to its fullest capacities—to strain vision until familiar things seem unfamiliar, new, and exciting. Then we might penetrate the "hidden meaning in everything." Then we will see the "invisible threads" which bind all things together—"with the entire world, with all the past and all the future." It should be noted that an idea of a bridge is implicit here—a metaphoric bridge which represents the true unity of all things. Moreover, Ouspensky held that art, especially poetry, was a means to attain this metaphoric bridge. To do so, however, poetry must develop a new language: "New parts of speech are necessary, an infinite number of new words." The function of poetry is to reveal the "invisible threads," to translate them into language which will "bind" the reader to the new perceptions. It is quite easy to see how attractive these ideas were to Hart Crane's poetic program. See Weber, 150-63.

Century Limited his vehicle, he moved westward out of the city to the Mississippi, the river of time. Borne backward on the stream, he found the goddess, joined her dance of union with nature and thus entered the archetype. Now he must return to the present, to bridge the personal vision of the goddess and the actuality of modern America. An older sailor (possibly Melville) in a South Street bar and an apparition of old clipper ships from Brooklyn Bridge in "Cutty Sark," are reminders of the quest. But the old has lost its direction; the age requires a renewal.

"Cape Hatteras" is the center of the span that leaps from Columbus to Brooklyn Bridge. The sea voyages are now done, the rondure accomplished. Now, a complacent age of stocks, traffic, and radios has lost sight of its goal; instead of a bridge, the age has created "a labyrinth submersed/ Where each sees only his dim past reversed." War, not peace and brotherhood, has succeeded the engineers, and flights into space are undertaken, not by poets but by war planes. "Cape Hatteras" poses the key questions of the poem: "What are the grounds for hope that modern history will not destroy itself?" "Where lies redemption?" "Is there an alternative to the chaos of the City?"

The answers are in Whitman's "sea eyes," "bright with myth." He alone has kept sight of the abstract form, the vision of ultimate integration. His perspective is geological; he stands apart, with "something green/ Beyond all sesames of science." Whitman envisioned the highest human possibilities within the facts of chaos. It was he who "stood up and flung the span on even wing/ Of that great Bridge, our Myth, whereof I sing." He is a presence: "Familiar, thou, as mendicants in public places." He has kept faith, even among the most disastrous circumstances of betrayal. With his help, the flight into space might yet become "that span of consciousness thou'st named/ The Open Road."

"Cape Hatteras" introduces the violence and the promise, the despair and the hope, of modern life. It argues for the effectiveness of ideals, for the power of Utopia over history. The poet places his hand in Whitman's, and proceeds upon his quest. Returning from the sea in "Southern Cross," he searches for love in "National Winter Garden" and "Virginia," for community and friendship in "Quaker Hill," and for art in "The Tunnel." He finds nothing but betrayal: the strip tease dancer burlesques Pocahontas, the office girl is a pallid Mary, the New Avalon Hotel and golf course mock the New England tradition, and the tunnel crucifies Poe. But throughout, the poet's hand is in Whitman's, and at last, having survived the terrors of "The Tunnel," he arrives at the bridge.

II

Brooklyn Bridge lay at the end of the poet's journey, the pledge of a "cognizance" that would explain and redeem history. To reach the bridge, to attain its understanding, the poet suffered the travail of hell. But he emerges unscathed, and ascends the span. In "Atlantis" he reaches Cathay, the symbol of sublime consciousness. The entire action implies a steady optimism that no matter how bad history may be, the bridge will reward the struggle richly. Such is its promise in the opening section of the poem, "Proem: To Brooklyn Bridge."

> How many dawns, chill from his rippling rest
> The seagull's wings shall dip and pivot him,
> Shedding white rings of tumult, building high
> Over the chained bay waters Liberty—
>
> Then, with inviolate curve, forsake our eyes
> As apparitional as sails that cross
> Some page of figures to be filed away;
> —Till elevators drop us from our day...
>
> I think of cinemas, panoramic sleights
> With multitudes bent toward some flashing scene
> Never disclosed, but hastened to again,
> Foretold to other eyes on the same screen;
>
> And Thee, across the harbor, silver-paced
> As though the sun took step of thee, yet left
> Some motion ever unspent in thy stride,—
> Implicitly thy freedom staying thee!
>
> Out of some subway scuttle, cell or loft
> A bedlamite speeds to thy parapets,
> Tilting there momently, shrill shirt ballooning,
> A jest falls from the speechless caravan.
>
> Down Wall, from girder into street noon leaks,
> A rip-tooth of the sky's acetylene;

All afternoon the cloud-flown derricks turn...
Thy cables breathe the North Atlantic still.

And obscure as that heaven of the Jews,
Thy guerdon...Accolade thou dost bestow
Of anonymity time cannot raise:
Vibrant reprieve and pardon thou dost show.

O harp and altar, of the fury fused,
(How could mere toil align thy choiring strings!)
Terrific threshold of the prophet's pledge,
Prayer of pariah, and the lover's cry,—

Again the traffic lights that skim thy swift
Unfractioned idiom, immaculate sigh of stars,
Beading thy path—condense eternity:
And we have seen night lifted in thine arms.

Under thy shadow by the piers I waited;
Only in darkness is thy shadow clear.
The City's fiery parcels all undone,
Already snow submerges an iron year...

O Sleepless as the river under thee,
Vaulting the sea, the prairies' dreaming sod,
Unto us lowliest sometime sweep, descend
And of the curveship lend a myth to God.

The setting of "Proem" in the harbor and lower Manhattan area is distinct, though the point of view shifts a good deal within this area, from a long view of the Bay and the Statue of Liberty, to an office in a skyscraper, down an elevator into the street, into a dark movie house, and then to the sun-bathed bridge. The view of the bridge also changes, from "across the harbor," in which the sun appears to be walking up the diagonal stays, to the promenade and towers as the bedlamite "speeds to thy parapets." Later the point of view is under the bridge, in its shadow. The shifting perspectives secure the object in space; there is no question that it is a bridge across a river between two concretely realized cities.

At the same time, the bridge stands apart from its setting, a world of its own. A series of transformations in the opening stanzas bring us to it. We begin with a seagull at dawn—a specific occurrence, yet eternal ("How many dawns"). The bird's wings leave our eyes as an "inviolate curve" (meaning unprofaned as well as unbroken) to become "apparitional as sails" (apparitional implies "epiphanal" as well as spectral and subjective). Then, in a further transmutation, they become a "page of figures." As the wings leave our eyes, so does the page: "filed away." Then, elevators "drop us" from the bird to the street. In the shift from bird to page to elevator, we have witnessed the transformation of a curve into a perpendicular, of an organism into a mechanism—wings into a list of numbers. "Filed away," the vision of the curve, identified with "sails" and voyages, has been forgotten ("How many" times?), like a page of reckonings. The quest for a vision of bird and sails resumes in the cinema, but, as in Plato's cave, the "flashing scene" is "never disclosed." Then, the eye finds a permanent vision of the curve in the "silver-paced" bridge.

The bridge has emerged from a counterpoint of motions (bird vs. elevator; sails vs. "multitudes bent") as an image of self-containment. Surrounded by a frantic energy ("some flashing scene... hastened to again"; "A bedlamite speeds...") the bridge is aloof; its motions express the sun. Verbs like drop, tilt, leak, submerge describe the city; the bridge is rendered by verbs like turn, breathe, lift, sweep. Established in its own visual plane, with a motion of its own, the bridge is prepared, by stanza seven, to receive the epithets of divinity addressed to it. Like Mary, it embraces, reprieves, and pardons. Its cables and towers are "harp and altar." The lights of traffic along its roadway, its "unfractioned idiom," seem to "condense eternity." Finally, as night has extinguished the cities and thereby clarified the shadow of the bridge, its true meaning becomes clear: its "curveship" represents an epiphany, a myth to manifest the divine. Such at least is what the poet implores the bridge to be.

In "Proem," Brooklyn Bridge achieves its status in direct opposition to the way of life embodied in the cities. Bridge and city are opposing and apparently irreconcilable forms of energy. This opposition, which is equivalent to that between myth and history, continues through the remainder of the poem; it creates the local tensions of each section, and the major tension of the entire work.

This tension is best illustrated in "The Tunnel," the penultimate section of the poem. After a fruitless search for reality in a Times Square theater, the protagonist boards a subway as "the quickest promise home." The short ride to Brooklyn Bridge is a nightmare of banal conversations and advertisements: "To brush some new presentiment of pain." The images are bizarre: "and love/ A burnt match skating in a urinal." Poe appears, his head "swinging from the swollen strap," his eyes "Below the toothpaste and the dandruff ads." The crucified poet, dragged to his death through the streets of Baltimore, "That last night on the ballot rounds," represents how society uses its visionary devotees of beauty.[7]

If the "Proem" promised deliverance, "The Tunnel" seems to deliver damnation; its chief character is a Daemon, whose "hideous laughter" is "the muffled slaughter of a day in birth." The Daemon's joke is that he has inverted the highest hopes and brightest prophecies: "O cruelly to inoculate the brinking dawn/ With antennae toward worlds that glow and sink." The presiding spirit in the tunnel, he represents the transvaluation of ideals in modern America.

At the end of "The Tunnel," the protagonist leaves the subway and prepares, at the water's edge, to ascend the bridge. His faith, like Job's, is unimpaired. Job endured the assault of Satan, uttered no complaints, and in the end profited by an enlightened understanding, albeit an irrational one, of the power of his God. It is

[7]It is wrong to assume that Poe and Whitman oppose each other in this work—one gloomy, the other cheerful. Poe in the tunnel does indeed represent the actuality of art in modern life, but the image is not meant to contradict Whitman's vision —perhaps to countervail it, and by so doing, to reinforce its strength. According to his friends—especially Samuel Loveman—Crane loved both poets, although he derived more substance for his art from Whitman (and Melville). To make this point may also be a good occasion to recall that Whitman himself was powerfully drawn to Poe. There is some evidence they knew each other as newspaper men in New York in the 1840's. Whitman was the only major American writer to attend the dedication of a Poe memorial in Baltimore in 1875, and sat on the platform as Mallarmé's famous poem was being read. In *Specimen Days,* Whitman wrote that Poe's verse expressed the "sub-currents" of the age; his poems were "lurid dreams." Thus, Poe presented an "entire contrast and contradiction" to the image of "perfect and noble life" which Whitman himself had tried to realize. But it is significant that Whitman concedes morbidity to be as true of the times as health. He tells of a dream he once had of a "superb little schooner" yacht, with "torn sails and broken spars," tossed in a stormy sea at midnight. "On the deck was a slender, slight, beautiful figure, a dim man, apparently enjoying all the terror, the murk, and the dislocation of which he was the center and the victim. That figure of my lurid dream might stand for Edgar Poe" (*Complete Prose Works,* 150). Whitman's "lurid dream" may very well be a source for Crane's nightmare in "The Tunnel"—where once more Poe is "the center and the victim."

revealing—although it has been largely unnoticed—that Crane's epigraph to *The Bridge* is taken from Satan's reply to God in Job, 1.7: "From going to and fro in the earth, and from walking up and down in it." The words might be read to indicate the theme of voyage, but their source suggests a richer interpretation: the omnipresence of evil, of the Daemon of "The Tunnel." Job's only defense is unremitting faith in his own righteousness and God's justice. And the same holds for the poet: faith in Whitman, his own powers, and in his bridge.

III

To keep the faith but not close his eyes to reality was Hart Crane's chief struggle in composing *The Bridge*. Reality in the 1920's— the age of jazz, inflated money, and Prohibition—did not seem to support any faith let alone one like Crane's. It was a period of frantic construction, of competition for the title of "Tallest Building in the World," won in 1930 by the Empire State Building. That tower had climbed the sky at the rate of a story a day to the height of a hundred and two floors. Elsewhere, Florida experienced a hysterical real-estate boom. In 1927 the first cross-country highway announced the age of the automobile. The same year, Lindbergh crossed the Atlantic. And in the same decade, the movie palacᵣ spread into neighborhoods.

In certain moods, Crane was possessed by the fever of the period: "Time and space is the myth of the modern world," he wrote about Lindbergh, "and it is interesting to see how any victory in the field is heralded by the mass of humanity. In a way my Bridge is a manifestation of the same general subject. Maybe I'm just a little jealous of Lindy!"[8] But the over-all effect of the direction of American life did not accord with his myth. From 1926 to 1929, years during which his own physical and emotional life deteriorated noticeably,[9] Crane searched for a way to acknowledge the unhappy reality of America without surrendering his faith. The changes he made in the final poem of the sequence—the poem he had begun in 1923 and altered time and again—disclose the accommodation he reached.

[8]Hart Crane to his father, June 21, 1927. Yale American Literature Collection.

[9]See Philip Horton, *Hart Crane: The Life of an American Poet* (New York: W.W. Norton and Company, Inc., 1937).

At first, as I have indicated, the finale projected an intense experience of harmony. As his conception of the bridge took shape, he changed the ending accordingly, weaving into it the major images developed earlier, which are mainly nautical and musical. He reorganized the section into a walk across the bridge, and incorporated many structural details of the cables and towers. "I have attempted to induce the same feelings of elation, etc.—like being carried forward and upward simultaneously—both in imagery, rhythm and repetition, that one experiences in walking across my beloved Brooklyn Bridge."

> Through the bound cable strands, the arching path
> Upward, veering with light, the flight of strings,—
> Taut miles of shuttling moonlight syncopate
> The whispered rush, telepathy of wires.
> Up the index of night, granite and steel—
> Transparent meshes—fleckless the gleaming staves—
> Sibylline voices flicker, waveringly stream
> As though a god were issue of the strings. ...
>
>   * * *
>
> Sheerly the eyes, like seagulls strung with rime—
> Slit and propelled by glistening fins of light—
> Pick biting way up towering looms that press
> Sidelong with flight of blade on tendon blade
> —Tomorrows into yesteryear—and link
> What cipher-script of time no traveller reads

Rhythm and imagery convey a real bridge as well as an "arc synoptic": the walk across the span recapitulates the experience of the concluding day.

In stanza six, at the center of the roadway, the poet attains his vision. It is midnight; night is lifted "to cycloramic crest/ Of deepest day." Now, as "Tall Vision-of-the-Voyage," the bridge becomes a "Choir, translating time/ Into what multitudinous Verb": it is "Psalm of Cathay!/ O Love, thy white pervasive Paradigm...!" This moment is the climax of the poem. In the six stanzas which follow, Crane interprets the "multitudinous Verb" as the explicit action of reaching Cathay. He achieves this through predominant images of voyage; the bridge becomes a ship which, in stanza seven, "left the haven hanging in the night." The past tense modulates the tone of the entire section, for we are now "Pacific here at time's end, bearing corn." We have left the physical bridge, and are transported to another realm, a realm which fuses land ("corn") and water ("Pacific")— or Pocahontas and Columbus. The implied image is clearly that of an island, much like the "insular Tahiti" of the soul which Ishmael discovers to his salvation in Melville's *Moby Dick*. The *Pequod* too had rushed ahead "from all havens astern." In stanza eleven, the poet, like the lone survivor of Ahab's madness, finds himself "floating" on the waters, his visionary Belle Isle (Atlantis) sustaining him. In the last stanza, still addressing the bridge, he floats onward toward Cathay. The passage has been made "from time's realm" to "time's end" to "thine Everpresence, beyond time." Like Melville, Crane began his spiritual voyage in the North Atlantic, plunged into older waters, and nearing Cathay, recovered the even older shores of Atlantis. East and West have merged in a single chrysalis.

The language of the closing six stanzas of the section has the resonance of a hymn; it includes some of Crane's most quoted epithets: "Unspeakable Thou Bridge to Thee, O Love." But the oracular tone is bought at an expense. The opening six stanzas were dominated by the physical presence of the bridge and the kinetic sense of moving across it; the last six, having left the "sheened harbor lanterns" behind, remove to a watery element. And as the bridge becomes a symbolic ship, we sense an underlying relaxation. It is true that the language remains rich, even rugged ("Of thy white seizure springs the prophecy"). But the hyperbolic imagery itself seems an effort to substitute verbal energy for genuine tension. The original tension, between the poet-hero and history, seems to be replaced by an unformulated struggle *within* the poet, a struggle to maintain a pitch of language unsupported by a concrete action. For the climactic action of the entire poem had already occurred, when, at the center of the span, the poet names the bridge as "Paradigm." The rest is an effort, bound to prove inadequate in the nature of the case, to say what it is a paradigm of. Thus the poet, full of ponderous (and, we sense, conflicting) emotions, sails away from the harbor, detaching the myth from its concreteness. And the bridge achieves its final transmutation, into a floating and lonely abstraction.

IV

The dissolution of the bridge as fact—and the subsequent drop in the poem's intensity—was perhaps an inevitable outcome of the poet's conflict between his faith and reality. In the summer of 1926, suffering an attack of skepticism about his "myth of America," Crane stated the problem in his own terms. "Intellectually judged," he wrote to Waldo Frank, "the whole theme and project seems more and more absurd." He felt his materials were not authentic, that "these forms, materials, dynamics are simply nonexistent in the world." As for Brooklyn Bridge: "The bridge today has no significance beyond an economical approach to shorter hours, quicker lunches, behaviorism and toothpicks." A month later he had recovered his faith. "I feel an absolute music in the air again," he wrote to Frank, "and some tremendous rondure floating somewhere." He had composed the "Proem," in which the bridge stands firmly opposed to the cities. He had beaten back the nightmarish view of the bridge, and could now proceed with his aim of translating a mechanical structure into a threshold of life.[10]

But Crane could not dismiss the nightmare. He had to account for it, and he did so in a subtle fashion. Later in 1926 he arrived at the title for his last section: "Atlantis." Until then, it had been "Bridge Finale." The destination of the protagonist's journey, like Columbus's, had been called Cathay, the traditional symbol of the East. Atlantis was the sunken island of the West—older even than the Orient. What does Crane intend by his new title? Does he mean to identify East and West? Or to introduce the idea of the decline of greatness at the very moment his hero's journey is accomplished?

[10]In light of Crane's efforts to sustain belief in his cultural symbol, Henry Miller's treatment of the bridge is significant. For Miller, Brooklyn Bridge was an intensely private experience—a means of release from his culture. It served him as it did John Marin, as a perspective upon the city. Only Miller found nothing in modern New York to celebrate. "Way up there," he wrote in *Tropic of Capricorn* (Paris, 1939), he seemed to be "hanging over a void": "up there everything that had ever happened to me seemed unreal…*unnecessary*" (p. 72). The bridge, he felt, disconnected him from the "howling chaos" of the shores. See also "The 14th Ward," *Black Spring* (Paris, 1936). In "The Brooklyn Bridge," the concluding essay in *The Cosmological Eye* (New York, 1939), he writes that the bridge had appeared to him with "splendour and illumination" in "violent dreams and visions." He recalled that he took to the bridge "only in moments of extreme anguish," and that he "dreamt very violently" at its center. In these dreams "the whole past would click"; he felt himself annihilated as an ego in space and time, but reborn in a "new realm of consciousness." Thus, he now realizes, the bridge was no longer "a thing of stone and steel" but "incorporated in my consciousness as a symbol." And as a symbol it was a "harp of death," "a means of reinstating myself in the universal

What precisely does Atlantis add to our "cognizance" of the bridge?[11]

The fable of Atlantis had been as important as Cathay to the discovery of the New World. Originally, it was a somewhat mystical legend told by Plato in *Timaeus* and *Critias,* concerning a land in the western ocean (the Atlantic), founded by Poseidon, god of the sea. Once all-powerful, the nation had grown lustful, and was punished for its pride with earthquakes and floods; in a single day it sunk forever. But the legend remained, and during the fifteenth century, was popular among sailors. The island was believed to be the place where seven Portuguese bishops, fleeing the Moors, had founded seven golden cities. Sailors hoped to rediscover this land, where Christians still lived in piety and wealth. To discover Atlantis, or to reach Cathay—these were the leading motifs among the navigators who sailed westward in the fifteenth century. No one, not

stream." Through it he felt "securely situated in my time, yet above it and beyond it." Crane's conception is similar, with this crucial difference: Miller stripped the bridge altogether of its ties with American life, but Crane wished to restore a meaningful relation between bridge and city, and to fuse the personal and the cultural. Moreover, Crane wished to incorporate the stone and steel into the symbol—to join meaning to fact.

Other treatments of the bridge versus the city theme appear in John Dos Passos, *Manhattan Transfer* (New York, 1925); Thomas Wolfe, *The Web and the Rock* (New York, 1938); Vladimir Mayakovsky, "Brooklyn Bridge" (1925), reprinted in *Atlantic* (June 1960); Federico Garcia Lorca, "Unsleeping City (Brooklyn Bridge Nocturne)" (1932), *Poet in New York* (New York, 1955). On May 26, 1923, the Sunday Brooklyn *Eagle* celebrated the fortieth birthday of the bridge with a poem by Martin H. Weyrauch, "The Bridge Speaks," in which the structure argues against modernization of itself in these words: "I think we ought to have/ At least one personality In this City of Wild Motion/ That stands for the solid,/ The poised,/ The quiet/ things of Life." It is likely that Hart Crane, already at work on his poem and living in Brooklyn Heights, read these lines.

[11]In May 1926 Crane recorded in a letter that he had been reading *Atlantis in America* by Lewis Spence. Spence, a leading student of mythology (he died in 1955), devoted much of his time and numerous books to "the Atlantean question." Crane found convincing his argument that there are traces of Atlantean civilization in American Indian culture: "it's easy to believe that a continent existed in mid-Atlantic waters and that the Antilles and West Indies are but salient peaks of its surface" (*Letters,* 255-6). It is, unfortunately, impossible to learn whether Crane knew *Atlantis: The Antediluvian World* (1882)—a remarkable work by Ignatius Donnelly, the fascinating Minnesotan, who tried to found a city in the 1850's, served many years in Congress, was an out-spoken Populist, a Baconian in the controversy over the identity of Shakespeare (he produced a massive argument in 1885, *The Great Cryptogram*), and something of an embittered prophet (*Caesar's Column,* 1890). His book on Atlantis was widely influential among students of the

even Columbus, dreamed that an entirely new world lay between the sunken world and the legendary riches of the Orient.[12]

Crane thus had historical grounds for identifying Atlantis and Cathay. As it turned out, the discovery of America proved both legends to be illusions: neither had the geographical position attributed to it by Renaissance navigators. Both, however, remained active myths—Cathay inspiring the revived theme of the Northwest Passage in the nineteenth century, and Atlantis even yet arousing speculation. Crane had indicated early in the composition of his poem that Cathay would stand for "consciousness, knowledge, spiritual unity"—material conquest transmuted into "an attitude of spirit." What does Atlantis stand for?

The answer is complex. When we learn from Plato that the Atlanteans possessed a land with a great central plain, "said to have been the fairest of all plains, and very fertile," the resemblance to America is striking. Further, we learn that they were a race of highly inventive builders, who intersected the island with a vast system of inland canals. They had invented basic tools, farming, and the alphabet. Their proudest creations, however, were bridges —a series of bridges, in fact, which led over the canals toward the exact center of the island. There, a monumental bridge opened upon the gate to a temple, the shrine of Poseidon.

This was Atlantis in its glory. But, Plato revealed, the glory did not last. The "divine portion" faded away, and human nature "got the upper hand." The people grew prideful, avaricious, imperialistic. And most of all, they grew blind to their own failings—blind to the loss of their true powers.

---

problem; Lewis Spence linked his name with Plato as the most prominent in "Atlantean science." Among the propositions Donnelly tried to prove were that Atlantis was "the true Antediluvian world; the Garden of Eden," and therefore, "the region where man first rose from a state of barbarism to civilization." To establish these—and other—"facts," would, he wrote, "aid us to rehabilitate the fathers of our civilization, our blood, and our fundamental ideas—the men who lived, loved, and labored ages before the Aryans descended upon India, or the Phoenicians had settled in Syria, or the Goths had reached the shores of the Baltic." Atlantis, in other words, provided mankind—and Americans in particular—with a historical tradition far older than any yet imagined. Donnelly's book was reissued, with revisions by Egerton Sykes, in 1949.

[12]See Boies Penrose, *Travel and Discovery in the Renaissance, 1420-1620* (Cambridge, 1952), 5, 19, 25; also, J. H. Parry, *The Age of Reconnaissance* (New York, 1964), 165.

Crane wove references to the sunken island throughout the fabric
of the poem. They appear in "Cutty Sark" as the old sailor's memory of "the skeletons of cities." They recur forcefully in "The
Tunnel" in two echoes of Poe's "The City in the Sea"; "And Death,
aloft,—gigantically down," and "worlds that glow and sink." And
they emerge explicitly in stanza eleven of the finale:

> Now while thy petals spend the suns about us, hold—
> (O Thou whose radiance doth inherit me)
> Atlantis,—hold thy floating singer late!

In the preceding line, the bridge was addressed as a sea creature—
"Anemone." Here, the poet invokes the floating form, now called
Atlantis, to sustain his faith. In the following stanza, the last of the
poem, the poet passes "to thine Everpresence, beyond time," as the
"orphic strings...leap and converge." Then:

> —One Song, one Bridge of Fire! Is it Cathay,
> Now pity steeps the grass and rainbows ring
> The serpent with the eagle in the leaves...?
> Whispers antiphonal in azure swing.

The question *may* indicate doubt that the bridge does in fact represent the "mystic consummation" of Cathay; more likely, it indicates wonder. The antiphonal whispers through the cables of the
disembodied bridge could hardly be negative. Atlantis, the bridge-
anemone, had answered the prayer and held the "floating singer
late."

How did the sunken island earn such a high function? Where did
it get the "radiance" to bestow upon the poet? The answer lies once
more in Plato's account. The people of Atlantis had indeed become
blind in their pride and materialism—but not all of them. "To those
who had no eye to see the true happiness, they still appeared glorious and blessed at the very time when they were filled with un-
righteous avarice and power." Some, however, retained "an eye
to see," and these few recognized baseness as baseness. The still
radiant ones kept their "precious gift" of the "divine portion."[13]

---

[13]It should be noted that Crane's epigraph to "Atlantis" is from *The Symposium:*
"Music is then the knowledge of that which relates to love in harmony and system."
This reinforces my view of his reliance upon the Platonic version of Atlantis—and
the Platonism of *The Bridge.* Harmony and system were central features of the island civilization—as they are of the Platonic cosmology. Love and music, moreover,
had been identified with the poet's quest throughout, and with the bridge in

It is now clear what Crane meant. His Cathay, his moment of supreme awareness, was a moment of Atlantean "radiance." With an "eye to see," he perceived the bridge as more than stone and steel, as a "mystic consummation." He perceived the gift embodied in the bridge. The inhabitants of the Daemon's dark tunnels could no longer see—no longer make out the shape of the future within the chaos of the present. These are the people for whom the bridge was nothing but "an economical approach." They represented the loss of radiance, the sinking of Atlantis.

Crane used the Atlantis legend, like the epigraph from Job, to maintain a double insight: the promise of redemption and the actuality of evil. As long as he held the double view, as long as he was able to affirm the myth while condemning the actuality of his culture, he would not sink. To this end he required a bridge to rise above the wreckage of history—to rise above itself—and be a pure curveship. The purity was essential; the bridge could harbor no ambiguities. Hence its symbolic radiance became the only enduring fact of Hart Crane's Brooklyn Bridge.

"Proem." The image of Atlantis, then, helps Crane draw these threads together in the finale.

Exile Guise:
Irony and Hart Crane

by Richard Hutson

In "Porphyro in Akron," one of his apprentice poems,[1] Hart
Crane outlined in a version that was new to him the inadequacy of
the world for the poet. Here the poet has become useless and an exile,
like the foreigners of Akron who dream of returning to their native
countries. Some of the people become reconciled to their new
environment; they "will be 'Americans.'" But there are others who
keep their memories of their native lands, whose memories and
imaginations will make them exiles. There is, for instance, the "host"
who welcomes the speaker and his friend with wine and the words:

> "One month,—I go back rich.
> I ride black horse...Have many sheep."

And there are other immigrants:

> The Greek grins and fights with the Swede,—
> And the Fjords and the Aegean are remembered.

Whereas in Crane's earlier poetry (for example, in "C 33" or "Interior" of the apprentice poems) the poet was a modest visionary
who had a certain efficacy before an unsympathetic world, now in
"Porphyro in Akron" the poet's exile leaves him impotent, useless,
unwanted:

"Exile Guise: Irony and Hart Crane," by Richard Hutson. From *Mosaic*, Vol. 2,
No. 4 (Summer, 1969), 71-86. Reprinted by permission of *Mosaic*.

[1]All quotations from the poetry of Hart Crane are from *The Complete Poems
and Selected Letters and Prose of Hart Crane*, ed. Brom Weber (New York, 1966).
The pagination of this edition is the same as the Anchor Book edition (Garden
City, N.Y., 1966). By the expression "apprentice poems" I refer to the group of
uncollected poems gathered by Brom Weber on pp. 122-152 of this edition. "Porphyro in Akron" is on pp. 144-146. All future references of this edition will be
incorporated into the text by the initials CP.

> O City, your axles need not the oil of song.
> I will whisper words to myself
> And put them in my pockets.

He has become a figure of irony, of humiliation and frustration. As Northrop Frye has reminded us, "the *eiron* is the man who deprecates himself,"[2] who finds ways of appearing to be less than he is. Crane's early personae or speakers clearly belong to the ironic mode. But, as Frye also suggests, there is something in irony that "moves steadily towards myth, and dim outlines of sacrificial rituals and dying gods begin to appear in it."[3]

Crane's discovery of the ironic mode, of the diminished hero, was no doubt inevitable, given the context of the twenties, but it is surprising how little this ironic side of Crane has been noted by his critics. Most recently, R. W. B. Lewis has done much to correct this view,[4] although his thesis that Crane transcends irony finally and becomes a pure visionary poet in his mature poetry I should like to call into question in my following remarks. Generally, Crane has been thought to have desired and expressed in his poetry only affirmation: "an exorbitant and utterly insupportable affirmation of the present and the future," as one critic lucidly states a prevalent view.[5] Of course, Crane is an affirmative poet, but we cannot allow ourselves to be too readily satisfied with this term. If Crane's affirmations seem exorbitant, part of the explanation may lie in what we have come to know as the negative mood of his time. Most critics draw upon Crane's remarks about his relationship to Eliot to show that he is predominantly a poet of the positive. But Crane remains of all Eliot's poetic contemporaries most personally and deeply impressed by the strength of Eliot's negations. His statements about using Eliot's poetry for his own poetic projects may be quickly recalled. There is his letter to Allen Tate in which he tries to console Tate for his shock of recognition upon reading Eliot's poetry and then goes on to advise Tate how to build an armor against Eliot by using his own experience as an example. "I flatter myself a little lately that I have discovered a safe tangent to strike which, if I can

[2]*Anatomy of Criticism* (Princeton, 1957), p. 40.

[3]*Anatomy of Criticism*, p. 42.

[4]*The Poetry of Hart Crane, A Critical Study* (Princeton, 1967).

[5]Sidney Richman, "Hart Crane's 'Voyages II': An Experiment in Redemption," *Wisconsin Studies in Contemporary Literature*, III (Spring-Summer, 1962), 65.

possibly explain the position,—goes *through* him toward *a different goal.* You see it is such a fearful temptation to imitate him that at times I have been almost distracted."[6] And there is the letter to Gorham Munson seven months later:

> There is no one writing in English who can command so much respect, to my mind, as Eliot. However, I take Eliot as a point of departure toward an almost complete reverse of direction. His pessimism is amply justified, in his own case. But I would apply as much of his erudition and technique as I can absorb and assemble toward a more positive, or (if [I] must put it so in a sceptical age) ecstatic goal.
>
> (*L*, pp. 114-115)

What critics generally emphasize in their notations of these statements is the contrast that Crane establishes between Eliot as an embodiment of the "skeptical" age's spirit of negation and his own push toward affirmation. But if we think for a moment about the implications in this contrast, we should see that the contrast is possible only within the feeling of similarity, that when Crane identifies his own poetic project with Eliot's he is irrevocably committed to an appropriation, at least in an oblique manner, of what he called the "vocabulary of damnations and prostrations." "The poetry of negation is beautiful—alas, too dangerously so for one of my mind. But I am trying to break away from it. Perhaps this is useless, perhaps it is silly—but one *does* have joys. The vocabulary of damnations and prostrations has been developed at the expense of these other moods, however, so that it is hard to dance in proper measure" (L, p. 89). The attractions of negation were always powerful for Crane.

In the early 'twenties, he was overwhelmed by Eliot; in the late 'twenties, he was "bowled over by Spengler" (*L*, p. 285). And if his own poetry is oriented toward an act of reversal, we must be willing to admit that he saw within negation, particularly in Eliot, a foundation of stability that allowed him his own creative flights. "You already know, I think," he wrote to Munson at the beginning of 1923, "that my work for the past two years (those meagre drops!) has been more influenced by Eliot than any other modern. He has been a

[6]*The Letters of Hart Crane, 1916-1932,* ed. Brom Weber (Berkeley and Los Angeles, 1965), p. 90. The pagination is the same in the hard cover and the paperback editions. It is also the same as the first edition published by Hermitage House (New York, 1952). All future references to these editions will be incorporated into the text by the initial *L*.

very good counter-balance to Matty's [Josephson] shifting morale and violent urgings" (*L*, p. 114). What this balance could mean for Crane is more clearly stated in his letter to Tate:

> In his own realm Eliot presents us with an absolute *impasse*, yet oddly enough, he can be utilized to lead us to, intelligently point to, other positions and "pastures new." Having absorbed him enough we can trust ourselves as never before, in the air or on the sea. I, for instance, would like to leave a few of his "negations" behind me, risk the realm of the obvious more, in quest of new sensations, *humeurs*.
>
> (*L*, p. 90)

I would place the emphasis here upon the maneuver of absorbing Eliot enough "so that we can trust ourselves as never before." Only after situating himself solidly upon what he considered to be the stable ground of Eliot's negations was Crane capable of risking his affirmations. And we distort beyond recognition the nature of his affirmations if we do not see the struggle within the complexity of the poetry, if we ignore the tensions, the fusions or the compromises created by the love of irrecncilables. Crane's personae in *White Buildings* and in *The Bridge* present themselves to us in a state of emaciation; their affirmations are the outcome of running a gaunt-let of negations—death, obstacles, fragmentations, voids, absence or distance, refusal, contradictions. If Crane's affirmations might seem exorbitant and insupportable, the reason cannot be that they are unacquainted with the conflicts of experience or that they do not encompass more than the naive and the innocent. "I am fond of things of great fragility, and also and especially of the kind of poetry John Donne represents, a dark, musky, brooding, speculative vintage, at once sensual and spiritual, and singing rather the beauty of experience than innocence" (*L*, pp. 67-68). In the poetry of experience, negations may contradict themselves, affirmations may cancel each other. In Crane's poetry, it is not the case that a "no" has simply and dialectically negated itself to form a "yes." Rather, the "no" and the "yes" are likely to be simultaneous and inextricable. It is not merely that Crane's poetry is able to "bear an ironical contemplation,"[7] to use I. A. Richards' test for poetry. In fact, we cannot even begin to understand it without an ironical contemplation. "Irony in this sense," Richards goes on to say in language that

---

[7] I. A. Richards, *Principles of Literary Criticism* (London, 1924), p. 250.

Crane would have found appropriate, "consists in the bringing in of the opposite, the complementary impulses."[8] Crane's mature work is unquestionably a poetry of irony in this sense.

Richards' whole notion of irony as synonymous with imagination is so consonant with Crane's poetic project that we might pause for a moment and recall the fact that Crane read *Principles of Literary Criticism* and thought that it was "a *great* book" (*L*, p. 314). I do not mean to imply that Crane was influenced by Richards' ideas, since he apparently read Richards rather late in his poetic development, and since, more importantly, he knew that ideas or categorizations of experience were irrelevant in moments of creation. Nevertheless, we may cautiously exploit Crane's enthusiasms for certain categorical formulations like, for instance, that by Richards. For Richards, irony is an "equilibrium of the opposed impulses" and thus allows for a kind of total, comprehensive poetry. It "brings into play far more of our personality than is possible in experiences of a more defined emotion." In irony, inhibitions are overcome, the impulses are liberated and widened, but they are opened toward a synthesis or a repose which quiets and maintains the oppositions while refusing to distort, suppress or exclude the heterogeneity of the terms which make up the oppositions. Poets may and do choose to express definite emotions, but a modern poet like Crane, as I have earlier suggested, strives for this fuller embodiment. "Every impulse which does not complete itself in isolation tends to bring in allied systems,"[9] says Richards. The language of such poetry becomes thus a vessel of suggestivity, full of "overnourishing signs,"[10] as Barthes has said, in his description of modern poetry. Crane will never allow an impulse, not even an affirmative impulse, to complete itself in isolation but allows it to become mingled with allied or opposing systems.

It may seem that in calling this poetry ironic I have used too large a concept of irony. But I am not so much concerned about securing my vocabulary as about the complexity of experience embodied within the actual poems. If, as Baudelaire said, there are "two funda-

[8]Richards, p. 250.
[9]Richards' ideas on irony are in the chapter on "The Imagination," *Principles of Literary Criticism*, pp. 239-253. I have used the whole chapter for my summary, but the quotations above are all from pp. 251-252.
[10]Roland Barthes, *Le dégre zéro de l'écriture* (Paris, 1953), p. 71.

mental literary qualities: supernaturalism and irony,"[11] Crane most characteristically tries to synthesize the two. Richards' sense of irony as synonymous with imagination may be large enough to include both of Baudelaire's terms. Northrop Frye's expression "ironic myth" would also be appropriate here, and Crane himself used the term "absolute"[12] to describe his kind of poetry. The issue here is not merely semantic, since it is a question of reading Crane's very complex poetry. I prefer the term "irony" for a number of reasons, not least of which is the fact that it might serve as a countervailing rhetoric to readers who tend to think that Crane's poetry represents an "exorbitant and utterly insupportable affirmation," or that irony was simply an early phase of Crane's development toward a visionary, non-ironic perspective. The term "irony" best describes, I think, what Crane refers to as trying "hard to dance in a proper measure." This synthesis or mingling of the No and the Yes can be found in all of Crane's poetry, from his earliest experiments to "The Broken Tower" which was completed shortly before his death. I should like to illustrate some of the features of this proper measure by turning to some instances of the poetry itself.

"Praise for an Urn" (*CP,* p. 8) represents an important version of Crane's kind of irony. In this poem as well as in two other poems written shortly before it—"Black Tambourine" and "Chaplinesque" —Crane tried to cultivate what he called a "graceful mask" (*L.,* p. 71) for his complaints against "the stupidity of American life" (*L.,* p. 93). A somewhat mythologized version of Crane's Cleveland friend, the Norwegian immigrant Ernest Nelson, is summarized in the first stanza:

> It was a kind and northern face
> That mingled in such exile guise
> The everlasting eyes of Pierrot
> And, of Gargantua, the laughter.

The poem is predominantly a meditation upon the speaker's relationship to his dead friend and the implications of this relation-

---

[11]Charles Baudelaire, "Fusées," *Oeuvres Complétes,* ed. Y.-G. Le Dantec, rev. Claude Pichois, Bibliothèque de la Pléiade (Paris, 1961), p. 1256.

[12]"General Aims and Theories," in Philip Horton, *Hart Crane: The Life of An American Poet* (New York: W.W. Norton and Company, Inc. 1937), p. 325.

ship for his poetry. It juxtaposes a number of disparate areas of experience beginning with the gentle violence in the coordination of two disparate adjectives to describe the dead man, "kind and northern." This pattern of modulated chaos or contradictoriness continues in such phrases as "exile guise," "crematory lobby," and, of course, in the mingling of Pierrot and Gargantua as well as in the paradoxical notion "of what the dead keep, living still" and in the larger contrast between exile and nativity, and between the moon and the sun. Pierrot's everlasting eyes and Gargantua's laughter are, in fact, excellent irreconcilables. The first suggest the possibility of sentimentality, of ennui, of an exquisite and melancholy idealism. Pierrot's eyes are the signs of his eternal search, of his eternal quest for love and for victory over death, of his intellectualizing and analyzing. Pierrot is the timid, repressed, delicate native of Platonic realms. Gargantua, on the other hand, represents a gigantesque and sovereign acceptance of the earthiness of the world. His laughter is a sign of gusto, of the greedy consumption of life and of a naturalistic transformation or eternalization of the human body. Pierrot's everlasting eyes are a kind of "no," Gargantua's laughter a definite "yes."

There is the suggestion that neither the prince of ennui and introspection nor the king of adventure and gusto nor the mingling of these two in the "kind and northern face" has a native place in the contemporary world of smoky suburbs. The dead man's face mingles the two as an "exile guise." Like the various workers in "Porphyro in Akron," the Norwegian born Nelson too suffers from a sense of loyalty to a different reality. And within the imaginary dimension of the poem, both Pierrot and Gargantua are survivals from an earlier and different world. They are "glories proper to the[ir] time" which have been transmitted to the contemporary world; they are, like the "thoughts" of the dead man, "inheritances—/ Delicate riders of the storm." The sense of exile is thus qualified both by the notion of inheritance and by the suggestion that this exile may be simply a mask or appearance, a "guise." These contradictory possibilities of alienation and participation may be only an extension of the Pierrot-Gargantua polarization. If the exile is merely a guise, the implication is that this richness of contradiction is the authentic native of the contemporary world because it is the legitimate native of an eternal world. Both the frank, heroic claim to the world and the humble, discrete and passive retreat before the world belong and do not belong to the "smoky spring."

The poem emerges from the speaker's meditation upon his relationship with the dead man:

> His thoughts, delivered to me
> From the white coverlet and pillow,
> I see now, were inheritances—
> Delicate riders of the storm.

These "thoughts" had apparently been lost to the speaker until the experience of death reclaimed them as "inheritances." But now he sees that the death has not simply implied discontinuity. And he recalls the occasion and nature of earlier experiences when Nelson was still alive:

> The slant moon on the slanting hill
> Once moved us toward presentiments
> Of what the dead keep, living still,
> And such assessments of the soul
>
> As, perched in the crematory lobby,
> The insistent clock commented on,
> Touching as well upon our praise
> Of glories proper to the time.

The power of the moon to affect the two men should remind us, perhaps, of Pierrot and his cult of the moon. But here, as in some of Crane's other poems—"Legende," for instance, of the early poems; "Chaplinesque"; "Lachrymae Christi"—there is nothing sentimental in the moon's efficacy. It is significant that the moon here incites a predominantly intellectual meditation of "presentiments" and "assessments." The sentimentality has become a presentimentality, as it were. But the reaction to the moon's initiative is not entirely intellectual either. The speculations of the two men seem modest enough; the "presentiment" of a continuity between death and life is only a provisional affirmation. And they have been taking stock, assessing the soul. But there is a sense that their meditations have overstepped the boundaries that reason can confirm, and the speaker qualifies these modest and provisional attempts to affirm a continuity or an everlastingness by acknowledging the commentary of the "insistent clock." The negative possibilities of this raven-like intrusion are also exceedingly modest. The clock does not deny their presentiments and assessments but simply comments upon them, like a polite, formal and rational judge, say, whose manner is insistent but also casual as it "touches upon" other matters related to the main issue.

The gentleness or modesty of the conflict here between the "us" and the "insistent clock" points to perhaps the poem's most important feature, its repose. There is no violent struggle between immortality and time apparently because the contradictions work toward a softening of each other. There is simply this very civilized dialogue between them. Besides, the "insistent clock" carries within it an important ambiguity. If it takes away through death, it appears also to have a hand in the creation of those "glories proper to the time." This is a poem of praise, and "praise" in this context—both the "praise for an urn" and the "praise of glories proper to the time"— represents, I think, a compromise between the melancholy and complaint of Pierrot and the raucous joy of Gargantua, the gusto transforming the complaint, the complaint tempering the gusto to form this tension of praise. There is nothing in this poem more striking or satisfactory than this "proper measure" of the "graceful mask," than the consistency and coherence of an almost impassive mood and elegant style. This mood begins with the word "kind" in the first line and pervades the poem. Crane will turn in many other poems to varieties of cruelty, but in "Praise for an Urn" all cruelties have been softened and the whole experience is articulated in "well-meant idioms." The violence of death has been greatly moderated in a number of ways. As usual in Crane's poetry, death is bountiful with its "inheritances," so bountiful that it tends almost to contradict itself. But in this poem, its bounty cannot be separated from the kindness of the northern face. Moreover, death seems to be no more terrible than a sleep, the body gently veiled and comforted by the "white coverlet and pillow." The speaker waits for the ashes of his dead friend in a "lobby," as if the crematorium were merely a hotel which, in "Porphyro in Akron," was a sign of exile, but which here suggests that the speaker is waiting for his friend to return as from his room. Even the moon, which is capable of some rather extraordinary violences in "Chaplinesque" or "Lachrymae Christi," has its force greatly mitigated here in its slantness. It is difficult to say whether the "slanting hill" has given its movement to the moon or whether the moon has imposed its slantness upon the hill, but the kind of reciprocity they establish is consonant with the other kindly activities of the poem.

The last two stanzas, while maintaining the mood and style of the kindness and well-meaning, change the direction of the poem considerably. The penultimate stanza points to a new version of "what the dead keep, living still":

> Still, having in mind gold hair,
> I cannot see that broken brow
> And miss the dry sound of bees
> Stretching across a lucid space.

Nelson's "gold hair" lives on now as a memory for the speaker. The poet qualifies everything that has been said before by acknowledging now the loss of his friend or second self. He acknowledges the loss, the absence, the brokenness of death, the loneliness. As in the apprentice poems, "Praise for an Urn" deals with the loss of a friend, and the problem is to be found in the nature of the survival, in working out some kind of a rapport with the fragmentary vestiges of an earlier intactness. Does something of the relationship survive as, for instance, the broken garden of "Postscript" or do all signs of it get carried away into total oblivion before an indifferent and smoky suburb, reminiscent of the "smoking hills" in "Porphyro in Akron":

> Scatter these well-meant idioms
> Into the smoky spring that fills
> The suburbs, where they will be lost.
> They are no trophies of the sun.

The smoke of the scene here is not a commentary upon the industrial and social environment as in "Porphyro in Akron," where it comes from the rubber factories. Instead, it has become something at once more general and specific, something mythic, the encroachment of death upon the season of renewal and upon the whole landscape, the volatilized survival—thanks to the crematory lobby—of the speaker's dead friend, a survival which is ironically enriched by the scattering of the "well-meant idioms."

The negations of this poem are such an essential aspect of its message that we have to perform some very careless reading to ignore them. But neither negation nor affirmation is likely to present its side definitively in such a way that we can state without hesitation what belongs to the one or to the other. The penultimate stanza begins with the word "still," for instance, which, as an adjective, implies a qualification or opposition to everything that has been said before, and I have suggested the negative emphasis of the last two stanzas. The last stanza almost drops the meditative tone with its insistent imperative opening. But as an adverb, the word "still" also implies a continuity between what has been said before and what comes after. These last stanzas also carry aspects of the earlier, more affirmative (actually, modulated, reposeful) tone. If the poet acknowledges his loss, he is also aware that he and his friend communicated so intimately that the space which separated them was a "lucid space." The messengers who bridge this space are not absent, and the speaker misses "the dry sound of bees/ Stretching across the lucid space." But the identification has already been achieved. The poet's words, his "well-meant idioms," are identical with the ashy remains of the dead man. And, although these idoms "will be lost," they will not necessarily be obliterated. Just as the poet has earlier reclaimed his friend's "thoughts" as "inheritances," so now these lost idioms carry the possibility of reclamation. Crane's imaginary landscapes, which tend, in the mature poetry, to be fairly elemental—composed of air, earth or water—may often be preservations. Just as the "thoughts" or "inheritances" were seen as "delicate riders of the storm," so now the "well-meant idioms" may be seen as delicate riders of the smoky spring air. The world itself has now become a kind of "urn" that preserves the body and thoughts transformed by fire into scattered idiom and smoke. The emptying of one kind of urn, as for instance the "broken brow" from which the thoughts have been delivered to the dead man's "brother in the half," helps to fill another kind of urn, the "suburbs," which will preserve them as lost. The "lucid space" has now become the "smoky spring," but the space still preserves a presence, although this presence can be neither seen nor heard.

"Praise for an Urn" is indeed a poem of praise, but the idea of praise here is extremely complex. Within the first section of the poem, we have seen the negative face of the experience subdued by the kindliness of tone. In the final two stanzas, we can find a positive element existing simultaneously with the negative, a partnership that continues in what I take to be a deeper implication of these stanzas, a more profound suggestion of the poem's negativity. Despite the fact that the scattering of the ashes in the spring suggests a kind of ritual sacrifice and cleansing for the world, as if this sacrifice were a necessary cause of the world's renewal, this ritual is presented with the acknowledgment of the merely personal and private significance of the scattering. Also the poet's own words, his "well-meant idioms," carry a severe qualification. This phrase, like those others I have mentioned ("exile guise," etc.), seems to juxtapose contradictories. "Well-meant" implies a gesture to a public, an intention to communicate. But the idea of "idioms" suggests the private quality, the idiosyncratic and strictly personal significance, of his words. The gesture to an audience is acknowledged to be only an intention, not really a full or satisfactory communication at all. Although, because of this ritual significance, the poet may be saying that the death and his celebration of it have an important function for the suburb, he recognizes that the suburb has no conscious use for such a sacrifice and consecration. The impulse to the elegy invokes the whole classical tradition of the elegy and, with the form of the poem itself, some of the ritual prerogatives of its earlier life. The form and the sovereignty of the ancient tradition of the poet subsist, but only obliquely, "lost," reduced to a private mourning with only echoes of the ancient tradition. The opposition between the private and the public nature of the poem can no longer be reconciled. The poem ends with the intensely lucid negative definition of the origin of the "well-meant idioms": "They are no trophies of the sun." The whole experience that the poem relates is immersed in this final qualification, the acknowledgment of a reticence, a confession of the darkness and the unheroic.[13]

Crane's "Chaplinesque" (*CP*, p. 11) was perhaps an even more important poem for him because in it he was able to crystallize in a public, American, modern myth a certain mode of response to a certain kind of world. Because the image of Chaplin had already been assimilated by the categories of art, Crane could achieve a new complexity and depth by taking what he wanted of this primary codification of the image and adding to it his own imaginary ob-

---

[13]Two good commentaries on this poem which have stimulated my own different approach and reading are Mark Van Doren, *Introduction to Poetry* (New York, 1951), pp. 102-107; and Samuel Hazo, *Hart Crane* (New York, 1963), pp. 28-31.

sessions. According to the poem, Chaplin transformed escape from the brutalities and arbitrary barriers of the world into a ballet of liberation. For Chaplin, or rather for the "we" of the poem, the self is the master of liberation. The person is an impotent, passive self before a world which cannot be budged. All of his energy, his spontaneity and imagination are expressed as reactions to the world. And he escapes the world by vision and by his magical transformation, because there is possible no other kind of transformation of the world. The world is not manipulable, but the self is, and so its powers are used to transform itself.

The self of "Chaplinesque" is a child of the random, whose great hunger and need as signified in his "too ample pockets" have only the wind for satisfaction. He would seem to be the repository of the wind's savings, almost as if his slithered pockets were a bank teller's window. His wealth consists in the ample emptiness of his tattered pockets, which are always opened to the world, ready to accept and receive in love what the world offers:

> For we can still love the world, who find
> A famished kitten on the step, and know
> Recesses for it from the fury of the street,
> Or warm torn elbow coverts.

Like his "slithered and too ample pockets," his "warm torn elbow coverts" provide an opening to the world, an opening hollowed out perhaps by all of the jostling in the fury of the street. This is the idea of an opened interior which is able to maintain its irreconcilable qualities of openness and enclosure. This is an openness which has been torn, but it is still hidden, still enclosed so that it can protect. Like the Brooklyn Bridge or the exploded tower of "The Broken Tower," the slithered and too ample pockets and the warm torn elbow coverts are interiorities which are completely open to the world and, thus, even in their protectiveness, available to the fury of the street.

This play between the world and self, between the world's initiative and the self's reactive powers is the essence of the poem. If the self is not strong enough to force its way, it can exploit, by its movement of adjustment, the world's energy to find the "recesses" of the world. The world of this poem prepares within the self the place for its acceptance. But it also prepares within itself the space by which its negativity can be relieved or transfigured. If it prepares the "ample pockets" and the "elbow coverts," it also provides the "step" upon which the kitten finds some respite from the "fury of the street." It also has the "recesses" and the "lonely alleys" within which the self can evade the full brunt of the fury. The solutions to the conflict have to be magical, visionary, at least in part. The self has to find its solutions within its own weakness. And this feat the Chaplinesque self performs elegantly. In his passivity he is a child of grace. He must hold himself open to something beyond his will, such as it is, even if his will should be concerned with legitimate objects. If he "finds" a kitten or sees the moon "make / A grail of laughter of an empty ash can," it is not because he has gone, like a modern Parzival, in quest of these insignificant or significant objects. His success lies in his vagabondage, in his ability to transcend any quest or even his own clownishness. He must be available to the wind, to its gratuitous and random consolations. The "game" of life, the clown's transformation of the world into a field of play, "enforces smirks." It demands the compromise, the partial expression, the repression of laughter in the "smirk" further distorted by its suggestion of an inauthenticity. But this Chaplinesque self is open to the pure gratuity of a vision of liberation. Beyond his need, his humiliations and hunger, he finds a spiritual fulfillment. Beyond the "empty ash can"—a new version of the empty receptacle and, in this case, a double negativity, since it is empty even of the burned down remains of the world's fury—there is the "grail of laughter," a purely naturalistic or secular redemption of the human body, the smirks and puckerings of both the cop and the clown achieving the full liberation, their consummate expressivity, in this vision. As in "Praise for an Urn," the moon initiates spiritual movements, in this case a visionary rather than a speculative reaction, and whatever affirmation the two poems have rests upon the significance of the urn emptied of Nelson's remains and the empty ash can of "Chaplinesque" as intensified signs of mortality and negativity. But there is the quick, spontaneous movement from a desolate reality to a visionary fulfillment.

None of the earlier poems captured such a complex relationship between the world and the self as "Chaplinesque." Both world and self are clearly demarcated, separate realms; they are engaged in such an intimate game, however, that there is really no suggestion of escape. But what if the world and the self should become even more intimate than in "Chaplinesque"? And what if the world of "Chaplinesque" should become more explosive, more violent and brutal? What if the "fury of the street" should become even more furious? Or what if the moon, in keeping with the intensified violence of the rest of the scene, should now not only transform but become so powerful as to obliterate, with a cruel chemical violence? We should then be living in the apotheosized violent world of "Lachrymae Christi" (*CP*, pp. 19-20). We would see the protagonist and the world undergo the "compulsion of the year," the initiative of time become so powerful now that it can renew the world and transform the persona into a complete martyr. Like the personae we have been viewing thus far, the complex figure of the Nazarene-Dionysus embodies a serious lack of initiative, but he has the capacity to stand before the world's violence and power and by this passive stance raise the earth above itself. Here, the intimacy between landscape and self that Crane expressed in the early poems and in "Chaplinesque" has become intensified and self-consciously mythologized. A poem like "Lachrymae Christi" indicates the deeper movement within the terms of the ironic mode itself, the "logical" emergence of the supernatural from the ironic. Crane's mature ironic personages, even the "black man" of "Black Tambourine" (*CP*, p. 4), all have this aura of the supernatural. With Nazarene-Dionysus, however, Crane allows this latency to become the foreground of the action although this new supernaturalism rests upon the usual ironic experience. If, as Frye has suggested, the movement from irony to myth has its own inner compulsion, the dialectic is clearly individualized in Crane's experience. In the image of Nazarene-Dionysus, Crane would find a consecration and a justification, which he renewed later in "The Broken Tower," of the suffering of the poet in the world.

In "Lachrymae Christi" the irreconcilables of the world have become more than usually wide and insistent. The title of the poem suggests the major irreconcilable: *Lachrymae Christi* means the tears of Christ, and *Lachryma Christi* is "the name of a strong, sweet wine grown in southern Italy."[14] The same irreconcilable is

---

[14]John C. McLaughlin, "Imagemes and Allo-images in a Poem by Hart Crane," *Folio,* XXII (Spring, 1958), 55.

expressed, of course, in the duality of the "Nazarene" and "Diony-sus." In this identification, Crane has extended one of his own favorite categories of experience. The Nazarene-Dionysus double identity is a mythologizing and sacralizing of the earlier mingling of Pierrot's everlasting eyes and Gargantua's laughter in the face of Nelson in "Praise for an Urn." In fact, this same contradictory identity is implicit in the protagonist of "Chaplinesque," in the spirituality and the naturalism yoked together in phrases like "grail of laughter" and "gaiety and quest." The complex activities of the Chaplinesque self represent a compromise between loyalties to two different responses to the world. In the mythologizing of "Lachrymae Christi," however, the contradictions between un-earthliness and earthliness which had mingled to form the repose of "Praise for an Urn" or the ballet of "Chaplinesque" seem to be much wider, harder to reconcile. John McLaughlin has set up the contra-dictories of the poem admirably. His structural investigation points to two sets of purification images within the poem, one a negative or Christian or repressive purity, as he thinks, and the other a positive, earthly, liberated purity of wine, body and emotion. The one kind of purity—"penitence"—represents a betrayal of the au-thentic spirituality, whereas the other—"song"—implies "an af-firmation of and glorification in the earthly quality of existence in contrast with the denial of that existence."[15] Some such transvalua-tion of spiritual values appears to be working in the poem, although McLaughlin's division of the poem's images and themes into these two categories seems sometimes arbitrary or unclear. Crane is clear-ly, in this poem as in others, secularizing and naturalizing his Christ image. It is significant that the sacrificial hero is never explicitly called Christ, but is always identified by his earthly existence, Nazarene, and in his identification with Dionysus he becomes as-sociated with a supernaturalism which is simply the natural itself in its ultimate truth as revelation. There is indeed a sense of be-trayal within the poem, but I find it difficult to know exactly what the betrayals and perfidies refer to unless they are related to the cruel transformations of the year itself:

> Immaculate venom binds
> The fox's teeth, and swart
> Thorns freshen on the year's

[15]McLaughlin, p. 54.

First blood. From flanks unfended,
Twanged red perfidies of spring
Are trillion on the hill.

Nor is there a sense that the violence has purified the world of this betrayal, since it would seem that the final image of the poem, the radiant but static "target smile," is not going to escape the "twanged red perfidies of spring." In any event, the contradictories have become wider, more violent. They have not been softened by the "kind and northern face" as in "Praise for an Urn." The "kind and northern face" has become, in "Lachrymae Christi," "Thy Nazarene and tinder eyes." In both lines, there is the peculiar yoking of geography and something quite different from geography, a condensed analysis of character in "Praise for an Urn," and a condensed characterization of the physicality of the eyes in "Lachrymae Christi," with the suggestion of emotional character. Commentators are quick to find in the word "tinder" the suggestion of "tender." But I think that Crane is suggesting that our normal expectations about Christ's eyes are going to be betrayed by his version of the "Nazarene." The word "tinder" does contain, I would say, the idea of tenderness, but keeps it latent, maintains the suggestion as rejected possibility. The "tears of Christ" in this poem seem to have nothing to do with tenderness. And the unsentimentality of this visage is perfectly consonant with the nature of the world's contradictions. Whereas the possibilities of contradiction in "Praise for an Urn" were mainly tentative and oblique, in "Lachrymae Christi" they tend to be excruciatingly open, at times even oxymoronic: "Immaculate venom," "inaudible whistle," "lilac-emerald" (organic-mineral), "undimming lattices." There is the contradiction that the Nazarene's eyes are both "perpetual fountains" and "undimming lattices of flame." The "world dimensional" is presented here with such ferocity because it has found the personage who will remain "untwisted" by all of these irreconcilables.[16]

This Nazarene-Dionysus is strangely victimized because he appears to be the end or goal of the earth. He is the *telos* of this compulsion of the year, his face the "grail of earth," the object of all spiritual quest. But this compulsion or quest is a brutal piercing of

---

[16]These two expressions are taken from "For the Marriage of Faustus and Helen" (*CP*, p. 28): "*There is the world dimensional for those untwisted by the love of things irreconcilable....*"

its goal. And the goal itself appears to emerge only by means of the brutality. Whether it is the "swart thorns," the "sable, slender boughs" or the "charred and riven stakes," the world always provides these arrow-like projectiles to twange toward the "target smile." The *telos* has become a target, the serenity suggested by the smile and by the static radiance of the target here containing clearly the possibility for further violence.

It is this violence of the world that saves it from the incomplete or muffled transformation of *The Waste Land*. And what Crane's protagonists lose in initiative they make up in their extreme passivity. In "Chaplinesque," the world has opened up only the clothes of the tramp, wearing them away, creating those spiritual hollows. In "Lachrymae Christi," the violence of the compulsion is so strong that the world and the self are both opened up. There is the chemical violence of the "benzine rinsings of the moon" which works upon the surfaces of things, but there is more characteristically a violence which penetrates—arrows, "swart thorns," the worms' "tunneling"— and opens up the various interiors of the world. The nights open and the worms tunnel so that the "sentient cloud of tears" can flock "through the tendoned loam." In this exchange between earth and sky we can see the mingling of Dionysus and the Nazarene. It is true that the Nazarene-Dionysus self seems to be accessible only from the outside—the names peel from his eyes, and the nights "Strike from Thee perfect spheres"; even the slitting of the eyes by the lattices does not mar their luminosity. He seems to have a very protected interior, like the serene interior within the first set of parentheses:

> (Inside the sure machinery
> Is still
> And curdled only where a sill
> Sluices its one unyielding smile).

It is impossible to say where or how this serenity originates, but it is present in the poem in the form of the "sure machinery" or the "compulsion of the year," the "unyielding smile" or the "unmangled target smile." He remains, unlike everything else in the poem, "unstanched." He appears to be the source of those simple negations of negations that pervade the poem with "un-" prefixes, translating the negations thereby into affirmations: "unyielding," "immaculate," "unfended," "innocence," "inaudible," "undimming," "unstanched," "unmangled." This kind of an affirmation maintains insistently and openly its dependency upon negation. And the "compulsion of the year" has nothing of the usual sentimentality of the conventional version of the savior or the purifier. By undergoing this brutal compulsion, the Nazarene-Dionysus becomes Crane's most obvious persona of the asceticism of his acceptance of the world. We may speak of this poem, with McLaughlin, as an "affirmation of and glorification in the earthly quality of existence," but we must recognize the pain, the martyrdom of such an affirmation.

The complexity of Crane's irony in its fullest expression is to be found in any of Crane's major lyrics and is, for instance, the spiritual foundation of *The Bridge*. I have chosen the examples in this essay not so much because they are representative in their individuality as because this is almost a random sampling that suggests something of the coherence of Crane's imagination, and together they have a certain representative descriptive value. Moreover, the speaker of "Chaplinesque," for instance, is a fairly obvious figure of irony, but most contemporary definitions of irony do not really account for his kind of "supernaturalism." And, on the other hand we may easily identify as "supernatural" the suffering protagonist of "Lachrymae Christi" but in doing so we tend to ignore his ironic side. The juxtaposition of these two poems illustrates, in a somewhat privileged manner, Crane's labors to "dance in a proper measure." Together, they illustrate a concept of irony that is undoubtedly classic, namely, as a scholar of Plato has said, that "Yes and No are peculiarly intertwined in the words of the ironic man."[17] But practically any of Crane's poems will express this most exciting and valuable feature of his imagination, his "love of things irreconcilable" that constitutes his irony.

---

[17]Paul Friedlander, *Plato: An Introduction* (New York, 1964), p. 139.

Hart Crane's Last Poem

by Marius Bewley

There is a literary superstition to the effect that the last work of
a good artist is likely to show a deeper insight or wisdom, a last
gathering of forces, as death comes on. There is enough corrobora-
tive evidence offered by the late work of artists who will immediately
spring to mind to suggest that the legend is sometimes true. The
manuscript of "The Broken Tower" is dated March 25, 1932. As Hart
Crane's death occurred on April 27, it is almost certainly his last
poem. Brom Weber wrote of it: "This poem is as personal as any
poem could be; it is unquestionably one of Crane's most magnificent
pieces." His judgment, if more enthusiastically expressed, echoes
the general opinion. Unfortunately, its magnificence seems to have
been blinding enough to have prevented anyone from looking very
closely at it, for I am not aware that the poem has ever been com-
mented on sufficiently to give more than the barest indication of its
meaning. It is one of the most difficult poems Crane ever wrote,
and the general response to it has been one of bafflement. Yet,
paradoxically, it is one of the most logically organized and coherent
among Crane's more difficult pieces, and the statement it makes is
more central to Crane's life and his view of poetry than any other
title in *The Collected Poems*. But its images come to life only when
we realize that they are the sheerest verbal integument for a meaning that perfectly informs every word and metaphor in the ten
quatrains. To understand that meaning verse by verse is to revive
the piety that, at the end, a poet may have a deeper intuition of the
meaning of his own creative effort and his life than he ever had
before.

If "The Broken Tower" is a deeply personal poem, it is also an objective and deliberately thought out expression of Crane's literary faith in his last months, and it expresses what he had learned of his own limitations by writing *The Bridge*. But it expresses most of all the anguish of that discovery, and it is from this center of pain that the poetry germinates. There is a letter that Crane wrote to Allen Tate acknowledging the latter's review of *The Bridge* in which he says:

> So many true things have a way of coming out all the better without the strain to sum up the universe in one impressive little pellet. I admit that I don't answer the requirements. My vision of poetry is too personal to "answer the call." And if I ever write any more verse it will probably be at least as personal as the idiom of *White Buildings* whether anyone cares to look at it or not.

Crane's early recognition (which is recurrent in his *Letters*) that *The Bridge* failed is behind this statement to Tate, for we find no such modesty in the notorious letter to Otto Kahn of September 12, 1927, outlining the design of his epic. After its publication, Crane's physical and moral decline allowed him little opportunity for serious composition. We have only "The Broken Tower" that merits serious attention, and if it is magnificent, it is also a little anomalous.

The best external clue to the meaning of the poem is Leslie Simpson's letter to the *New English Weekly*, which Philip Horton quotes in his biography of Crane:

> I was with Hart Crane in Taxco, Mexico, the morning of January 27, this year, when he first conceived the idea of "The Broken Tower." The night before, being troubled with insomnia, he had risen before daybreak and walked down to the village square. It so happened that one of the innumerable Indian fiestas was to be celebrated that day, and Hart met the old Indian bellringer who was on his way down to the Church. He and Hart were old friends, and he brought Hart up into the tower with him to help ring the bells. As Hart was swinging the clapper of the great bell, half drunk with its mighty music, the swift tropical dawn broke over the mountains. The sublimity of the scene and the thunder of the bells woke in Hart one of those gusts of joy of which only he was capable. He came striding up the hill afterwards in a sort of frenzy, refused his breakfast, and paced up and down the porch impatiently waiting for me to finish my coffee. Then he seized my arm and bore me off to the plaza, where we sat in the shadow

of the Church. Hart the while pouring out a magnificent cascade of
words. It was a Hart Crane I had never known and an experience I
shall never forget.

If the experience which began the chain of subjective associations
was an intensely personal one, the final meaning which the reader
should take from the poem is far more public than the imagery in
which it is expressed, and which seems at first so inscrutably private,
as if only meant for the eyes of initiated illuminati.

While "The Broken Tower" is self-contained as a poem, it will
aid understanding if it is read with *The Bridge,* and particularly
with "For the Marriage of Faustus and Helen," freshly in mind. In
some ways "The Broken Tower" is a return on Crane's part, after
the grandiose aspiration of *The Bridge,* to the more modest intention of the earlier sequence of three poems that composes "Faustus."
In the earlier sequence Crane asserts that in the interaction between
the abstract ideal and the degrading encroachments of the world that
seek to destroy it, the life of the imagination is necessarily con-
demned to death. Part III ends:

> Distinctly praise the years, whose volatile
> Blamed bleeding hands extend and thresh the height
> The imagination spans beyond despair,
> Outpacing bargain, vocable, and prayer.

But if the imagination persists beyond despair, its final victory
is not a complete triumph. "Faustus and Helen" has shown us the
ideal of beauty, symbolized by the Helen of Part I, swaying to jazz
tunes and exposed to modern lust in the skyscraper roof garden of
Part II. Finally, in Part III, the imaginative life and the ideal
world towards which it aspires seem utterly destroyed by the catastrophe of the First World War, which Crane unsuccessfully attempts to merge with images of the Trojan siege. But always
Anchises escapes to the sea and founds a new city. The imaginative
ideal cannot, perhaps, be achieved in a permanent form, but the
transient intimations it gives us are all we have of life:

> A goose, tobacco and cologne—
> Three-winged and gold-shod prophecies of heaven,
> The lavish heart shall always have to leaven
> And spread with bells and voices, and atone
> The abating shadows of our conscript dust.

These lines are damaged a little poetically by the awkward obscurity of the opening trio of images, but they express an attitude basically more mature than the mystagogic, self-induced levitation that is attempted in the "Atlantis" section of *The Bridge*. The creative imagination struggles against odds in the world, but it carries an implicit promise with it that makes life endurable. When we look at a goose we are much aware of the part the duck plays in its ancestry, but it also has a good deal of the swan. The reference to tobacco as a prophecy of heaven is unfortunate because it merely suggests the daydreaming escape of the tobacco trance, while the introduction of cologne is too private a reference to deserve discussion. As human beings, we are conscripted to the dust; our spiritual and emotional stature lessens in secular shadow, but the word of the poet, ringing out like a bell, prevents the ultimate encroachment of despair.

It was to this attitude that Crane returned in "The Broken Tower," but he was able to express it in his last poem with far greater concision; and the ordeal of having composed *The Bridge,* in which he tried to transcend his "conscript dust" towards some vaguely conceived cosmic consciousness, gives this poem the weight of a felt, a suffered, experience. It is coherent and emotionally realized in a degree that "Faustus and Helen" is not, but a similarity of imagery indicates the relation between the two pieces.

The first four stanzas of "The Broken Tower" comprise a movement that may be considered as a unit:

> The bell-rope that gathers God at dawn
> Dispatches me as though I dropped down the knell
> Of a spent day—to wander the cathedral lawn
> From pit to crucifix, feet chill on steps from hell.
>
> Have you not heard, have you not seen that corps
> Of shadows in the tower, whose shoulders sway
> Antiphonal carillons launched before
> The stars are caught and hived in the sun's ray?
>
> The bells, I say, the bells break down their tower;
> And swing I know not where. Their tongues engrave
> Membrane through marrow, my long-scattered score
> Of broken intervals....And I, their sexton slave!
>
> Oval encyclicals in canyons heaping
> The impasse high with choir. Banked voices slain!

> Pagodas, campaniles with reveilles outleaping—
> O terraced echoes prostrate on the plain!

In my last quotation from "Faustus and Helen" Crane gives us a hint of the meaning of the bells and the tower. And there is Leslie Simpson's letter. Bells had already been established in his consciousness as the poet's voice, carrying, as we gather from the "Faustus" passage cited and from Simpson's account of the genesis of the poem, an insistent religious connotation. Such a connotation would be agreeable to Crane as the disciple of Whitman, for whom the poet was prophet and priest. If this is the meaning of the bells, then the tower that supports them must necessarily be the poet's vision. Helen of Part I stood for such a faith or vision in the earlier poem. It adds little to the grace of one's reading at this point to suggest that the bell-rope of the first line is the creative impulse of the poet: but that is what it is. Just as the rope of a great bell tyrannically exacts the coordinated response of its ringer's whole body, so are the exactions of the creative impulse on the poet equally tyrannical. And as a church bell calls worshipers to prayer, and rings out divine praises, so the poet endeavors to celebrate his imaginative vision in song. But for the poet of imperfectly realized vision, poetic creation is as much of a struggle as bell-ringing is for the sexton who does not understand the life and rhythm of his bell. So, momentarily relinquishing his grasp, the poet wanders disconsolately between the hell of creative sterility and the heaven of imaginative fulfillment in his art.

In the second verse, the shadows in the tower of vision are the poet's imperfect efforts to create. They recall "The abating shadows of our conscript dust" in "Faustus and Helen," and they suggest the shades of the dead. The sun is Apollo, the god of poetry and music, who enters appropriately here after the dawn image of the poem's opening line. Although the god is not named in the poem, the reference to "that tribunal monarch of the air/ Whose thigh embronzes earth" leaves us in no doubt. Moreover, the complex metaphorical development that so closely attends the unfolding argument makes the identification inevitable. The shadow-songs in the poet's tower have been created in darkness, not under the patronage of Apollo, and they are imperfect. In Part II of "Faustus and Helen" Crane spoke of "the siren of the springs of guilty song," and these songs, swaying their shoulders as if in dance, invoke the siren, not the god. They are the songs of lust and darkness that (to quote "Faustus" once more) lead only to

> metallic paradises
> Where cuckoos clucked to finches
> Above the deft catastrophe of drums.

In one of Crane's most impressive metaphors they are contrasted with the light and sweetness that poetry is capable of achieving. In *The Bridge,* stars were employed as a symbol of vision on the point of realization. To take a single instance, one might cite the seventh verse of "The Dance." The protagonist, before leaving his canoe near the headwaters of the river up which he has made his excursion backward in time to achieve mystic identification with the Indian heritage of the past, sees the morning star fading into light. It is not necessary to believe that Crane realized his vision in "The Dance" to recognize the symbolic role the morning star is called upon to play. It is the herald of that mystical immersion in his vision that follows almost immediately in the ritual dance and death. In "The Broken Tower" the stars that fade into the light of morning represent perfect poems that are totally assimilated in the vision they express. Their light is absorbed by the sun, the god of perfect poetry, and in one of his finest lines Crane implements the star imagery with a suggestion of bees returning laden with sweetness to a great Platonic hive of absolute song. Perhaps it is worth remarking that Crane speaks of them in the second verse in terms of a hypothetical future, and, in any case, as beyond his reach. His tower is still inhabited with shadows.

In the third verse Crane gives us the poet's grapple with meaning. The torturing urgency to express what may even be inexpressible sometimes comes near to destroying the vision altogether:

> The bells, I say, the bells break down their tower.

This had happened, or had come dangerously near to happening, in Crane's own case when he wrote *The Bridge.* But even among the fragments of a vision no longer intact, the creative urgency of the poet continues. The bells swing, surrealistically, even without a supporting faith. This constitutes agony for the poet, and recalls his earlier lines,

> There is the world dimensional for
> those untwisted by the love of things
> Irreconcilable...

The commonplace dimensional world of things is only for those who accept its conventional boundaries; it cannot be for the poet, even when his vision is broken. His poetry may be imperfect, but he must continue to make it.

But imperfect or not, there is a sanctity about poems. They are the poet's encyclicals. They are described as oval because, since the metaphor is that of bells, sound radiates outward from its source in circles; and because, since they attempt to embody the poet's vision of the ideal and perfect, they suggest the circle of perfection, yet are imperfectly circular in themselves. Life is an enclosed and low-lying place from which the poet cannot free himself, and by the walls of which his vision is cut off. In the first verse the poet had been "dropped down the knell of a spent day," just as in the "Proem" of *The Bridge* elevators had dropped him from the skyscraper tower of his vision into the city streets where cinemas invite humankind to the pursuit of appearance rather than reality. The poet who seeks an absolute, as Crane had done in *The Bridge,* becomes more than ever aware of the shadow-filled impasse of this "world dimensional." The struggle to escape from its denials towards vision is across a battlefield scattered with the evidences of creative defeat—"Banked voices slain!" But it is a holy struggle, and the voices are a choir's.

The "Atlantis" section of *The Bridge* celebrated high buildings and towers, which became a symbol of aspiration and achieved vision. Returning to this imagery in pagodas and campaniles, eastern temples and bell towers for churches, Crane continues to insist on the religious and aspiring nature of poetry by the introduction here of religious architecture in a surrealistic scene that faintly recalls the "Falling towers" passage in "What the Thunder Said." As the reveille (continuing the battlefield imagery of the preceding lines) is a summons to rise, the word emphasizes here, in a line of frenzied excitement bordering on delirium, the desperate quality of the poet's aspiration. It was a desperation Crane had learned in his struggle with *The Bridge,* seeing the vision elude him and its promises turn to ashes.

But if his vision was fragmentary, it was all he had of life; it was both his love and his hell:

And so it was I entered the broken world
To trace the visionary company of love, its voice
An instant in the wind (I know not whither hurled)
But not for long to hold each desperate choice.

My word I poured. But was it cognate, scored
Of that tribunal monarch of the air
Whose thigh embronzes earth, strikes crystal Word
In wounds pledged once to hope—cleft to despair?

There is a reference here to the lovers Paolo and Francesca, hurled aimlessly in infernal winds, clasped in each others arms. The cruelty of the line

But not for long to hold each desperate choice

exists in Crane's growing belief that he had betrayed his vision and his powers. What seemed to him his creative inconstancy is expressed here in imagery that wells up from the growing frustration, in his last years, of his increasingly aimless sexual encounters. He envied the lovers the eternity of their embrace, even in hell.

The sixth verse gives us what are possibly the most moving lines of the poem. Crane handles the dual Christian and pagan implications of his verse with much skill. "My word I poured." "Word" here has a theological significance that is almost immediately developed. The "tribunal monarch," as I have already said, is Apollo. Were his poems, Crane asks, embodiments of that vitality or life force of the sun, suggested here in the reference to Apollo's embronzing thigh? Then, capitalizing Word, he shifts it to its Christian meaning, associating, in a fine act of compression, the word of the poet with the creative fiat of God. As the wounds of Christ brought hope, must the ordeal of the poet be hopeless? Is it (returning to Apollo in the musical term) "cleft to despair"?

The last four verses are technically the most original, as they are also the most difficult and the most personal. They provide us with Crane's final comment and judgment on his own practice as a poet, and on the possibilities of vision:

The steep encroachments of my blood left me
No answer (could blood hold such a lofty tower
As flings the question true?)—or is it she
Whose sweet mortality stirs latent power?—

> And through whose pulse I hear, counting the strokes
> My veins recall and add, revived and sure
> The angelus of wars my chest evokes:
> What I hold healed, original now, and pure...
>
> And builds, within, a tower that is not stone
> (Not stone can jacket heaven)—but slip
> Of pebbles—visible wings of silence sown
> In azure circles, widening as they dip
>
> The matrix of the heart, lift down the eye
> That shrines the quiet lake and swells a tower...
> The commodious, tall decorum of that sky
> Unseals her earth, and lifts love in its shower.

To recapitulate briefly: the poet, dedicated to an absolute, a Platonic vision, must necessarily fail to achieve it in his art. Crane had learned that the tower of absolute vision was much too lofty for him to climb in his poetry, and he realized this was peculiar clairvoyance at the close of his life when he seemed to be running down in a frenzy of neurotic debauchery. The steep encroachments of his blood seemed to be not only qualifying but destroying his poetic vision. Crane turns, therefore, from Apollo, whose fierce exactions he cannot satisfy, to the instruction of a lowlier, more human, guide, "she/ Whose sweet mortality stirs latent power." This woman is not merely an abstract personification like the Pocahontas of *The Bridge,* she is a gracious evocation from the very center of Crane's own being, and she beckons him back to an acceptance of those creative limitations no poet can escape, but which *The Bridge* had desperately tried to deny. Crane is intimately aware of her in ways that suggest she is not, indeed, physically separable from Crane himself, but is an emblematic concentration of the feminine qualities of submission and humility in his own nature. Crane counts the beats of her pulse, but it is important to observe that the throbbing is in his own veins. She faintly recalls, in her identification with Crane, the nostalgic, nameless yearning he had expressed in "Southern Cross" and embodied in his picture of

> homeless Eve,
> Unwedded, stumbling gardenless, to grieve
> Windswept guitars on lonely decks forever.

This rather exceptional Eve, unwedded and an outcast (Crane's own condition), he describes as "docile, alas, from many arms/..."

wraith of my unloved seed!" She is less the object of his desire than his feminine counterpart and (in the guitar image) the burden of his songs. In what Brom Weber has called Crane's "womanless life," this focusing of the female elements in his nature—acceptance, passivity, acquiescence, humility—in terms of a symbolic woman is an astonishingly original way of encompassing the full circle of human experience which is necessary to achieve the final vision towards which the poem is directed, and which is explicitly described in the tenth verse. Crane's technical achievement here is more startling and original than Eliot's invention of using the male-female consciousness of Tiresias in *The Waste Land* to attain a somewhat similar goal.

The woman of "The Broken Tower" is differentiated at once from the swaying shadows of the second verse. Her "sweet mortality" relates to the bee and honey imagery of perfect song, but simultaneously qualifies the reference by the idea of limit implicit in "mortality." The presence of the qualities she represents provides a regenerating influence on Crane's vision: "What I hold healed, original now, and pure." The agony he has endured so long subsides before the Angelus, which teaches submission to the creative Word: "Be it done unto me." This is the lesson that he can only learn from woman, and the sweet lady of his poem suddenly looks towards him in the guise of the Virgin.

From this new feeling of wholeness and integrity the poet builds a new vision in which there is an interaction between heaven and earth—a vision in which both the Apollo of absolute song and the lady of "sweet mortality" play their parts. The Angelus, prayer of prophecy and submission, rings the key of the last two stanzas, and they are verses composed of humilities and quiet acceptances. A slip is a pier to which ships come for docking and unloading. The word suggests here Crane's willingness to accept what his vision brings to his poetry without the frenetic attempt to force his experience, as he had done for so long. It is worth noting that the circling wings of the ninth verse recall the circling gull of the "Proem," which was a metaphorically successful prophecy of vision in *The Bridge* before that vision collapsed. In a sense Crane has returned in almost the last lines he ever wrote to a new beginning and a better vision than the old.

There are two aspects to poetry, then: its godlike aspiration, symbolized by the sun imagery, and its human limitations, embodied in the evoked lady of the seventh and eighth verses. Neither aspect can exist successfully without the other. The last verse deals in opposites which, in the imagery, live harmoniously together. Thus, "lift down" represents a poised balance between the two directions and tendencies. The "eye" is both the eye of the poet and the eye of heaven, the sun. Now that Crane understands that absolute vision can be approached only through the limiting and perhaps distorting perspectives of mortal vision, he draws closer to the possibility of genuine vision than he had ever been before, and one word does service both for the poet's eye and for the sun. This eye, or symbol of vision, shrines a lake—feminine symbol of acquiescence and passivity; but it also swells a tower—a masculine, aggressive symbol. Both symbols are sexual and implicitly contain the images of the god and the earth-bound lady, between whom union is now seen as possible. The blending of these constitutes the resolution, and the heaven of the poet's imagination. The last two lines show the interaction once again of the two tendencies, but it is the god imagery, the sky and the sun, which remains the stronger, though only complete in its acceptance of earth and limitation.

There is something oddly unsatisfactory about the state of Crane criticism today. Crane is readily accorded the rank of "major" American poet, but, the accolade having been given, usually in the most general terms, the talk then continues to anatomize the structural defects of *The Bridge,* the threadbareness of Crane's intellectual tradition, the inadequacy of his myth, or the occult obscurity of his imagery. One wonders how anyone dare call such a fellow, whom everyone is engaged in showing up, a "major" poet. The practical result has been that Crane is less read today than any other American poet of comparable importance. It is essential to understand the large defects of his poetry, and the critics who have outlined them have only performed their function in doing so. But on the positive side there is still a good deal to be said, and this is largely concerned with the complex beauty of Crane's best imagery, and the effectively original organization of his best poems. Yet on these points there has been comparative silence.

Crane himself is largely responsible for this state of affairs. His early admiration for P. D. Ouspensky and the higher consciousness, and his scattered remarks about a new dynamics of metaphor, and a use of symbols outside the rational order, have not encouraged a close scrutiny of what he was doing on the level of practice. Crane's poetry shows an unusually strong rational bias, which his blueprints for the structure of *The Bridge* should indicate, even if other evidence were lacking. Through most of his career it is probable that he misunderstood the nature of his own genius, for his theoretical statements on logic and metaphor sometimes seem to apply more aptly to *Ash Wednesday* or to Wallace Stevens' work than to his own, which is essentially different from either. The importance and beauty of "The Broken Tower" partly arise from the new depth of Crane's intuition into the creative process of his own mind, and from his willingness to accept it at last without forcing it into something larger than itself. It shows us Crane working his way into a new wisdom.

The organization of the poem clearly employs no new order of logic, no suprarational use of symbols. It is an extremely difficult piece to cope with at first, but it gradually becomes clear that its difficulty is similar to what an early reader of Hopkins would have experienced. It is chiefly a matter of extraordinary verbal and syntactical compression, and the occasional elimination of nonessential words. In Hopkins' case such metaphorical compression has been called Shakespearean, and the term seems to me no less applicable to certain verses of this poem. Nor do I find a strained relationship between Crane's symbols and the reality they signify. The bells and the tower correspond at least as naturally and as tautly to the poet's voice and vision as Hopkins' windhover corresponds to Christ. Allen Tate has written: "...with a poetry which is near us in time, or contemporaneous, much of the difficulty that appears to be in the language as such, is actually in the unfamiliar focus of feeling, belief, and experience which directs the language from the concealed depths that we must laboriously try to enter." The difficulty of much of Crane's language is easily resolved by an application of those disciplines with which critics have been so ready and so adept in the case of Crane's contemporaries. Crane's poetry will not again have many readers until we cease to take Crane at his word and forget all that he said about the new dynamics of poetry and its new logic, its new use of symbols, and P. D. Ouspensky. These are will-o'-the-wisps, and only distract us from the more deeply traditional ways in which the originality of Crane's poetry, at its very best, enlarged and enriched the resources of language.

Lyricism and Modernism:
The Example of Hart Crane

by Sherman Paul

Hart Crane was nothing if not a lyric poet, a poet of intensity, and to some of the critics who meant most to him, nothing but a lyric poet. That is the crux of the matter. [...]

Crane was not untroubled, as his friend Susan Jenkins Brown says, by the critical response to *The Bridge*. He did not begin to study Dante for idle reasons — he took up the corrective so highly regarded by his critics. Nor was the following remark, in a letter written shortly before his death asking for an opinion of "The Broken Tower" ("about the 1st [poem] I've written in two years"), merely casual: "I'm getting too damned self-critical to write at all any more."[1] Criticism, we must remember, was part of the milieu of his work, and he closely attended it because much of it, written by poets and writers (Pound, Eliot, Williams, Tate, Winters, Frank), addressed the difficulties of poets in the modern world. Having learned so much from it — having made the issues it defined so much the substance of his work — he could not easily dismiss its strictures, and all the more so since his intelligence was of the healthy kind that admitted doubt.

To read the criticism of *The Bridge* — of Hart Crane — from our present vantage is, to say the least, an astonishing experience. How could Allen Tate, Yvor Winters, and R.P. Blackmur, the critics

"Lyricism and Modernism: The Example of Hart Crane" [abridged by the editor] by Sherman Paul. From *English Symposium Papers III* (Fredonia, New York: 1972), 47-105. Copyright 1972 by Department of English, State University of New York at Fredonia. Reprinted by permission of Sherman Paul.

[1]*Robber Rocks* (Middletown: Wesleyan University Press, 1967), p. 120; *The Letters of Hart Crane,* ed. Brom Weber (Berkeley: University of California Press, 1965), pp. 356, 406 (September 30, 1930; Easter Sunday, 1932); hereafter cited as *Letters.*

whose opinions of Crane and his work went almost uncontested until recently, have been so unaware of the merits of the *poem* and the tough genius of its maker? How could critics so well versed in Eliot's work find it so difficult to make formal sense of *The Bridge*, and, being poets themselves, to enter the dimensions of the poem? They had the "time and familiarity" that, Crane told a reviewer of *The Bridge*, had helped him discover the unity of *The Waste Land* and would help others discover the unity of his "complicated" poem. But then, though Tate and Winters knew Crane's "too well-known biography," of more importance in understanding their response is the fact that criticism is always of its moment—that the criticism as much as the writing of *The Bridge* belongs to the history of modernism.[2]

Crane never disputed Eliot. Eliot was his teacher, a "beloved predecessor," to borrow Pasternak's generous phrase. As Crane told Tate at the beginning of their correspondence, Eliot, "our divine object of 'envy,' " was not someone to reject but to "absorb," to work *"through...*toward a *different goal."* He was especially pleased when Eliot accepted "The Tunnel" for *The Criterion*, and Eliot. he said, inspired his reading of Dante. By placing him within his poem —and from the beginning he is a significant voice in Crane's work— Crane honored him.[3] Yet, Eliot, ironically, had prepared the generation of critics who discounted Crane's achievement.[4] He had given them the idea of dissociation of sensibility, a psychological idea that served the purposes of immediate cultural description—it was witnessed by much in "modern" life—and of historical interpretation. Like "lowbrow" and "highbrow," Van Wyck Brooks' terms for what Santayana called the "two mentalities" in America, it was a ready critical instrument and equally useful in dramatizing the "ordeal" of the artist. Adopting this idea, Tate and Winters, Crane's

[2]*Letters*, p. 350 (April 22, 1930); *The Complete Poems and Selected Letters and Prose of Hart Crane*, ed. Brom Weber (Garden City: Doubleday & Co., 1966), p. 21. Hereafter cited as P. Nine sections of *The Bridge* appeared in periodicals prior to the publication of the book. There is no evidence that time and familiarity altered the early opinions of these critics.

[3]*Letters*, pp. 90, 308, 356.

[4]Crane anticipated their response when, speaking of Eliot, he told Munson: "But in the face of such stern conviction of death on the part of the only group of people whose verbal sophistication is likely to take an interest in a style such as mine—what can I expect?" *Letters*, p. 236 (March 5, 1926).

first critics, treated him as a representative figure whose "ordeal"—
he was said to suffer the limitations and failure of the romantic
sensibility—provided an instructive, "cautionary" example.

The chief objection to *The Bridge* is already present in Tate's
Foreword to *White Buildings*. It is Crane's ambitiousness, which we
learn by the end of the essay has nothing to do with a poetry "at
once contemporary and in the grand manner" but with a fault
"common to ambitious poets since Baudelaire," the fact that "the
vision often strains and overreaches the theme." What this means
exactly, in terms of the poems in *White Buildings*, is never made
clear because Tate, as his reference to Whitman indicates, is looking
ahead to Crane's uncompleted poem ("The great proportions of the
myth [of America] have collapsed in its reality. Crane's poetry is a
concentration of certain phases of the Whitman substance, the fragments of the myth"). But what he means in this respect is clear, at
least to readers of *The Sacred Wood*, in his conclusion: "It [the
common fault] appears whenever the existing poetic order no longer supports the imagination. It appeared in the eighteenth century
with the poetry of William Blake."[5]

Eliot's short essay on Blake is in some ways the model for much of
the criticism of Crane. Take, for example, the assignment of praise
and blame: Blake is "only a poet of genius" where Dante is a "classic."
This distinction rests on Eliot's view of Blake as a "naked man," one
whose "philosophy, like his visions, like his insight, like his technique, was his own"; it rests, even when Eliot acknowledges the historical necessity, on his distrust of the poet who "needs must create a
philosophy as well as a poetry." Dante wisely "borrowed" his philosophy and so was spared "the certain meanness of culture" Eliot notes
in Blake, a poet outside "the Latin traditions." Blake remained only
a genius because "what his genius required, and what it sadly lacked,
was a framework of accepted and traditional ideas which would
have prevented him from indulging in a philosophy of his own"—a
deficiency that contemporary poets may avoid because, as Eliot
observes, "we are not really so remote from the Continent, or from

our own past, as to be deprived of the advantages of culture, if we wish them."[6]

If we wish them. Crane's early critics seem as much disturbed by what they consider needless balkiness as by the challenge of his genius. They address him as a schoolboy who, as Munson, citing Arnold and Eliot, says, "'did not know enough.'" Blackmur summarizes their objection when he says that Crane was an extreme case of the "predicament of immaturity." His genius is indubitable ("of a high order," Winters says) but its "flaws"—in a muddy yet transparent statement—"are...so great as to partake, if they persist, almost of the nature of a public catastrophe." "Poetic order" (Tate), "system" (Munson), "adequate ideational background" (Winters)—deficient in these, Crane, according to Munson, is "a 'mystic' on the loose," and his work, according to Winters, is "a form of hysteria."[7] So much, in sum, for individual talent without tradition.

Of course it was not that Crane was wholly without learning—though his meager formal education is usually noted—but that he had, as Blackmur claims, the "wrong masters," had submitted to deleterious influences. Yes, he had read Eliot but "not, so to speak, read the Christianity from which Eliot derives his ultimate strength...." The advantages of culture, of all that Crane might have gained from the Continent, from Latin traditions, from philosophy, are reducible to Christian culture—the kind of culture or "system of disciplined values" that would have provided him the "faith [and] discipline to depend on" he was said to lack.[8] And that Crane, whose poem has its foundation in an awareness of the bankruptcy of all "systems"—he said that "the great mythologies of the past (including the Church) are deprived of enough façade to even launch good raillery against"—that he refused the advantages and subscribed instead to the radical American modernism associated

[6]"William Blake," *Selected Essays* (London: Faber and Faber, 1951), pp. 317-22; originally published in *The Sacred Wood* (1920).

[7]Munson, "Hart Crane: Young Titan in the Sacred Wood," *Destinations* (New York: J. H. Sears and Co., 1928), pp. 160-77; Blackmur, "New Thresholds, New Anatomies," *Language as Gesture: Essays in Poetry* (New York: Harcourt, Brace and Co., 1952), pp. 301-16 (originally published in 1935); Winters, "The Progress of Hart Crane," *Poetry,* XXXVI (June, 1930), 153-65.

[8]Blackmur, "New Thresholds, New Anatomies"; Tate, "American Poetry Since 1920," *Bookman,* LXVIII (January, 1929), 507; F.O. Matthiessen, "Harold Hart Crane," *Dictionary of American Biography,* Supplement One, Vol. XXI (New York: Charles Scribner's Sons, 1944), p. 207.

with the "tradition" of Whitman and Stieglitz is chiefly what accounts for the vehemence of his critics.[9] More than a decade ago, Gordon Grigsby put the matter of orthodoxy in criticism with salutary directness: "Criticism of *The Bridge* has been strongly affected from the start by the simple fact that Crane does not share the ethics or the religion of the majority of his critics."[10] And not only the ethics and the religion but allegiance of place. For Crane stands with Paul Rosenfeld, a cosmopolitan critical spokesman of the Stieglitz circle, who concluded *Port of New York* by offering another reading than Eliot's of the "Falling towers" of *The Waste Land,* one more in accord with Crane's "Atlantis": "We had been sponging on Europe for direction instead of developing our own, and Europe had been handing out nice little packages of spiritual direction to us. But then Europe fell into disorder and lost her way, and we were thrown back on ourselves to find inside ourselves sustaining faith."[11]

Now this is heresy too, and fatal, as Tate argues in an obituary essay on Crane. Alluding to Brooks' thesis about the failure of American artists, Tate maintains the contrary:

> If there is any American life distinct from the main idea of western civilization, their failure has been due to their accepting it too fully. It is a heresy that rises in revolt against the traditional organization of the consciousness—for which the only substitute offered is the assertion of the will. We hear that Americans are not rooted in the soil, that they must get rid of the European past before they can be rooted. That is untrue: the only Americans who have ever been rooted in the American soil [Southerners, according to Southern Agrarians] have lived on the European system, socially and spiritually.

That Crane was not a Southerner Tate points out elsewhere, though he may have had this in mind when he said that Crane's early life and education fitted him to be the "archetype of the modern American poet"—a role, we are told, he filled with admirable "integrity" and "courage" by carrying his work to "its logical conclusion of

[9]"General Aims and Theories" (1925-26), P, 218.

[10]*The Modern Long Poem,* doctoral dissertation, University of Wisconsin, 1960, p. 251.

[11]*Port of New York: Essays on Fourteen American Moderns* (New York: Harcourt, Brace and Co., 1924) p. 295. In reply to Munson, with whose awareness of "spiritual disintegration" he was in sympathy, Crane said that he doubted "if any remedy will be forthcoming from so nostalgic an attitude as the Thomists betray, and moreover a strictly European system of values, at that." *Letters,* p. 323 (April 17, 1928).

personal violence." Crane's suicide, Tate believes, was "morally appropriate" and significant as "a symbol of the 'American' mind," because, like Crane's, this mind, as the quotation marks indicate, is dissociated or isolated from *the* tradition. And Tate believes—it is the real point of contention—that Crane misunderstood the grounds of Eliot's pessimism and that instead of refuting him exemplified Eliot's "major premise": "that the integrity of the individual consciousness has broken down."[12]

This conclusion was arrived at in another way by Winters, who said that Crane's master and model was Whitman and that "Mr. Crane's wreckage" *(The Bridge)* demonstrates "the impossibility of getting anywhere with the Whitmanian inspiration." Tate attributes the failure of *The Bridge* and Crane's inability to continue his work to the "framework" of the poem, which, he believes, Crane himself knew was "incohèrent." Such views, even granting Winters' and Tate's attention to the poem, are compromised by the threefold assumption that a poem (especially one of epic proportions) must have a framework, presumably outside of itself, that there is a correct framework ("framework of accepted and traditional ideas," to cite Eliot again), and that in choosing the wrong framework (if anything romantic or Whitmanian can be called a framework) one is sure to fail. *(The Bridge,* Winters said, not knowing he was pointing in the direction of a different truth, "has no more unity than the *Song of Myself....")* Tate assumes an "intellectual order"; like the "framework," it is there for those disposed to take it. And his account of Crane's place in recent literary history, where Crane is set against but in a succession from Rimbaud, follows from it. For Crane, he says, coming "at the end of the romantic movement, when the dissociation [of the inherited intellectual order] is all accomplished, struggles with the problem of finding an intellectual order. It is the romantic process reversed, and the next stage in the process is not romanticism at all." The futility and failure of misdirection are the burden of these remarks on the struggle of the modern. Yet seen from another side these remarks might be said to define and

---

[12]"American Poetry Since 1920"; "Hart Crane and the American Mind," *Poetry,* XL (July, 1932), pp. 211-16. Tate had also developed these views in reviewing *The Bridge:* see "A Distinguished Poet," *Hound and Horn,* III (July-September, 1930), 580-85.

approve the courageous enterprise of one who understood and fully accepted the modern condition.[13]

Crane's sensibility, aesthetics, and poetry are decidedly modern, for they are all characterized by distrust of absolutes (intellectual orders or systems) and respect for experience and by an intelligence both intelligent and resilient enough to remain skeptical and to include skepticism in its "stab at a truth."[14] The "confusion" in Crane's work is not inadvertent, as Tate and others believe, but deliberate; it belongs to that "extraordinary insight into the foundations of his work" that in other respects Tate said Crane had.[15] To those in quest of certainty, Crane's vision is disturbing because it is "doubtful" or double; it is not a vision of either/or but of both/and. As Gordon Grigsby maintains, in a study of *The Bridge* that in many ways remains the essential pioneering work, "this doubtful vision, far from ruining the poem, is in fact one of its chief sources of strength"; and as Eugene Nassar insists, in a recent study that considers only the "posture toward experience" presented in the verbal texture of *The Bridge,* the poem "dramatizes a dualistic experience of life," a complex response to complexity that is not "'idealistic,' or 'affirmative,' or 'platonic,' or 'mystic,' or 'epic,' or, for that matter, wholly 'tragic,'"—though these elements may be included in it.[16] [...]

Crane's summary statement of this crucial issue is his best, delivered with the declarative force of a poet for whom aesthetics and ethics, poetry and being are one, and with the assurance of a poet

[13]"The Progress of Hart Crane" by Yvor Winters. From *Poetry* XXXVI (June 1930), pp. 153-65. Copyright ©1930 by the Modern Poetry Association. Reprinted by permission of the Editor of *Poetry* and Ms. Janet Lewis, executrix of the estate of Yvor Winters; Tate, "Hart Crane and the American Mind." Leslie Fiedler points out that "the failure of *The Bridge* was interpreted not as Crane's failure, but as Whitman's" and that Whitman was regarded "not only as a bag 'influence' but even as a bad poet, the founder of an inferior tradition." "Images of Walt Whitman," *Leaves of Grass: One Hundred Years After,* ed. by Milton Hindus (Stanford University Press, 1955), p. 70. See also Karl Shapiro, *Essay on Rime* (New York: Reynal & Hitchcock, 1945), pp. 51, 66.

[14]P, 220. Crane may be said to be modern in the sense employed by Irving Babbitt, who identified the modern spirit with "the positive and critical spirit, the spirit that refuses to take things on authority." *Rousseau and Romanticism* (Boston: Houghton Mifflin, 1919), p. xi.

[15]"Hart Crane and the American Mind." P. 211.

[16]*The Modern Long Poem,* p. 254; *The Rape of Cinderella* (Bloomington: Indiana University Press, 1970), pp. 144-45.

who has informed himself and put what he knows to the test. The third paragraph in an article on "Modern Poetry," this statement is the logical conclusion to brief descriptions of the situation in poetry — of the rebellion, already over, that had moved in "a classic direction," and of the tradition of rebellion (he has in mind the early phases of what Harold Rosenberg calls "the tradition of the new") that is now, he feels, of little importance to the "serious artist." What matters to the serious artist is outlined in the following:

> The poet's concern must be, as always, self-discipline toward a formal integration of experience. For poetry is an architectural art, based not on Evolution or the idea of progress, but on the articulation of the contemporary human consciousness *sub specie aeternitatis,* and inclusive of all readjustments incident to that consciousness and other shifting factors related to that consciousness. The key to the process of free creative activity which Coleridge gave us in his *Lectures on Shakespeare* exposes the responsibilities of every poet, modern or ancient, and cannot be improved upon. "No work of true genius," he says, "dares want its appropriate form, neither indeed is there any danger of this. As it must not, so genius can not, be lawless: for it is even this that constitutes its genius—*the power of acting creatively under laws of its own origination.*"[17]

This is Crane's reply to his critics, to those who perhaps did not appreciate, as much as he did, the view of poetry advanced by I. A. Richards in *Principles of Literary Criticism;* who had not fully grasped, as he had, that the "architectural" aspect of poetry, like that of a cubist painting, refers not only to the way an art-work is made but to the artist's conception, the imagination of the work, which Coleridge's notions of genius and organic form confirm; and who did not value, to the extent that he did, the "process of free creative activity" nor accept so willingly as a responsibility of art the "articulation"—the double meaning is intended—of "the contemporary [immediate, always changing] human consciousness."[18] Here, as in the work of Williams, whom Crane's declaration calls to

[17]P, 260. The quotation is accurate except for the italics.
[18]For Crane's appreciation of Richards' book, see *Letters,* p. 314 (December 19, 1927).

mind, the poet is given the fundamental tasks of "unbound thinking" and of bringing the immediate world to form.[19]

Crane's definition of the poet's concern—"self-discipline toward a formal integration of experience"—also tells us of the function poetry had for him. He was a poet by necessity, having need of a discipline, not of denial but of inclusion, that provided enough security to permit the risk of growth. The first lesson of art and psychology he reports having been taught by Carl Schmitt was one of balance ("There is only one harmony, that is the equilibrium maintained by two opposite forces, equally strong"), a lesson, it seems, that did not omit the caution to maintain the vital or dynamic condition of constant "inward struggle."[20] For the discipline respected experience, required, as he told William Wright, the "development of one's consciousness even though it is painful."[21] The moments of equilibrium that Crane reports are those ecstatic ones of love (a "thrilling and inclusive" experience that "reconciled" him), of "inspiration" (as, when under ether, he "felt the two worlds ...at once"), and of art, when, by inward struggle, he achieved a "consistent vision of things."[22] Balance, integration, synthesis—interchangeable words for Crane—characterize these moments and provide the touchstone of his appreciation of Donne ("at once sensual and spiritual, and singing rather the beauty of experience than innocence") and, to cite another example, of Fielding, whose attitude toward society and life he found "more 'balanced'" than Hardy's.[23] They explain his quarrel with Matthew Josephson, who

[19]*Selected Essays of William Carlos Williams* (New York: Random House, 1954), p. 163. For Williams, "the poet thinks with his poem...." see *The Autobiography of William Carlos Williams* (New York: Random House, 1951), pp. 390-91, and for a characteristic criticism of systems, pp. 360-61. And see Stanley Burnshaw, who says that poetry is "an open area...the only field of discourse in which thought can participate in its entirety." *The Seamless Web: Language-Thinking, Creature-Knowledge, Art-Experience* (New York: George Braziller, 1970), p. 107.

[20]*Letters*, p. 5 (January 5, 1917).

[21]*Letters*, p. 19 (June 17, 1919). Giving up the therapy of Christian Science and having fewer "denials" was part of it. See *Letters*, pp. 14, 15 (March 11; April 2, 1919).

[22]*Letters*, pp. 49, 92, 267 (December 22, 1920; June 1922; July 16, 1926). See also, on the need for "a strong critical faculty," *Letters*, p. 245 (April 5, 1926).

[23]*Letters*, pp. 68, 300.

refused "to admit the power and beauty of emotional intensity" (both means and end where "fury fused"). And they also explain his reservations concerning Eliot, whose "poetry of negation [was] beautiful" but one-sided in not acknowledging that "one *does* have joys," that there are "positive" emotions.[24] To balance Eliot's pessimism by presenting "these other moods" was one of Crane's objectives in *The Bridge*. "I tried to break loose from that particular strait-jacket, without however committing myself to any oppositional form of didacticism," he told Selden Rodman, who had reviewed it. "Your diffidence in ascribing any absolute conclusions in the poem is therefore correct, at least according to my intentions. The poem, as a whole, is, I think, an affirmation of experience [that is, of the possibility of a more inclusive experience and of experience itself as an 'absolute'], and to that extent is 'positive' rather than 'negative' in the sense that *The Waste Land* is negative."[25]

How well this statement substantiates itself by demonstrating the quality of mind it declares—a quality of mind that put Crane in opposition to most of his friends and critics. What he objected to early in Josephson became the prominent theme of his letters and essays on art: "he tries to force his theories into the creative process....[26] To Munson, who asked that his poems provide philosophical and moral "knowledge," Crane answered that he had misunderstood his "poetic purpose" and had proposed "such ends as poetry organically escapes...." For poetry, he said, does not provide knowledge unless by knowledge one means simply "the concrete *evidence* of the *experience* of a recognition." His intention was neither to oppose "any new synthesis of reasonable laws which might provide a consistent philosophical and moral program for our epoch" nor to use poetry "to delineate any such system." But he was disinclined to follow Munson in search of system because system itself was, in fact, the chief obstacle to poetry. "The tragic

---

[24]*Letters*, pp. 106, 89, 71 (November 1922; May 16, 1922; November 26, 1921); P. 46. In the passage on Eliot, Crane may be referring, in "it is hard to dance in proper measure," to Williams' *Kora in Hell,* an appropriate book. For intensity, see *Letters,* p. 302.

[25]*Letters*, p. 351 (May 22, 1930). For "absolute" experience, see P, 221; *Letters,* p. 302.

[26]*Letters*, p. 65.

quandary...of the modern world," he said in a statement that accords with the central idea of Ortega's *The Modern Theme,* "derives from the paradoxes that an inadequate system of rationality forces on the living consciousness."[27] When Crane told his mother— this context is also significant—that "the freedom of my imagination is the most precious thing that life holds for me.—and the only reason I can see for living," he spoke his deepest truth. For system, too, betrays, and poetry is prior to all system.[28]

Crane's replies to Winters and Tate cogently argue this point. To Tate he protests Winters' "arbitrary torturings—all for the sake of a neat little point of reference," and to Winters he protests Munson's desire for "some definite ethical order." He tells Winters that in his own case he has not attempted "to reduce" his code of ethics "to any exact formula"; that he cannot trust, as Winters does, "to so methodical and predetermined a method of development"; that to do so makes a "commodity" of experience and frustrates "the possibility of any free realization...." In response to Tate's review of *The Bridge,* he tells him that critics like Genevieve Taggard and Winters are no longer interested in "poetry as poetry" but in finding some "cure-all," and, with evident weariness, simply remarks that "so many things have a way of coming out all the better without the strain to sum up the universe in one impressive little pellet."[29]

Though Crane withstood the arguments of his friends, he never convinced them that "truth has no name," a lesson they might also have learned from his poetics and, explicitly, from "A Name for All," a late poem available to them in *The Dial.* In this neglected poem he treats the naming, inevitable to writing, whose limitations the "logic of metaphor"—or more evocatively, the "dynamics of inferential mention"—enabled him to overcome.[30]

> Moonmoth and grasshopper that flee our page
> And still wing on, untarnished of the name
> We pinion to your bodies to assuage
> Our envy of your freedom—we must maim
>
> Because we are usurpers, and chagrined—
> And take the wing and scar it in the hand.

[27]*Letters,* pp. 237-240.
[28]*Letters,* p. 189 (September 14, 1924).
[29]*Letters,* pp. 288, 298-302, 353 (February 24, 1927; May 29, 1927; July 13, 1930).
[30]*Letters,* p. 240; P, 221-222.

Names we have, even, to clap on the wind;
But we must die, as you, to understand.

I dreamed that all men dropped their names, and sang
As only they can praise, who build their days
With fin and hoof, with wing and sweetened fang
Struck free and holy in one Name always.

In this poem the poet's dream of redeemed mankind is a dream of
poetry as a liberating field of natural life. We name, but what we
name, having the winged life of spirit and imagination, escapes us,
cannot be fixed. We name—in the name of rationality—out of envy
of freedom, for rationality is vindictive, a will to power feeding on
what Nietzsche called *ressentiment*. We even try to imprison the
wind! And as the negative condition implied by "sweetened fang"
tells us, our own fury to name makes nature red in tooth and claw.
And only when we ourselves become the objects of a similar death
do we begin to "understand"—not know, but understand—an understanding, alas, that, coming too late, is irremediable. And so the poet
dreams of a better world and a better poem, of the peaceable king-
dom of life ("For every thing that lives is Holy"),[31] where men drop
their names or chains, or, rather, are "Struck free" by doing so *and*
by entering a different realm of being and language, the totality of
interpenetrated freely living things, or the poem whose form, paradoxically, is all-inclusive, a "Name" for all.[32] [...]

The central importance of Crane's quarrel with his friends becomes clearer when we realize that he is repudiating the notions of
mimetic form and correspondence truth. For him the poem is not
to be judged by anything external to it: its form is organic in the
primary sense of self-originating and its "truth" is nothing absolute
but the coherence of meanings generated by its language. He explained this to Munson when he told him that "Plato doesn't live
today because of the intrinsic 'truth' of his statements: their only
living truth today consists in the 'fact' of their harmonious relationship to each other in the context of his organization. This grace par-
takes of poetry." And he indicated what he meant by "architecture"

[31]Blake, "A Song of Liberty," *The Marriage of Heaven and Hell.*
[32]This poem—what its vision both enables and is of—is closely related to "The
Wine Menagerie."

—how it relates to organic form, to "logic of metaphor," to the use of "build" in "A Name for All"—when he spoke of the "architecture of [Plato's] logic" as "poetic construction."[33]

Crane first employed the phrase "logic of metaphor" in a letter to Stieglitz, the import of whose work for his own he had begun to understand at the time he was beginning *The Bridge*. The phrase occurs in a passage praising Stieglitz for being an "indice of a new order of consciousness" and is connected with freedom of the imagination and the need, in using the imagination to transform "the great energies about us," of "perfecting our sensibilities" and thereby "contributing more than we can realize (rationalize)...." [...] Crane complained to Stieglitz that he had "to combat every day those really sincere people, but limited, who deny the superior logic of metaphor in favor of their perfect sums, divisions and subtractions." [...]

The phrase "superior logic of metaphor" refers to an earlier letter in which Crane had tried to describe Stieglitz's art—how he used the camera as an instrument of "apprehension," how the speed of the shutter enabled him to make the moment eternal, to arrest the essences of things by suspending them on "the invisible dimension whose vibrance has been denied the human eye at all times save in the intuition of ecstasy." He, too, by means of this logic, would make poetry an instrument of "consciousness," of an "absolute" experience, of radiant apprehension or illumination—that "peculiar type of perception" which, he said, was capable of "apprehending some absolute and timeless concept of the imagination with astounding clarity and conviction." In the previously cited passage on Plato the "fact" is just this presentness, the direct communication of the thing itself made possible by "poetic construction," or by the two aspects of the "logic of metaphor" that permit the poet who employs it to make this stunning impact: the fact that this logic is "organically entrenched in pure sensibility"—in the reader's as well as the poet's—and the fact that the poem it constructs is "a name for all"—strikes the reader as "a single, new *word*, never before spoken and impossible to actually enunciate, but self-evident as an active principle in the reader's consciousness henceforward." This logic operates at a deeper level than "pure logic" and transcends its limits. By using it

[33]*Letters*, p. 238.

the poet not only serves the "truth of the imagination" and gives form to its "living stuff" but lives, like the soaring bird of "Forgetfulness," in the fullness of its freedom.[34]

The overreaching and incoherence that Tate found in Crane's poetry—in particular in *The Bridge*—have their ground in Tate's failure to appreciate or grant the nature of the "logic of metaphor." This logic is the means by which the poet builds the poem from the inside out, creates the field of meaning upon which its coherence depends—the field of meaning, however, whose "expanding resonances of implication" also keeps the poem forever open.[35] Whether excluded from the poem by their own beliefs or by insufficient attention, Crane's early critics were confused by the fact that "poems...are steadily engaged in the work of con-fusing, for the paradigm of poetry—metaphor—pervades its every act." They forgot, it seems, that what Crane called the "logic of metaphor" is the logic of the imagination and that the imagination, expressing our deepest being, always seeks unification, always seeks "a name for all," for the reason Crane did: because "The poetries of speech/ Are acts of thinking love...."[36]

Even before the assumptions underlying the early criticism of *The Bridge* were questioned, close examination of the poem proved untenable the verdict of its incoherence. The poem was found to have the structural elements of other large modern works: a persona or central subjective consciousness, lyric design or thematic form, and symbolic narrative. Crane himself called it an "epic of the modern consciousness," spoke of its symphonic form, identified the architectural aspect of the "logic of metaphor" ("reflexes and symbolisms," "interlocking elements," "strands...interwoven") and of its episodic construction, and noted in the sequence of poems "a

[34]*Letters*, p. 132; P, 263, 235, 221-22. In an introductory comment on Mina Loy, William Carlos Williams speaks of making poems and recalls "the time of James Joyce's *Ulysses* when the Word was made." *Lunar Baedeker & Time-Tables: Selected Poems of Mina Loy* (Highlands, N.C.: Jonathan Williams, 1958). See also, for its relevance to this argument, Roland Barthes, "Is there any Poetic Writing?" *Writing Degree Zero*, trans. by Annette Lavers and Colin Smith (London: Jonathan Cape, 1967).

[35]I am indebted to J. Hillis Miller for this phrase and for the lecture on Wordsworth from which I gleaned it on February 11, 1971.

[36]Burnshaw, *The Seamless Web*, pp. 182, 194. The concluding lines are from Burnshaw's *Caged in an Animal's Mind* and so doubly reminds us of "The Wine Menagerie."

certain progression." Criticism has substantiated him and shown him to be "'a master builder,'" as Otto Kahn hoped he would be, "'in constructing *The Bridge* of your dreams, thoughts and emotions.'"[37]

Though such characterizations of *The Bridge* as Otto Kahn's or Crane's ("epic of the modern consciousness") have embarrassed critics, they are accurate and valuable in indicating the deliberate building-up or construction of the conception of the poem—that in which its form is cubist or "synthetic"—and its special modernity— that, say, where it differs from *The Waste Land*, a poem in which modern elements of form are also employed.[38] The poem is an epic of *modern* consciousness. It is that epic, first, in an antiepical sense, for the modern poet is no more the hero of an epic action than he is a discoverer like Columbus. If we follow the progression of the epic hero from the *Aeneid*, with which Crane compared *The Bridge*, to recent "epic" works, we arrive, as Thomas Whitaker says, "at the modern poet's often ironic celebration of himself as hero-everyman, who performs universal imaginative acts...in an ambiguous cosmos where history must be discovered and values renewed."[39] But the very scope of this enterprise deserves to be called epic. The space in which the poet journeys is an infinitely larger space than any traversed before—the space of consciousness, at once of self, world, and word, a new field of discovery. Here the heroic deed, the culturally redemptive act, the particularly modern exploit is performed. Crane called it the "conquest of consciousness," meaning also that the conquest is achieved by consciousness alone.[40]

The poem itself is the imaginative action that performs this daring exploit. By means of the "logic of metaphor" the poet creates the space or world of the poem, the field of meaning through which he journeys. "Proem," which establishes the bridge as an artifact of the

[37]Stanley Coffman, Bernice Slote, and Lawrence Dembo were among the first to appreciate the poem's coherence. Grigsby, *The Modern Long Poem,* is the fullest early study and the most useful. *Letters,* pp. 306, 125, 176, 241, 305, 340, 232.

[38]Crane noted the synthetic form of *Winesburg, Ohio* and of Stieglitz's photographs, and pointed out the relation of poetry and cubism in "Modern Poetry." Here the important statement for his own work is the following: "...both media were responding to the shifting emphasis of the Western World away from religion toward science. Analysis and discovery, the two basic concerns of science, became the conscious objectives of both painter and poet." P, 212, 260; *Letters,* p. 139.

[39]*Letters,* p. 309; *William Carlos Williams* (New York: Twayne, 1968), p. 129.

[40]P, 222.

real world as well as the center of the space of the poem, calls the field of meaning into being. As the poet moves within the field, which he also continues to create (explore) as he goes and which, in turn, permits us at each stage to possess all of the poem at once, each episode, or state of consciousness, is actualized (like a Whiteheadian "event") out of the field.[41] (Crane was true to the nature of the poem when he said that there might be additional episodes: the materials are already there, in the field of meaning.) Each episode presents directly rather than symbolizes a different kind or stage of consciousness. All contribute to the "world dimensional" of the poem, the world in which the poet, after the fashion of Satan in the epigraph from *The Book of Job* that prefaces *The Bridge*, goes to and fro in the earth and up and down in it, enacting in his movement the doubleness and balance that distinguish so many elements of the poem. To follow him is to learn of heaven and hell, of vast continents and seas, of immense elemental energies (nebular, volcanic, meteorological) and processes (diurnal, seasonal, vegetative), of evolutionary and human history.[42] It is indeed to know the constituents of chaos—and of cosmos.

[...] When we recall "Porphyro in Akron" and "The Bridge of Estador"—even "For the Marriage of Faustus and Helen"—we realize better the difficult resolution of modernist allegiance Crane achieved in *The Bridge*. To be reminded by it so often of Williams is a measure of the distance Crane had come as well as an indication of his particular modernity. We think of *The Bridge* less in relation to *The Waste Land* than to *Paterson* and chiefly for the reason that both offer us a myth of the imagination, and one that is inalienable from place: the "myth" of America is itself "modern," for it is a myth of discovery, of discovering (entering) our world, the ground of our being—or recovering it, making new. Like *Paterson, The Bridge*

---

[41]Crane read Whitehead's *Science and the Modern World* early in 1926, when he was beginning *The Bridge. Letters,* p. 235 (March 5, 1926).

[42]Again, because he was concerned with "framework," Tate was mistaken about Crane's use of American history. He did not see that it functioned within consciousness and not as plot, and that Crane actually included—was aware of—the decisive, representative events. ("A Distinguished Poet," 582.) Denis Donoghue perpetuates Tate's view in *Connoisseurs of Chaos* (New York: Macmillan, 1965), p. 48. Like Williams, in *In the American Grain,* Crane shows us, in *The Bridge,* how the poet takes up tradition, makes the past "usable."

reminds us that "again is the magic word" and that for a culture as for art the difficult thing is "to begin to begin again,/ turning the inside out...." Both poems represent the making by which we begin ("To make, that's where we begin"); they invite "the recreators."[43]

[...] For neither poet, finally, are the imperatives of imagination religious or visionary. Cubist better describes them. The poet of *A Voyage to Pagany*, who, in meditating on making new, not only remembers Whitman but confesses his envy of modern French painters might as readily be Crane as Williams. For Crane employs the "logic of metaphor" more in the manner of a cubist than a symbolist.[44] Condensed metaphor is not used to evoke a reality beyond the senses but to present an object clearly to the senses by way of simultaneous perspectives of meaning. In this fashion Crane moves around the object. (Ideally, by completing the circle, he would make the word a Word—though not quite in Mallarmé's sense.) Or he uses this logic to achieve the "interpenetration of dimensions" one finds in cubist painting.[45] And Crane's vision is also cubist, comporting with the kind of apprehension and presentation he found in Stieglitz's photographs, the kind of vision for which he turned for corroboration to Blake, and, in considering his lyricism, we may too: "vision represents the total imagination of man made tangible and direct in works of art."[46] [...]

---

[43][William Carlos Williams], *Paterson*, Book III. Copyright 1949 by William Carlos Williams. Reprinted by permission of New Directions. [Williams], *A Voyage to Pagany*, pp. 129-30. Philip Furia interprets both poems in terms of Williams' aesthetic in *The Beast That Was and Is Not and Yet Is: A Study of the Imagery of Hart Crane's The Bridge and William Carlos Williams' Paterson*, doctoral dissertation, University of Iowa, 1970.

[44]*A Voyage to Pagany* (New York: Macaulay Co., 1928) pp. 131-32. For Crane's turning from the symbolist tradition, see Haskell Block, "The Impact of French Symbolism on Modern American Poetry," *The Shaken Realist: Essays in Modern Literature in Honor of Frederick J. Hoffman*, ed. by Melvin J. Friedman and John B. Vickery (Baton Rouge: Louisiana State University Press, 1970), p. 216. For Crane's painterly description of *The Bridge* see *Letters*, p. 305.

[45]See Mina Loy, "Communications" [on Gertrude Stein], *The Transatlantic Review*, II (September, 1924), 307.

[46]Alfred Kazin, "Introduction," *The Portable Blake* (New York: Viking Press, 1946), p. 17.

"Inventive Dust": The Metamorphoses of "For the Marriage of Faustus and Helen"

by Philip R. Yannella

There are good reasons for it, but the fact remains that compared to *The Bridge* or even to the six "Voyages," Hart Crane's "For the Marriage of Faustus and Helen" has been severely underread. Of course, it is generally recognized that the poem marks an important stage in Crane's career. Its completion was really the second major event of the poet's development; the first was the composition and publication of the altogether different "Chaplinesque" in 1922. Yet "Faustus and Helen" is significant in several other ways; indeed it is a major work not only in terms of Crane's poetry but in terms of the history of modernist and postmodernist poetry in the United States. This is a rather spectacular claim for a poem which, it must be admitted at the outset, is deeply flawed and at times rhetorically pompous. The evidence is there, however.

In the first place, I should like to argue that "For the Marriage of Faustus and Helen" sets forth clearly one of the characteristic dichotomies of twentieth-century American poetry, the diametrical opposition of Eliot and Blake. For whatever reasons, our poets have persistently felt it necessary to choose one or the other as master and inspiration; Blake and Eliot have come to represent the polarization of standards in our poetics. One of the essential features of postmodernist poetry has been its rejection of Eliot, often to the chagrin of his convinced followers.[1] But at the same time a large number of poets (for example, Patchen, Rexroth, Ginsberg, and Robert Duncan) have taken up the banner of Blake. For aficionados of the little magazines it should come as no surprise to learn that Blakean epigraphs and Blake-inspired diatribes are now as common as quotations from Eliot were, say, in 1925 or 1940. So far as I know, Hart Crane was the first American poet to make what turned out to be the historically "right" choice. His "Faustus and Helen," while it obviously owes something to Eliot's efforts to popularize the metaphysical poets (like others, Crane finds it difficult to bury Eliot), is the first distinctively Blakean poem published in the United States.[2]

Secondly, "For the Marriage of Faustus and Helen" is one of the earliest American poems (after Whitman) to express a renewed hope in the American city [...] Crane establishes, through the central metaphor of Helen, an urbanism and an accessory technology (the connections between the two are absolutely necessary) which is the last hope of modern man. [...]

"For the Marriage of Faustus and Helen" had its inception in Crane's desire to affirm his age against what he saw as the shallow pessimism of his contemporaries. The negativism he identified particularly with Eliot's *The Waste Land,* and his comments on Eliot's despair are scattered in letters he wrote in 1922 and 1923. His most significant elaboration of his position, and one which bears importantly on "Faustus and Helen," is contained in a letter written in early January, 1923, to Gorham Munson, who with Waldo Frank served as his most receptive audience at the time. He first admits his respect for Eliot's work but then goes on to write:

> I feel that Eliot ignores certain spiritual events and possibilities as real and powerful now as, say, in the time of Blake. Certainly the man has dug the ground and buried hope as deep and direfully as it can ever be done. He has outclassed Baudelaire with a devastating humor that the earlier poet lacked.

[1]See, for example, the recently published book of Russell Kirk, *Eliot and His Age: Eliot's Moral Imagination in the Twentieth Century.* (New York: Random House, 1972). Kirk argues, seriously I think, that all of literature collapses after the demise of the poet.

[2]A case could be made for the similarities of Blake and Whitman, but there is no evidence of direct influence.

...All I know through very much suffering and dullness (somehow I seem to twinge more all the time) is that it interests me to still affirm certain things. That will be the persisting theme of the last part of "F and H" as it has been all along.[3]   [...]

There are so many incidental similarities between "Faustus and Helen" and *The Waste Land* that it is possible to conclude that Crane meant his poem to provide an oblique "answer" to Eliot's. He may have been mistaken, at least partly, about *The Waste Land* but the evidence suggests his fervent seriousness. The opening of "Faustus and Helen" parallels in meaning and tone the "London Bridge" passage of "The Burial of the Dead," though of course Eliot's image of modern urban man never takes the turn Crane provides for his. Both poems at one point deal with one of the popular phenomena of the postwar years, jazz, though again to different ends. In "A Game of Chess" and elsewhere Eliot provides a number of exemplary anecdotes about debauched sexuality; in the second part of "Faustus and Helen" a coupling more ambiguous in nature and consequences occurs. Finally, both poets employ mythological figures, most importantly as a means of commentary, though again the directions of the two are quite opposite. Of course, *The Waste Land* and "For the Marriage of Faustus and Helen" are very different poems—the point must be stressed—despite their substantive parallels and despite the fact that Crane seems to have utilized Eliot's method of kaleidoscopic presentation.

Their essential differences are nowhere made clearer than in their treatments of one of the central images they share. In a pivotal stanza of the first part of "Faustus and Helen" the prophetic voice proclaims of Helen:

> Inevitable, the body of the world
> Weeps in inventive dust for the hiatus
> That winks above it, bluet in your breasts.[4]

[3]*The Letters of Hart Crane: 1916-1932*, ed. Brom Weber (Berkeley and Los Angeles: Univ. of California Press, 1965), p. 115. Parenthetical page references will be preceded by *L*.

[4]Hart Crane, "For the Marriage of Faustus and Helen," *The Collected Poems of Hart Crane*, ed. Waldo Frank (New York: Liveright, 1946), p. 94. Subsequent references in the text will be from this edition (pp. 93-99).

Like much of the poem, the passage suffers from a sputtering rhetoric which draws attention to the idiom and away from the subject. It is readily apparent, however, that the world's body is mired in "*inventive* dust," that, somehow, a metamorphosis of circumstances is possible. The dust of *The Waste Land,* on the other hand, is only dust, the sign of a culture reduced to a state of utter decay. Along with the accessory images of dryness and "stony rubbish," Eliot's dust offers no possibilities for renascence (or so Crane would have believed). Its only use is to produce a kind of minor catharsis through contemplation and recognition; as Tiresias announces, "I will show you fear in a handful of dust."[5] To this awful prophecy of doom Crane responds with his assertions of the potentialities of a culture which even though it is in a state of deterioration will rise triumphant from its own dust. Against what he took to be Eliot's resignation and pessimism he provides a vision which, in one bombastic and sweeping formulation, insists that we "greet naively —yet intrepidly/ New soothings, new amazements."

It is possible to see transformation as the center of "Faustus and Helen." In fact, the poem is composed of a hierarchy of extravagant metamorphoses which establish a variety of possibilities and radical reconciliations. The most important member of the hierarchy is Helen. In a statement of intentions Crane wrote to Waldo Frank He says, "The whole poem is a kind of fusion of our own time with the past. Almost every symbol of current significance is matched by a correlative, suggested or actually stated, 'of ancient days'" (*L,* p. 120). It would therefore seem that the conventional meanings of the mythological figure Helen are significant. However, I should like to suggest that those meanings are relatively insignificant. Crane's Helen provokes the action of the poem; she appears as a symbol of supernal beauty and is given a special status as spirit of her culture. But in most particulars she bears little resemblance to the historical or mythological Helen. In Crane's clearest formulation of her character and role she represents the speed, intensity, and dynamism of modern industrial-technological culture. [...]

The dialectic of the poem is set in motion in Part I through the broad contrast between the world characterized in the first two

[5]T. S. Eliot, *Collected Poems: 1909-1935* (New York: Harcourt, Brace, 1936), p. 70.

stanzas and the discovery of Helen. Crane spoke of the process as
a movement from the "quotidian" to the "abstract" (*L*, p. 120). It
is perhaps more inclusive and more enlightening to see it as a movement from excessive, coercive discipline to energy.[6] As is usually
the case in Crane's major accomplishments, this movement is
achieved largely as the result of the multiple suggestions of diction.
The first two stanzas assert the constrictions imposed on the "mind"
by the urban environment. The speaker perceives division, fragmentation, sharply angular lines, and an overall linear quality (all
of this is summarized by the phrase "world dimensional" in the
prose gloss which follows). The conception is conveyed through
words such as "divided," "partitions," "margins," "curbs," "numbers," "memoranda," "baseball scores," "stenographic," "stock
quotations," and "convoying." Each reinforces the others so that the
sense of an extremely constricted environment is established. There
is no individuation; the emphasis falls on mass man, "multitudes,"
and "numbers." As the opening of the poem indicates, the individual mind, including the poet's, is totally suppressed. In ways
reminiscent of Elmer Rice's *The Adding Machine*, selfhood has
been replaced by cipher-hood. It is a thoroughly conventional conception of modern man.[7]

The images of the two stanzas are beautifully integrated and
deeply resonant. On the one hand, they provide an evocative, precise description of the reality which is to be metamorphosed in the
rest of the poem; on the other hand, one line in particular, "Smutty
wings flash out equivocations," serves to foreshadow some of the
characteristics of the metamorphosis. The "wings" anticipates the
actual movement of the poem. That is, the word establishes an idea
of flight which is developed later on when the speaker contemplates
Helen on a "plane" above the rest of the world, then joins her on a
Manhattan rooftop, and then, in the final section, considers a crucial
twentieth-century phenomenon, the airplane. The idea of flight, of a

[6]The terms "discipline" and "energy" as they are used here are drawn from the
discussion of literature and technology in Thomas Reed West, *Flesh of Steel: Literature and the Machine in American Culture* (Nashville: Vanderbilt Univ. Press,
1967).

[7]More frequently than not, Crane shared in the conception. Hence, his career,
I think, can be seen as oscillating between a fear of the city and a "belief" in it.
While "Faustus and Helen" and certain sections of *The Bridge* express hope, several poems express despair. See, for example, "Possessions," "Repose of Rivers,"
and "The Tunnel."

movement upward and away from the quotidian, is of course appropriate to the visionary basis of the poem and to the emphasis the poet places on the transforming powers of the imagination. Secondly, the word "flash" anticipates the primary characteristic of Crane's reconstituted Helen. Here it is used to underscore the impotence of the sullied, retarded possibilities of modernity, but there is also the implication of potential energy.[8] The idea of a rapid, sharp evocation of light is developed on a number of occasions through the active verbs used to describe Helen. When she is first seen on a streetcar, her eyes are said to be *"flickering"* with "prefigurations." In the first extended description of her functions, she is said to *"count* the nights/ Strippled with pink and green advertisements." When in the crucial "inventive dust" passage the speaker comments on her role as a conveyance to new realities, one of the verbs he uses is *"winks."* (In each instance these are my italics.)

On one level the verbs point to Helen's metamorphic qualities and to her good humor, her gaiety. It is more significant, however, that each of the verbs suggests, however obliquely, the electrical quality possessed by Helen and developed as the major motif of the poem. One of the difficulties of "Faustus and Helen" arises from the variety of surprising transformations we are expected to accept and credit. Perhaps the most surprising is that the poem is worked out through a series of images which suggest electricity. In his use of "flickering," "counts," and "winks" Crane has begun to explore the idea and to convey Helen's primary qualities. As I indicated before, this is no mythic or historic Helen, though it should be remarked that in his transformation Crane has attempted to create a new mythology which attempts to give credence to the notion that cultural energy resides in technology and industry. The initial placement of Helen on a streetcar stresses her involvement with modern culture and her commonplaceness. These suggestions are reinforced in the opening sentence of the next stanza when in the first metamorphosis of the poem Helen is said to be above the quotidian, marking the time of the neon signs of the night. The beginning of the fifth stanza clarifies and extends the concept:

[8]It is also possible that Crane is again remembering *The Waste Land,* in particular the ambiguous and provocative "flash of lightning" in "What the Thunder Said."

> Reflective conversion of all things
> At your deep blush, when ecstasies thread
> The limbs and belly, when rainbows spread
> Impinging on the throat and sides...

Helen is so thoroughly mythicized that she not only takes on extra-human capabilities but in a very real sense becomes a mechanic being. Her chromatic qualities obviously set her apart from the quotidian. Her capacity to initiate change in "all things" establishes her as a kind of numen of the modern world. The question might well be asked, exactly what has Helen become at this juncture in the poem? As preposterous as the answer may seem, it appears that we are expected to believe that she has been metamorphosed into a neon sign.

Her transformation into one of the basic advertising gimmicks of the age is shocking,[9] but no more so than are her later transformations into a rather vulgar flapper and into a "religious gunman" presiding magisterially over a violent landscape. We are prepared for this initial transformation through the previous application of certain key verbs. In the same way these verbs are prefigurations, Helen's newly asserted status anticipates the language of some of the poem's later significant events. The transformation is not capricious. At the end of Part I the speaker's praise is described as a "glowing orb," which while it suggests the speaker's eyes is a strikingly apt metaphor for an electric bulb. At the end of Part II the relationship between Helen and the speaker is consummated on the "incandescent wax." In Part III mythological analogies to the present are described in terms of "voltage." In a final crescendo of apocalyptic praise (one is tempted to call it the hysteria of a person contemplating the millennium) the imagination's transforming power is said to be "volatile." The use of the word is a perfect example of Crane's multilevel meanings. First, it suggests the ability to fly; second, it indicates the ability to erupt into explosive action; and third, it indicates lightheartedness. Needless to say, each of the three levels has a great deal to do with the ultimate meanings of "For the Marriage of Faustus and Helen."

[9]In point of fact, the first neon tubes, perfected by the French inventor Georges Flaude, were installed over a movie marquee on Times Square in early 1923. See Christopher Tunnard and Henry Hope Reed, *American Skyline* (New York: Mentor, 1956), p. 119.

To apprehend these meanings it is necessary to consider the influences of Waldo Frank and Gorham Munson on the poem. In early 1923 Crane read Munson's *Waldo Frank: A Study*. [...] Munson's *Study* is ostensibly an appreciative appraisal of Frank's work up until 1923. In this regard it is an oftentimes ecstatic, hyperbolic account of Frank's contributions to American fiction and social criticism. However, the method of the book is not simply descriptive and evaluative. Munson extrapolates from his subject to indicate directions for literature. One of his primary considerations is the use of machinery in art. Frank's *Our America* is seen as a great work of visionary social criticism but its failure is that it accepts machinery only as a "necessary evil," if not as an encroachment upon human possibilities:

> *Our America* has but a limited future and neglects and underestimates certain phenomena of American civilization that may seem more significant and healthy later on, such phenomena as our skyscrapers, bridges, motion pictures, jazz music, electric light displays, advertising. It may have missed completely the peculiar genius of the American people thrusting up into a new age.[10]

The emphasis here is on absorbing the various manifestations of modern technology. Elsewhere in his *Study* Munson comments on prior attempts to create a Machine Art. Futurists and dadaists have achieved some moderate successes but theirs are "minor aesthetic thrills." In a passage that must have struck a responding chord in Crane, he says,

> Up to now, it [Machine Art] has refused to channel emotional profundities, to take up love and desire and religion into its form. But while thus so patently limited, it should still be encouraged. For if my tentatives should prove to be sound, then we are in the childhood of a new age. We are, by the accident of our birth, chosen to create the simple forms, the folktales and folk-music, the preliminary art that our descendants may utilize in the vast struggle to put glowing spiritual content into machinery.[11]

That such hortatory statements as these were a direct influence on the conception and execution of "Faustus and Helen" and played

[10]Gorham Munson, *Waldo Frank: A Study* (New York: Boni and Liveright, 1923), p. 25.

[11]*Ibid.*, p. 20.

a large part in the early projections of *The Bridge* is attested to by Crane in a letter to Munson dated February 18, 1923:

> I am even more grateful for your very rich suggestions best stated in your *Frank Study* on the treatment of mechanical manifestations of today as subject for lyrical, dramatic, and even epic poetry. You must already notice that influence in "F and H." It is to figure even larger in *The Bridge*. The field of possibilities literally glitters all around one with the perception and vocabulary to pick out significant details and digest them into something emotional. (*L,* p. 125)

Certain of the particulars considered in "Faustus and Helen"— most notably, jazz, electric light displays, and advertising—are also stressed by Munson. The new art asserted by Munson is exactly the kind of art that Crane seemed to have in mind when he spoke of himself as "the *Pindar* of the dawn of the machine age." Like the Greek poet's hymns and dithyrambs, the new voice Crane achieved in "Faustus and Helen" is wildly (and naively) enthusiastic; and if Pindar can be seen as a poet of cultural pieties, so too can Crane in "Faustus and Helen." The poet who speaks to us here is no longer the figure of "Chaplinesque," living a set of rather precious ironies on the fringes of orthodox society; he is, like Pindar, the voice of the popular culture of the age. Of course, the popular culture is radically metamorphosed in "Faustus and Helen"—as Munson would say, the poet is attempting "to put glowing spiritual content into machinery"—but this is a process of discovery, not repudiation. Munson's desire for a "preliminary art" is at least partially fulfilled by Crane's mythicization of the commonplace.

In *Salvos,* his 1924 collection of miscellaneous essays, Waldo Frank also had something to say about this kind of art. Discussing the function of the poet in the twentieth century, he remarks that "The great primal artists [of the past, Dante, Blake, and Whitman] were creators, prophets, and sustainers of religion.[12] The comment is strikingly similar to remarks scattered through Crane's letters. Two of the three poets in Frank's pantheon of visionary seers, Blake and Whitman, are also the two foremost in Crane's. There are other affinities between Frank and Crane, of course, and some of these have been pointed out by other commentators. The most useful

[12]Waldo Frank, *Salvos: An Informal Book about Books and Plays* (New York: Liveright, 1924), p. 17.

discussion, as well as the most extended, is contained in Robert L. Perry's *The Shared Vision of Waldo Frank and Hart Crane*. Though Perry at times pays undue attention to shared "philosophies" at the expense of shared aesthetics, his monograph is crucial in two respects. First, his final chapter on the "Mystical Geometry" which the two writers share suggests much about the meanings of the curvilinear lines which often dominate Crane's mature poetry. Second, Perry points to the affinities between Frank's story "Hope" and "Faustus and Helen." [...]

Perry points out a number of similarities between poem and story. The young man in "Hope" resides in a meaningless urban environment at the start of the initiation, as does the speaker at the beginning of "Faustus and Helen"; Frank's character finds his salvation in a woman, as does Crane's; the denouements of both come in sexual union.[13] There are other and ultimately more significant affinities. Both figures achieve renewal after an enforced obliteration of the past. When he first sees Helen on a streetcar Crane's speaker is apparently in a semicomatose state, a rather purposeless repose in motion. He has

> ...forgot
> The fare and transfer, yet got by that way
> Without recall,—

The past of Frank's character is "beingless and thoughtless."[14] The strategy of both writers, in short, is to enforce and emphasize the new beginnings by placing their characters in a temporal vacuum from which they can emerge totally transformed. They both insist on the absolute necessity of starting anew. Consonant with this are the kinds of fusions which bring about the metamorphoses. They are not merely the sexual unions of male and female; they are the fusions of radically disparate entities. In "Hope" a sensitive young man whose thoughts at first indicate great refinement couples with a crude and vulgar Negro prostitute. In "Faustus and Helen" the partners are even more opposed.

The similarities between "Hope" and "Faustus and Helen" are illustrative of two writers coming to the same conclusions indepen-

[13]Robert L. Perry, *The Shared Vision of Waldo Frank and Hart Crane*, University of Nebraska Studies, n.s., No. 33 (May 1966), passim.
[14]Waldo Frank, "Hope," *Secession*, 3 (August 1922), 1.

dently. Just as Crane responded sympathetically to Frank's story, Frank responded enthusiastically to Crane's poem and became with Gorham Munson one of its two intelligent readers. As Crane wrote Frank, "It is a new feeling, and a glorious one, to have one's inmost delicate intentions so fully recognized as your last letter to me attested" (*L*, p. 127). Fortunately, the letter Crane referred to has been preserved. In it Frank says the poem "is a sort of marriage of heaven and hell...the hell of our modern mechanized world suddenly bearing as its essence an antique beauty which certain Elizabethans glimpsed for our language: and which you will also find fleshed in Racine."[15] In his criticism Frank is rarely as shrewd as he is here. First of all, his comment rightly emphasizes the Elizabethan quality of "Faustus and Helen." Essentially, the poem's idiom is comprised of ejaculations, bizarre diction, heavy stress patterns, and shocking syntactical distortions. Its ostentation, its oftentimes baroque quality, seems calculated to call attention to itself. It resembles nothing so much as seventeenth-century strong-lined verse. Secondly, and more to the point of my discussion, Frank has hit upon Crane's basic conception, the poem's "marriage of heaven and hell." He is using the phrase loosely but, nevertheless, his remark is extraordinarily suggestive.

The title of Crane's poem clearly echoes the title of Blake's *The Marriage of Heaven and Hell*, and in its radical fusion of disparate things it seems to be working in the same direction. Like Blake's *Marriage*, Crane's poem is an attempt to assert new possibilities by penetrating beyond quotidian realities, by sloughing off conventional responses to sensory experience, and by asserting the existence of extra dimensions which can somehow be apprehended if only the potential seer will discard the shackels of reason. Of course, these methods and aims are to be found elsewhere in visionary literature and philosophy. Other critics have suggested a variety of sources for Crane's "mysticism," including Nietzsche, Whitman, Rimbaud, P. D. Ouspensky, Samuel Greenberg, even the teachings of Christian Science.[16]   While Crane "absorbed" each of these

[15]From an unpublished letter quoted by Unterecker, p. 281.

[16]Perhaps the most suggestive discussion of these influences is by R. W. Butterfield, *The Broken Arc: A Study of Hart Crane* (Edinburgh: Oliver and Boyd, 1969), pp. 49-52.

writers, and knew of Christian Science through his mother, he would
have been hard put to say what he had learned from each. [...]

   Under these circumstances, it is difficult to disengage the influence of any one writer in the tradition of Crane's poetry. However,
I would still suggest that if there is a literary analogue to "For the
Marriage of Faustus and Helen" it is Blake's *The Marriage of
Heaven and Hell*. Beyond the similarities of title and aim there are
several important substantive parallels. Taken as a whole, Crane's
poem can be seen as working out the same philosophical contention
that serves as premise for Blake. At the beginning of the *Marriage*
the prophet declares, "Without Contraries is no progression. Attraction and Repulsion, Reason and Energy, Love and Hate, are
necessary to human existence."[17] He then goes on to audaciously
bring about the marriage of the contraries of heaven and hell, just
as Crane presides over the marriage of Faustus and Helen. The
heroes of the two poems are likewise similar. Blake's speaker actually descends into hell to learn of the new order. Crane's Faustus,
the man of imagination, is first located in the "hell" of the quotidian,
then meets his Helen in the eternal flames of Purgatory:

> I meet you, therefore, in that eventual flame
> You found in final chains, no captive then—
> Beyond their million brittle, bloodshot eyes;

His position assures that he is far removed from the commonplace,
that he has entered the realm of mythology to discover reality. In
Crane's work such a voyage is not peculiar. Faustus is like the very
Blakean figure in "Legend," a poem which, as I have tried to show
elsewhere,[18] serves as prologomena to *White Buildings*. There the
poet-lover-sacrificial idol commits himself to the flames in order to
discover a "constant harmony," a post-*Symboliste* Word which yields
changes of apocalyptic proportions.

   The last stanza of "Legend" reads:

[17]William Blake, *The Marriage of Heaven and Hell*, *The Poetry and Prose of
William Blake*, ed. David V. Erdman (Garden City, N.Y.: Doubleday, 1965), p. 34.
   [18]See "Toward Apotheosis: Hart Crane's Visionary Lyrics," *Criticism*, 10 (Autumn 1968), 313-33.

> Then, drop by caustic drop, a perfect cry
> Shall string some constant harmony,—
> Relentless caper of all those who step
> The legend of their youth into the noon.[19]

The idea of the "cry," the Dionysian utterance analogous to Whitman's "barbaric yawp," being "caustic" is significant. It points to a number of things, the most important among which is that poetry functions as a corrosive. This is perfectly appropriate to Crane's poetics; on many occasions he would insist that all great art serves to penetrate the surfaces of reality in order to reveal new possibilities. A similar attitude toward poetry is apparent in "Faustus and Helen" as, through the penetrating and transforming powers of the speaker's art, the dust of the beginning is changed to become, near the end, "The abating shadows of our conscript dust." In the process of the poem a series of magical transformations has been made, so that the achromatic grays and whites and blacks of the quotidian described in the first stanzas are replaced by the golds and reds of the last three stanzas. Here again "Faustus and Helen" is illustrative of one of the key assertions of Blake's *Marriage*. In his prophecy Blake discusses his own poetics and suggests much about his methods and goals as an engraver. In his attempt to reconcile body and soul he declares:

> But first the notion that man has a body distinct from his soul, is to be expunged; this I shall do, by printing in the infernal method, by corrosives, which in Hell are salutary and medicinal, melting apparent surfaces away, and displaying the infinite which was hid.
> If the doors of perception were cleansed everything would appear to man as it is, infinite.
> For man has closed himself up, till he sees all things thro' narrow chinks of his cavern.[20]

The passage recalls certain manifestoes in the writings of the alchemical mystics Jacob Boehme and Paracelsus; Blake's use of what he calls the "infernal method" can be regarded as a kind of modified alchemy. So too can Crane's method in "Faustus and Helen. [...]

In a sense, "Faustus and Helen" aims to bring about the same kind of transformation sought after futilely by Renaissance alchemists.

[19]Hart Crane, "Legend," *The Collected Poems of Hart Crane*, p. 62.
[20]Blake, *The Marriage*, pp. 38-39.

Its "inventive dust" is the dross with which the alchemist begins his machinations; its "gold-shod prophecies of heaven" and "shadow of gold hair" are the equivalents of the precious metals yielded by the dross when the chemicals, the corrosives, do their work. The process is not completed in "Faustus and Helen," however. At the end we are clearly asked to carry out the speaker's directions by lifting our voices with his. In one of many rhetorical flourishes at the close, the speaker remarks that he has survived "To saturate" his Helen, the modern world, "with blessing and dismay." As on so many other occasions in the poem, Crane here uses the word which carries with it the perfect connotation. "Saturate" at first appears to be an over-statement, another instance of the poet's rhetoric exceeding his thought. But with the parallels to alchemy in mind, the word takes on a nice sharpness. On the one hand, it connotes the way the dross of modernity is to be treated. On the other hand, it indicates the chemical process by which two elements (in this case, Faustus and Helen) are caused to combine until there is no further tendency to combine. The word serves the double function of recalling the hyperbole of traditional love poetry even while it calls to mind scientific technology. And, of course, the fusion of the traditional and the technological is the ultimate aim of the poem.

The shock of the strange, magical transformations is somewhat mitigated by Crane's use of lines from Jonson's *The Alchemist* (IV, 3) as the epigraph for the poem. In the play the lines are spoken by the shrew (and shrewish) whore, Dol Common, when she is in her "fit of talking." R.W.B. Lewis has called the lines "pure Jabberwocky," rejecting the idea that Crane may have been hinting at an image of the poet as magician-alchemist. In doing so he asserts that the inclusion of them was a mistake, though he does concede that Crane "may have kept the lines for their rhetorical exuberance."[21] Lewis is quite correct in calling attention to the fact that Jonson's scene, in which Dol is continuing her attempt to gull Sir Epicure Mammon, is a raucous parody of the meeting of Faustus and Helen in Marlowe's *Doctor Faustus*. But that is precisely the point of Crane's use of the lines. "For the Marriage of Faustus and Helen" does many things—at times one may feel it attempts to do *too* many things—but it is clear that it is first and foremost an attempt to trans-

---

[21]R. W. B. Lewis, *The Poetry of Hart Crane, A Critical Study* (Princeton: Princeton Univ. Press, 1967), p. 91.

mute commonplace reality to the point where it becomes vibrant with promise. The personages employed are drawn from tradition, but it should be clear by now that they are representative of the twentieth century. Though not entirely appropriate, the Helen of the poem is akin to Dol Common (indeed, the tag name might well apply to Crane's female in her guises of streetcar-rider, neon sign, and flapper) and Faustus, at least the early Faustus of the poem, is akin to Sir Epicure Mamon. Crane is fully participating in Jonson's parody of Marlowe's scene; he is pointing, in effect, to a new version of the Faustus-and-Helen myth. Rather than being "a bewildering complex of ironies,"[22] the poem's epigraph is quite direct (that is perhaps too strong a phrase: the epigraph is really no more and no less bewildering than the rest of the poem). It serves as a fitting entrance to the sense of "Faustus and Helen." In its reference to "Talmud skill/ And profane Greek" as the methods by which renewal is to be achieved it anticipates the severely arcane quality of the idiom Crane employs. So too does it identify the forces of the enemy, the outcasts and exotic, pagan furies who would no doubt be opposed to Crane's assertions. Finally, the mere fact that *The Alchemist* is referred to at all sets a framework within which the poem is to be understood. It matters little that Jonson's play is in part a satire on alchemy; in Crane's hand, Dol Common's speech is transformed to become an entirely positive statement. It may be "pure Jabberwocky" but that is not to say that Crane's use of it is similar.

As I have indicated, "Faustus and Helen" is a synthesis of several different traditions, urges, convictions, beliefs, hopes. Understanding it depends on understanding the circumstances of its composition, the influences Crane was feeling at the time, and the degree of integration of its image patterns. Were these the only problems, however, it could be concluded that we are merely dealing with another classic text (or rescuing it from obscurity), another complex, multifaceted poem which must be seen totally. There is more to it than that.

What is implicitly at stake in "Faustus and Helen" is of vastly greater import: the crucial issue which emerges is the conflict between an aesthetic and a metaphysic based on a Newtonian concep-

[22]*Ibid.*

tion of the universe and an aesthetic and metaphysic which is probably best characterized as relativistic and atomist. I do not wish to overstate the case. Despite some evidence that Crane was aware of developments in modern science, his knowledge was most likely not more than that of a reasonably well-educated layman.[23] But, like many postmodernist poets, his interest in Blake and his quarrel with Eliot were based on a keen recognition that the one was simply more *contemporary* than the other. To put the point another way, Crane recognized that the notion of a neatly dimensional, material, ordered, comprehensible universe (the universe as it is described in the opening stanzas of the poem) was a thing of the past, a thing held to, ironically, by a modern poet, Eliot, and thoroughly repudiated by a poet of the early nineteenth century, Blake. [...]

The entire history of modern science, from the great nineteenth-century geometers forward, demonstrates a stance toward reality quite at odds with Eliot's and, not too surprisingly, quite in keeping with Blake's. It argues continuity, the relativity of measuring sticks, the existence of an endless variety of orders, the fact that to measure something is to change it, the kinetic structure of the universe, the indeterminacy of physical events, the unpredictability of the future, the lack of evidence for cause and effect. Translated into aesthetic terms, it suggests that Aristotelian ideas of order are outmoded, irrelevant. Charles Olson, who so far as I know is the only contemporary writer to articulate what amounts to a quantum aesthetics based on non-Euclidean geometry and modern physics, has asserted much of this. [...]

Olson's own poetry is clearly based on these conceptions of reality. So too is the work of Robert Creeley; a reading of his large collec-

[23]Others have discussed Crane's knowledge of modern science. Among specialized studies, see Frederick J. Hoffman, "The Technological Fallacy in Contemporary Poetry: Hart Crane and Macknight Black," *American Literature,* 21 (1949), 94-107; Margaret LeClair Foster, "Hart Crane: Poet of the Machine Age," *Carnegie Studies in English,* II (Pittsburgh: Carnegie Institute of Technology, 1955), pp. 4-23; Peter Viereck, "The Poet in the Machine Age," *Dream and Responsibility: Four Test Cases of the Tension Between Poetry and Society* (Washington: Univ. Press of Washington, D.C., 1953), pp. 47-65; Hyatt Howe Waggoner, "Hart Crane's Bridge to Cathay," *American Literature,* 16 (1944), 115-30. The most satisfying discussion of the subject, at least in terms of its theoretical framework, is also the most recent: James C. Cowan, "The Theory of Relativity and *The Bridge,"* *Hartford Studies in Literature,* 3 (1971), 108-15.

tion of essays, reviews, and notes, *A Quick Graph,* confirms that. Even the title is suggestive of the degree to which the analogies to geometry are at issue. My purpose here is not to establish the aesthetic basis of Black Mountain poetry, or of postmodernism in general. Nor is it my intention to argue the veracities of Olson and Creeley. The point of all this is that there are connections to Hart Crane's "For the Marriage of Faustus and Helen." that Crane's 1923 work is anticipatory of much recent poetry in the United States (it should be understood, of course, that in speaking of Olson and Creeley we are in fact talking of the two most influential contemporary poets).[24] Aside from the establishment of Blake as opposed to Eliot as the master, Crane does several important things. First, he relies heavily on an attitude toward scientific technology which is at odds with the attitudes of the major writers of the period. Obviously, he has moved far beyond the fracture of the "two cultures." Second, like Olson, Crane makes an effort to rescue a city from the grasp of the wastelanders, to make the dust "inventive. [....] Third, if I am correct in suggesting that Crane's aesthetic, like Olson's, is basically non-Aristotelian, non-Newtonian, and non-Euclidean, then we are dealing with entirely new matters. Questions of rational structure have haunted Crane's critics, particularly those critics who have discussed *The Bridge;* the structure of "Faustus and Helen" is equally problematic. [...] The crux of these discussions, however, is in a stance toward reality not shared by the poet. In other words, primarily Newtonian, Aristotelian questions have been asked of works which are relativistic and atomist. Mechanical order of a traditional nature is demanded of poems which reject mechanical order. As Olson would say, and, I believe, as Crane would echo, one kind of manifold, the discrete, is pitted against another and more credible manifold, the continuous.

The idea of poetry being on the order of a continuum places us, of course, in an entirely different universe. But that universe, first

---

[24]Creeley has written very sympathetically of Crane. In "Hart Crane and the Private Judgment," a 1953 essay collected in *A Quick Graph,* he cites James B. Conant's *Modern Science and Modern Man.* He quotes Conant quoting J. J. Thompson's *The Corpuscular Theory of Matter* as a means of distinguishing *The Bridge* from *The Waste Land:* "From the point of view of the physicist, a theory of matter is a policy rather than a creed; its object is to connect or coordinate apparently diverse phenomena and above all to suggest, stimulate, and direct experiment" (p. 79). Eliot's poem is a "creed"; Crane's, a "policy."

entered by Crane in "Faustus and Helen," is the universe as seen in postmodern American poetry. Metamorphosis is at its center; the transforming, synthesizing imagination is its kingpin; the idea of the absolute freedom of the will to create anew is its basis. Hart Crane's "mysticism" is by now a well-worn concept. In closing, I should like to suggest that his mysticism is no more mysterious than many of the perceptions of modern geometry and modern physics. To suggest that Helen changes so, or that there is a "fourth dimension" (a phrase Crane was fond of quoting from Ouspensky), is, finally, no more and no less "mystical" to the Newtonian imagination than to say that the universe is a four dimension space-time continuum, or that bodies contract in direct ratio to their velocity, or that an endless number of parallel lines pass through a given point. It is just that, as Olson says, "The new world of atomism offered a metrical means as well as a topos different from the discrete."[25]

[25]"Equal, That Is, To the Real Itself," *Selected Writings of Charles Olson*, ed. Robert Creeley (New York: New Directions, 1966), p. 46. Copyright © 1966 by Charles Olson. Reprinted by permission of New Directions Publishing Corporation.

Hart Crane's Gnosis

by Harold Bloom

O Thou steeled Cognizance whose leap commits
The agile precincts of the lark's return...

    I remember reading these lines when I was eleven years old, crouched over Crane's book in a Bronx library. They, and much else in the book, cathected me onto poetry, a conversion or investment fairly typical of many in my generation. I still have the volume of Crane that I persuaded my older sister to give me on my twelfth birthday, the first book I ever owned. Among my friends there are a few others who owned Crane before any other book. Growing up in the thirties, we were found by Crane's poetry, and though other poets followed (I went from Crane to Blake) the strength of first love still hovers whenever they, or I, read Crane.

    The Marlovian rhetoric swept us in, but as with Marlowe himself the rhetoric was also a psychology and a knowing, rather than a knowledge, a knowing that precisely can be called a gnosis, transcending the epistemology of tropes. What the Australian poet Alec Hope, echoing Tamburlaine, perceptively called: "The Argument of Arms," is as much Crane's knowing and language as it was Marlowe's. "Know ye not the argument of arms?" Tamburlaine calls out to his protesting generals before he stabs his own son to death for cowardice. As Hope expounds it, "the argument of arms" is poetic warfare, the agonistic interplay of the Sublime mode:

> There is no middle way and no compromise in such a world. Beauty is the rival of beauty as force of force, and only the supreme and perfect survives. Defeat, like victory, is total, absolute, final.

This is indeed Marlowe's knowing, and it would be pointless for a humanist critic to complain that such a vision is human-all-too-human. *Power* is the central poetic concept in Marlowe as it will be in Milton, and as it came to be in the American Milton, Emerson (a prose Milton, granted) and in Crane as a kind of American Marlowe. Hope rightly points to Hazlitt on *Coriolanus* as the proper theorist of the union of the Argument of Arms and the Argument of Poetry. Hazlitt also would not gain the approval of the natural super-naturalist kind of critical humanist:

> The principle of poetry is a very anti-leveling principle. It aims at effect, it exists by contrast. It admits of no medium. It is everything by excess. It raises above the ordinary standard of sufferings and crimes.

But Crane is a prophet of American Orphism, of the Emersonian and Whitmanian Native Strain in our national literature. His poetic of power is therefore best caught by the American theorist proper:

> ...though Fate is immense, so is Power, which is the other fact in the dual world, immense. If Fate follows and limits Power, Power attends and antagonizes Fate. We must respect Fate as natural history. For who and what is this criticism that pries into the matter? Man is not order of nature, sack and sack, belly and members, link in a chain, nor any ignominious baggage; but a stupendous antagonism, a dragging together of the poles of the Universe...

This might be Melville, meditating upon his own Ahab, but of course it is the uncanny Sage of Concord, satirized by Melville as Plotinus Plinlimmon and as Confidence Man, yet the satire was uneasy. Crane is not very easy to satirize either, and like Shelley, with whom his affinities were deep, Crane goes on burying his critical undertakers. Whitman and Dickinson, Frost and Stevens all had time enough, but Crane, perhaps more gifted than any of them, was finished at an age when they had begun weakly or not at all. A gnosis of Man as a stupendous antagonism, Orphic and Promethean, needs time to work itself through, but time, reviled by all gnostics with a particular vehemence, had its literal triumph over Crane. As with Shelley and Keats, we have a truncated canon, and yet, as with them, what we have is overwhelming.

I am concerned here with Crane's "religion" *as a poet* (not as a man, since that seems an inchoate mixture of a Christian Science background, an immersion in Ouspensky, and an all but Catholic yearning). But by poetic "religion" I mean American Orphism, the Emersonian or national religion of our poetry, which Crane inherited, quite directly, from his prime precursor Whitman. True precursors are always composite and imaginary, the son's changeling-fantasy of the father that his own poetry reinvents, and there is usually a near-contemporary agon as well as a struggle with the fathering force of the past. The older contemporary antagonist and shaper for Crane was certainly Eliot, whose anti-Romantic polemic provoked in Crane an answering fury of High Romanticism, absurdly undervalued by Crane's critical contemporaries, but returning to its mainstream status in the generation that receives the recent abundance of poetic maturation in Ashbery, Merrill, Ammons and others.

The governing deities of American Orphism, as of the ancient sort, are Eros and Phanes, Dionysus or Bacchus, and Ananke, the Necessity who appears as the maternal ocean in Whitman and Crane most overtly, but clearly and obsessively enough in Stevens also. Not so clear, though just as obsessive, must be our judgement upon Melville's representations of an Orphic Ananke in the great shroud of the sea. Melville's "that man should be a thing for immortal souls to sieve through!" is the apt epigraph of a crucial chapter on Greek Shamanism in E. R. Dodds' great book, *The Greeks and the Irrational*. Dodds traced to Scythia the new Orphic religious pattern that credited man with an occult self of divine origin. This self was not the psyche, but the daemon; as Dodds says, "the function of the daemon is to be the carrier of man's potential divinity and actual guilt." Crane's daemon or occult self, like Whitman's, is the actual hero and victim of his own poetry. Crane as American Orpheus is an inevitable image, exploited already by writers as diverse as Winters in his elegy for Crane and Tennessee Williams in *Suddenly Last Summer*. The best of the Orphic hymns to Crane is the astonishing "Fish Food" of John Brooks Wheelwright, except that Crane wrote his own best Orphic elegy in "Atlantis," his close equivalent of Shelley's *Adonais*. But I narrow my subject here, of Crane's "Orphism," down to its visionary epistemology or Gnosis. Crane's Eros, his Dionysus, above all his Whitmanian Ananke, remain to be explored, but in these pages

I concern myself only with Crane as "daemon," a potential divinity knowing simultaneously its achievement and its guilt.

The assumption of that daemon, or what the poets of Sensibility called "the incarnation of the Poetic Character," is the inner plot of many of the lyrics in *White Buildings*. The *kenosis* or ebbing-away of the daemon is the plot of the "Voyages" sequence, where the other Orphic deities reduce Crane to a "derelict and blinded guest" of his own vision, and where the "ocean rivers" churn up the Orphic heritage as a "splintered garland for the seer." Certainly the most ambitious of the daemonic incarnations is the sequence "For the Marriage of Faustus and Helen," which is Crane at his most triumphantly Marlovian, but so much else is at play there that I turn to two lesser but perfect hymns of Orphic incarnation, "Repose of Rivers" and "Passage."

Crane is a great master of transumptive allusion, of achieving poetic closure by a final trope that reverses or sometimes even transcends both his own lyric's dominant figurations and the poetic tradition's previous exploitations of these images. So, "Repose of Rivers" concludes:

> ...There, beyond the dykes
> I heard wind flaking sapphire, like this summer,
> And willows could not hold more steady sound.

The poem's opening stanza gives a more complex version of that "steady sound" because the synaesthetic seeing/ hearing of "that seething, steady leveling of the marshes" is both an irony and an oxymoron:

> The willows carried a slow sound,
> A sarabande the wind moved on the mead.
> I could never remember
> That seething, steady leveling of the marshes
> Till age had brought me to the sea.

Crane is recalling his version of a Primal Scene of Instruction, a moment renewing itself discontinuously at scattered intervals, yet always for him a moment relating the inevitability of sexual orientation to the assumption of his poethood. The slow-and-steady dance of the wind on the marshes became a repressed memory until "age" as maturation brought the poet to the sea, central image of necessity in his poetry, and a wounding synecdoche here for an acceptance of one's particular fate as a poet. The repressed reveals itself as a grotesque sublimity, with the second stanza alluding to Melville's imagery in his story, "The Encantadas";

> Flags, weeds. And remembrance of steep alcoves
> Where cypresses shared the noon's
> Tyranny. They drew me into hades almost.
> And mammoth turtles climbing sulphur dreams
> Yielded, while sun-silt rippled them
> Asunder…

The seething, steady leveling of the mammoth turtles, their infernal love-death, is a kind of sarabande also. In climbing one another they climb dreams of self-immolation, where "yielded" means at once surrender to death and to one another. The terrible slowness of their love-making yields the frightening trope: "sun-silt rippled them/ Asunder," where "asunder" is both the post-coition parting and the individual turtle death. Crane and D. H. Lawrence had in common as poets only their mutual devotion to Whitman, and it is instructive to contrast this stanza of "Repose of Rivers" with the Tortoise-series of Lawrence in *Birds, Beasts and Flowers*. Lawrence's tortoises are crucified *into* sex, like Lawrence himself. Crane's Melvillean turtles are crucified *by* sex. But Crane tells a different story about himself: crucified *into* poetry and *by* poetry. The turtles *are* drawn into a sexual hades; Crane is *almost* drawn, with the phrase "hades almost" playing against "steep alcoves." Embowered by steep alcoves of cypresses, intensifying the dominant noon sun, Crane nearly yields to the sexual phantasmagoria of "flags, weeds," and the sound play alcoves/ almost intensifies the narrowness of the escape from a primary sexuality, presumably an incestuous heterosexuality. This is the highly oblique burden of the extraordinary third stanza:

> How much I would have bartered! the black gorge
> And all the singular nestings in the hills
> Where beavers learn stitch and tooth.
> The pond I entered once and quickly fled—
> I remember now its singing willow rim.

What he would have bartered, indeed did barter, was nature for poetry. Where the second stanza was a *kenosis,* an emptying-out, of the Orphic self, this stanza is fresh influx, and what returns from repression is poetic apperception: "I remember now its singing willow rim," a line that reverberates greatly against the first and last lines of the entire poem. The surrendered Sublime here is a progressive triad of entities: the Wordsworthian abyss of birth of "the black gorge"; "the singular nestings" instructive of work and aggression; most memorably the pond, rimmed by singing willows, whose entrance actually marks the momentary daring of the representation of Oedipal trespass, or perhaps for Crane one should say "Orphic trespass."

If everything heretofore in "Repose of Rivers" has been bartered for the antithetical gift of Orpheus, what remains is to represent the actual passage into sexuality, and after that the poetic maturation that follows homosexual self-acceptance. Whether the vision here is of an actual city, or of a New Orleans of the mind, as at the end of "The River" section of *The Bridge,* the balance of pleasure and of pain is left ambiguous:

> And finally, in that memory all things nurse;
> After the city that I finally passed
> With scalding unguents spread and smoking darts
> The monsoon cut across the delta
> At gulf gates...There, beyond the dykes
> I heard wind flaking sapphire, like this summer,
> And willows could not hold more steady sound.

The third line of the stanza refers both to the pathos of the city and to Crane's own sexual initiation. But since "all things nurse" this memory, the emphasis must be upon breakthrough, upon the contrast between monsoon and the long-obliterated memory of sarabande-wind: "like this summer," the fictive moment of the lyric's composition, the monsoon of final sexual alignment gave the gift of an achieved poethood, to hear wind synaesthetically, flaking sapphire, breaking up yet also distributing the Shelleyan azure of vision. In such a context, the final line massively gathers an Orphic confidence.

Yet every close reader of Crane learns to listen to the wind for evidences of *sparagmos,* of the Orphic breakup, as omnipresent in Crane's winds as in Shelley's, or in Whitman's. I turn to "Passage," *White Buildings'* particular poem of Orphic disincarnation, where the rite of passage, the movement back to unfindable and fictive origins, is celebrated more memorably in the opening quatrain than anywhere else even in Crane, who is clearly the great modern poet of *thresholds,* in the sense definitively expounded in Angus Fletcher's forthcoming book of that title:

> Where the cedar leaf divides the sky
> I heard the sea.
> In sapphire arenas of the hills
> I was promised an improved infancy.

The Fletcherian *threshold* is a daemonic crossing or textual "image of voice," to use Wordsworth's crucial term. Such a chiasmus tends to hover where tropes collide in an epistemological wilderness. Is there a more outrageously American, Emersonian concept and phrase than "an improved infancy"? Crane presumably was not aware that "Passage" centered itself so directly at the Wordsworthian heart of the crisis poem, in direct competition with "Tintern Abbey" and the "Intimations of Immortality" ode. But the American version as established in the *Seadrift* poems of Whitman was model enough. Crane, inland far though he finds himself, hears the sea. The soft inland murmur promised Wordsworth so improved an infancy that it became an actual intimation of a more-than-poetic immortality. But for Whitman the secret of the murmuring he envied had to be listened for at the water-line. Crane quests for the same emblem that rewarded "Repose of Rivers," but here the wind does not flake sapphire in the arenas of these inland hills, where the agon with the daemon, Whitman's dusky demon and brother, is to take place.

In Whitman's great elegy of Orphic disincarnation, "As I Ebb'd with the Ocean of Life," the daemon comes to the poet in the shape of a sardonic phantom, "the real Me," and confronts Whitman, who may hold his book, *Leaves of Grass,* in hand, since the phantom is able to point to it:

> But that before all my arrogant poems the real Me
>   stands yet untouch'd, untold, altogether unreach'd
> Withdrawn far, mocking me with mock-congratulatory
>   signs and bows,
> With peals of distant ironical laughter at every
>   word I have written,
> Pointing in silence to these songs, and then to the
>   sand beneath.

> I perceive I have never really understood any thing,
> not a single object, and that no man ever can.
> Nature here in sight of the sea taking advantage of me
> to dart upon me and sting me,
> Because I have dared to open my mouth to sing at all.

In Crane's "Passage" the sulking poet, denied his promise, abandons memory in a ravine, and tries to identify himself with the wind, but it dies, and he is turned back and around to confront his mocking daemon:

> Touching an opening laurel, I found
> A thief beneath, my stolen book in hand.

It is deliberately ambiguous whether the real Me has stolen the book, or whether the book of Hart Crane itself is stolen property. Unlike the abashed Whitman, Crane is aggressive and his phantom is lost in wonderment:

> "Why are you back here—smiling an iron coffin?"
> "To argue with the laurel," I replied:
> "Am justified in transience, fleeing
> Under the constant wonder of your eyes—."

But nature here, suddenly in sight of the sea, does take advantage of Crane to dart upon him and sting him, because he has dared to open his mouth to sing at all:

> He closed the book. And from the Ptolemies
> Sand troughed us in a glittering abyss.
> A serpent swam a vertex to the sun
> —On unpaced beaches leaned its tongue and drummed.
> What fountains did I hear? What icy speeches?
> Memory, committed to the page, had broke.

The Ptolemies, alluded to here as though they were a galaxy rather than a dynasty, help establish the pyramid image for the serpent who touches its apex in the sun. The glittering abyss belongs both to time and the sun, and the serpent, drumming its tongue upon the beach where no Whitmanian bard paces, is weirdly prophetic of the imagery of Stevens' "The Auroras of Autumn." The penultimate line glances obliquely at Coleridge's "Kubla Khan," and the poem ends appropriately with the broken enchantment of memory, broken in the act of writing the poem. It is as though, point for point, "Passage" had undone "Repose of Rivers."

The Bridge can be read as the same pattern of Orphic incarnation/ disincarnation, with every Sublime or daemonic vision subsequently undone by an ebbing-out of poethood. That reading, though traditional, seems to me a weak misreading, inadequate to *The Bridge's* strong misreadings of its precursors. Nietzsche and Pater, both of whom Crane had pondered, taught a subtler *askesis,* and *The Bridge* advances upon *White Buildings* (except for "Voyages") by mounting a powerful scheme of transumption, of what Nietzsche called the poetic will's revenge against time and particularly against time's proclamation of belatedness: "It was." Crane shrewdly wrote, in 1918: "one may envy Nietzsche a little; think of being so elusive,— so mercurial, as to be first swallowed whole, then coughed up, and still remain a mystery!" But veteran readers of Crane learn to observe something like that when confronted by the majesty of *The Bridge* at its finest, as here in the final quatrains of the "Proem":

> Again the traffic lights that skim thy swift
> Unfractioned idiom, immaculate sigh of stars,
> Beading thy path—condense eternity:
> And we have seen night lifted in thine arms.
>
> Under thy shadows by the piers I waited;
> Only in darkness is thy shadow clear.
> The City's fiery parcels all undone,
> Already snow submerges an iron year...
>
> O Sleepless as the river under thee,
> Vaulting the sea, the prairies' dreaming sod
> Unto us lowliest sometime sweep, descend
> And of the curveship lend a myth to God.

Crane in *White Buildings* is wholly Orphic, in that his concern is his relation, as poet, *to* his own vision, rather than *with* the content of poetic vision, to utilize a general distinction inaugurated by Northrop Frye, following after Ruskin. The peculiar power of *The Bridge,* at its strongest, is that Crane succeeds in becoming what Pater and Nietzsche urged the future poet to be: an ascetic of the spirit, which is an accurate definition of a purified Gnosis. Directly before these three final quatrains of "To Brooklyn Bridge," Crane had saluted the bridge first as Orphic emblem, both harp and altar, but then as the threshold of the full triad of the Orphic destiny, Dionysus or prophet's pledge, Ananke or prayer of pariah, and Eros, the lover's cry. It is after the range of relations to his own vision has been acknowledged and accepted, that a stronger Crane achieves the Gnosis of those three last quatrains. There the poet remains present, but only as a knowing abyss, contemplating the content of that knowing, which is a fullness or presence he can invoke but scarcely share. He sees "night lifted in thine arms"; he waits, for a shadow to clarify in darkness; he knows, yet what he knows is a vaulting, sweep, descent, above all a curveship, a realization of an angle of vision not yet his own.

This peculiarly effective stance has a precursor in Shelley's visionary skepticism, particularly in his final phase of *Adonais* and *The Triumph of Life*. Crane's achievement of this stance is the still-unexplored origin of *The Bridge*, but the textual evolution of "Atlantis," the first section of the visionary epic to be composed, is the probable area that should be considered. Lacking space here, I point instead to the achieved stance of "Voyages VI" as the earliest full instance of Crane's mature Orphism, after which I will conclude with a reading of "Atlantis" and a brief glance at Crane's testament, "The Broken Tower."

The governing deities of the "Voyages" sequence are Eros and Ananke, or Emil Opffer and the Caribbean as Whitmanian fierce old mother moaning for her castaways. But the Orphic Dionysus, rent apart by Titantic forces, dominates the sixth lyric, which like Stevens' "The Paltry Nude Starts upon a Spring Journey" partly derives from Pater's description of Botticelli's Venus in *The Renaissance*. Pater's sado-masochistic maternal love-goddess, with her eyes smiling "unsearchable repose," becomes Crane's overtly destructive muse, whose seer is no longer at home in his own vision:

> My eyes pressed black against the prow,
> —thy derelict and blinded guest
>
> Waiting, afire, what name, unspoke,
> I cannot claim: let thy waves rear
> More savage than the death of kings,
> Some splintered garland for the seer.

The unspoken, unclaimed name is that of Orpheus, in his terrible final phase of "floating singer." Crane's highly deliberate echo of

Shakespeare's Richard II at his most self-destructively masochistic is assimilated to the poetic equivalent, which is the splintering of the garland of laurel. Yet the final stanza returns to the central image of poetic incarnation in Crane, "Repose of Rivers" and its "hushed willows":

> The imaged Word, it is, that holds
> Hushed willows anchored in its glow.
> It is the unbetrayable reply
> Whose accent no farewell can know.

This is the achieved and curiously firm balance of a visionary skepticism, or the Orphic stance of *The Bridge*. It can be contrasted to Lawrence again, in the "Orphic farewell" of "Medlars and Sorb Apples" in *Birds, Beasts and Flowers*. For Lawrence, Orphic assurance is the solipsism of an "intoxication of perfect loneliness." Crane crosses that intoxication by transuming his own and tradition's trope of the hushed willows as signifying an end to solitary mourning and a renewal of poetic divination. "Voyages VI" turns its "imaged Word" against Eliot's neo-orthodox Word, or Christ, and Whitman's Word out of the Sea, or death, death that is the Oedipal merging back into the mother. Crane ends upon "know" because knowledge, and not faith, is his religious mode, a Gnosis that is more fully developed in *The Bridge*.

The dozen octaves of the final version of "Atlantis" show Crane in his mastery of the traditional Sublime and are wholly comparable to the final seventeen stanzas of Shelley's *Adonais*. Crane's absolute music, like Plato's, "is then the knowledge of that which relates to love in harmony and system." but Crane's love is rather more like Shelley's desperate and skeptical outleaping than it is like Diotima's vision. For six stanzas, Crane drives upward, in hyperbolic arc whose burden is agonistic, struggling to break beyond every achieved Sublime in the language. This agon belongs to the Sublime, and perhaps in America it *is* the Sublime. But such an agon requires particular contestants, and "Atlantis" finds them in *The Waste Land* and, yet more repressedly, in Whitman's "Crossing Brooklyn Ferry," the great addition to the second (1856) *Leaves of Grass,* and Thoreau's favorite poem by Whitman.

Much of Crane's struggle with Eliot was revised out of the final "Atlantis," but only as overt textual traces, and the deep inward-

ness of the battle is recoverable. Two modes of phantasmagoria
clash:

> Through the bound cable strands, the arching path
> Upward, veering with light, the flight of strings,—
> Taut miles of shuttling moonlight syncopate
> The whispered rush, telepathy of wires.
> Up the index of night, granite and steel—
> Transparent meshes—fleckless the gleaming staves—
> Sibylline voices flicker, waveringly stream
> As though a god were issue of the strings....
>
> A woman drew her long black hair out tight
> And fiddled whisper music on those strings
> And bats with baby faces in the violet light
> Whistled, and beat their wings
> And crawled head downward down a blackened wall
> And upside down in air were towers
> Tolling reminiscent bells, that kept the hours
> And voices singing out of empty cisterns and exhausted wells.

The latter hallucination might be called an amalgam of *Dracula*
and the Gospels, as rendered in the high style of Tennyson's *Idylls
of the King,* and obviously is in no sense a source or cause of Crane's
transcendental opening octave. Nevertheless, no clearer contrast
could be afforded, for Crane's lines answer Eliot's, in every meaning
of "answer." "Music is then the knowledge of that which relates to
love in harmony and system," and one knowledge answers another
in these competing and marvelous musics of poetry, and of visionary
history. Crane's bridge is to Atlantis, in fulfillment of the Platonic
quest of Crane's Columbus. Eliot's bridge is to the Inferno, in fulfillment of the neo-Christian condemnation of Romantic, Tran-
scendentalist, Gnostic quest. Crane's Sibylline voices stream upward; his night-illuminated bridge becomes a transparent musical
score, until Orpheus is born out of the flight of strings. Eliot's
Sibyl wishes to die; her counterpart plays a vampiric score upon
her own hair, until instead of an Orphic birth upwards we have an
impotent triumph of time.

This contrast, and others equally sharp, constitute the context of
Crane's aspiration in "Atlantis." But this aspiration, which is for
knowledge, in the particular sense of Gnosis, yields to Eliot, as it
must, much of the world of things-as-they-are. The closing images of

"The Tunnel," the section of *The Bridge* preceding "Atlantis,"
combine *The Waste Land's* accounts of loss with Whitman's darker
visions of those in "Crossing Brooklyn Ferry":

> And this thy harbor, O my City, I have driven under,
> Tossed from the coil of ticking towers....Tomorrow,
> And to be....Here by the River that is East—
> Here at the waters' edge the hands drop memory;
> Shadowless in that abyss they unaccounting lie.
> How far away the star has pooled the sea—
> Or shall the hands be drawn away, to die?
>
> Kiss of our agony Thou gatherest,
>   O Hand of Fire
>   gatherest—

Emerson's was a Gnosis without Gnosticism; Crane's religion, at
its darkest, shades from Orphism into Gnosticism, in a negative
transcendence even of the Whitman who proclaimed: "It is not upon
you alone the dark patches fall,/ The dark threw its patches upon
me also." The negative transcendence of "Atlantis" surmounts the
world, history, and even precursors as knowing, in their rival ways,
as Eliot and Whitman. Crane condenses the upward intensities of
his first six octaves by a deliberate recall of his own Columbus
triumphantly but delusively chanting: "I bring you back Cathay!"
But Crane's Columbus invoked the Demiurge under Emily Dickinson's name for him, "Inquisitor! incognizable Word/ of Eden."
This beautiful pathos of defeat, in "Ave Maria," was consonant with
Whitman's "Prayer of Columbus," where the battered, wrecked old
mariner denied all knowledge: "I know not even my own word past
or present." Crane's American burden, in the second half of "Atlantis," is to start again where Dickinson and Whitman ended, and
where Eliot had sought to show no fresh start was possible. Knowledge is precisely the Gnostic sense—a knowing that knows the
knower and is, *in itself,* the form of salvation—becomes Crane's
formidable hymn addressed directly to itself, to poem and to bridge,
until they become momentarily: "—One Song, one Bridge of Fire!"
But is this persuasively different from the "Hand of Fire" that
gathers the kiss of our agony?

The dialectic of Gnosticism is a triad of negation, evasion, and
extravagance. Lurianic Kabbalah renders these as contraction,
breaking-of-the-vessels, and restitution. Fate, freedom, power is the

Emersonian or American equivalent. All of these triads translate aesthetically into a dialectic of limitation, substitution, and representation, as I have shown in several critical books starting with *A Map of Misreading*. Crane's negation or limitation, his contraction into Fate, is scarcely different from Eliot's, but then such rival negative theologies as Valentinian Gnosticism and Johannine Christianity are difficult to distinguish in their accounts of how to express Divinity. Gnostic evasion, like Crane's notorious freedom and range in troping, is clearly more inventive than authorized Christian modes of substitution, just as Gnostic extravagance, again like Crane's hyperbolical Sublime, easily surpasses orthodox expressions of Power.

Crane's elaborate evasiveness is crucial in the seventh stanza of "Atlantis," where the upward movement of the tropology has ened, and a westward lateral sweep of vision is substituted, with the Bridge no longer confronted and addressed but seen now as binding the continent:

> We left the haven hanging in the night—
> Sheened harbor lanterns backward fled the keel.
> Pacific here at time's end, bearing corn,—
> Eyes stammer through the pangs of dust and steel.
> And still the circular, indubitable frieze
> Of heaven's meditation, yoking wave
> To kneeling wave, one song devoutly binds—
> The vernal strophe chimes from deathless strings!

The third line implies not merely a circuit of the earth, but an achieved peace at the end of days, a millennial harvest. When the Bridge returns in this stanza's last four lines, it has become heaven's own meditation, the known knowing the human knower. And such a knowing leads Crane on to the single most central stanza of his life and work:

> O Thou steeled Cognizance whose leap commits
> The agile precincts of the lark's return;
> Within whose lariat sweep encinctured sing
> In single chrysalis the many twain,—
> Of stars thou art the stitch and stallion glow
> And like an organ, Thou, with sound of doom—
> Sight, sound and flesh Thou leadest from time's realm
> As love strikes clear direction for the helm.

Contrast the precise Shelleyan equivalent:

> The One remains, the many change and pass;
> Heaven's light forever shines, Earth's shadows fly;
> Life, like a dome of many-colored glass,
> Stains the white radiance of Eternity,
> Until Death tramples it to fragments.—Die,
> If thou wouldst be with that which thou dost seek!
> Follow where all is fled!—Rome's azure sky,
> Flowers, ruins, statues, music, words, are weak
> The glory they transfuse with fitting truth to speak.

Superficially, the two stanzas are much at variance, with Crane's tone apparently triumphal, Shelley's despairing. But the pragmatic or merely natural burden of both stanzas is quite suicidal. The Bridge, as "steeled Cognizance," resolves the many into One, but this music of unity is a "sound of doom" for all flesh and its senses living in time's realm. Love's "clear direction," as in Shelley's climatic stanza, is towards death. But Shelley is very much involved in his own relation, as poet, to his own vision. Crane's role, as known to the Bridge's knower, forsakes that relation, and a terrifyingly free concentration on the content of poetic vision is the reward. "Of stars Thou art the stitch and stallion glow," Marlowe himself would have envied, but such both terms of the trope, bridge and stars, exclude the human, Crane is impelled onwards to extraordinary achievements in hyperbole. When the bridge is "iridescently upborne/ Through the bright drench and fabric of *our veins,*" then the human price of Gnosticism begins to mount also. Crane insists that all this is "to our joy," but that joy is as dialectical as Shelley's despair. And Crane, supremely intelligent, counts the cost, anticipating all criticism:

> Migrations that must needs void memory,
> Inventions that cobblestone the heart,—
> Unspeakable Thou Bridge to Thee, O Love
> Thy pardon for this history, whitest Flower,
> O Answerer of all,—Anemone,—
> Now while thy petals spend the suns above us, hold—
> (O Thou whose radiance doth inherit me)
> Atlantis,—hold thy floating singer late!

Would it make a difference if this read: "Cathay,—hold thy floating singer late!" So that the prayer of pariah would belong to

Columbus and not to Orpheus? Yes, for the final stanza then would have the Orphic strings leap and converge to a question clearly different:

> — One Song, one Bridge of Fire! Is it Atlantis,
> Now pity steeps the grass and rainbows ring
> The serpent with the eagle in the leaves...?

Crane's revision of the Orphic stance of *White Buildings,* of lyrics like "Repose of Rivers" and "Passage," here allows him a difference that is a triumph. His serpent and eagle are likelier to be Shelley's than Nietzsche's, for they remain at strife *within* their border of covenant, the ring of rainbows. Atlantis is urged to hold its Orpheus late, as a kind of newly fused Platonic myth of reconcilement to a higher world of forms, a myth of which Gnosticism was a direct heir. "Is it Cathay?" repeating the noble delusion of Columbus, is not a question hinting defeat, but foreboding victory. Yet Orphic victories are dialectical, as Crane well knew. Knowledge indeed is the kernel, for Crane astutely shows awareness of what the greatest poets always know, which is that their figurations intend the will's revenge against time's "it was" but actually achieve the will's limits, in the bewilderments of the abyss of troping and of tropes.

The coda to Crane's poetry, and his life, is "The Broken Tower," where the transumption of the Orphic quest does allow a final triumph:

> And so it was I entered the broken world
> To trace the visionary company of love, its voice
> An instant in the wind (I know not whither hurled)
> But not for long to hold each desperate choice.

Crane mentions reading other books by Pater, but not the unfinished novel, *Gaston de Latour.* Its first few chapters, at least, would have fascinated him, and perhaps he did look into the opening pages, where the young Gaston undergoes a ceremony bridging the spirit and nature:

> Gaston alone, with all his mystic preoccupations, by the privilege of youth, seemed to belong to both, and link the visionary company about him to the external scene.

The "privilege of youth" was still Crane's when he died, and "The Broken Tower" remains as one of those links.

Chronology of Important Dates

1899   Harold Hart Crane born July 21, in Garretsville, Ohio.

1908   Moved to Cleveland, Ohio, where his father started candy business.

1913   Began to write verse while in high school.

1916   "C 33" published in *Bruno's Weekly*. Moved to New York to write and prepare for college.

1917   Began to use name "Hart Crane" for published work.

1918   Returned to Cleveland, tried to enlist in armed services, was turned down as underaged. Worked briefly as a riveter, then as a reporter for the Cleveland *Plain Dealer* after World War I ended.

1919   Returned to New York, became advertising manager for *The Little Review*. Became a close friend of Gorham Munson. In November moved to Akron, Ohio, to work in one of father's candy stores. Had first homosexual affair.

1920-1921   Worked for father in Cleveland and Washington, D.C. Quit in April, 1921, after quarrel. Wrote "Black Tambourine" in February, 1921, "Chaplinesque" in September.

1922   Hired as copywriter by Cleveland advertising agency. Wrote "Praise for an Urn" in spring.

1923   Completed "For the Marriage of Faustus and Helen" in January. Formed idea of *The Bridge*. Returned to New York. Met Waldo Frank. Worked for J. Walter Thompson advertising agency. Spent end of year in Woodstock, New York.

1924   Employed by Sweet's Catalogue Service. Moved to 110 Columbia Heights, Brooklyn, rented room once occupied by Roebling, architect of the Brooklyn Bridge. Met Allen Tate.

1925 Completed "Voyages" in April. Received $1,000 from Otto Kahn and promise of $1,000 more to enable him to work on *The Bridge*. Spent part of summer in Patterson, New York.

1926 Winter and spring in Patterson, New York with Tates. Left after quarrel. Went to Isle of Pines, completed much of *The Bridge*. Returned to New York and Patterson for autumn and winter. *White Buildings* published by Liveright.

1927 Spent five months in California as traveling secretary to Herbert Wise. Met Yvor Winters.

1928 Left California after quarrel with mother. Grandmother died, leaving $5,000 legacy. Quarrel over bequest led to final estrangement from mother. Left for Europe in November.

1929 While in Paris met Harry and Caresse Crosby, who wished to publish *The Bridge*. Returned to New York in July to complete the poem.

1930 *The Bridge* published in February by The Black Sun Press (Paris), in April by Liveright (New York).

1931 Lived with father in Chagrin Falls, Ohio, for several months. Won a Guggenheim Fellowship, went to Mixcoac, Mexico, in April. Father died. Lived with Peggy Baird, former wife of Malcolm Cowley.

1932 Completed "The Broken Tower" on March 25. Sailed April 24 from Vera Cruz on the S.S. *Orizaba,* returning to New York. On morning of April 26, leapt overboard and was lost at sea.

1933 *The Collected Poems of Hart Crane* published by Liveright.

Notes on the Editor and Contributors

ALAN TRACHTENBERG, the editor of this volume, is Professor of American Studies and English at Yale University. He is the author of *Brooklyn Bridge: Fact and Symbol* (1979) and other works on American literature and culture.

JOSEPH WARREN BEACH (1880-1957) was Professor of English at the University of Minnesota for many years. His works include *The Comic Spirit in George Meredith* (1911), *The Technique of Thomas Hardy* (1922), and *American Fiction, 1920-1940* (1941).

MARIUS BEWLEY (1915-1973) was Professor of English at Rutgers University. He is the author of *The Complex Fate* (1952) and *The Eccentric Design* (1959).

R. P. BLACKMUR (1904-1965), critic and poet, was Professor of English at Princeton University. He is the author of *The Double Agent* (1935), *Language as Gesture* (1952), and *Form and Value in Modern Poetry* (1957).

HAROLD BLOOM is Professor of Humanities at Yale University. His works include *The Visionary Company* (1961), *The Anxiety of Influence* (1973), and *Wallace Stevens* (1977).

WALDO FRANK (1889-1967), novelist and critic, was a founder and editor of *The Seven Arts*. His numerous books include *Our America* (1919), *Virgin Spain* (1926), and *The Rediscovery of America* (1929).

RICHARD HUTSON is Professor of English at the University of California at Berkeley.

R. W. B. LEWIS is Professor of English at Yale University. He is the author of *The American Adam* (1955), *The Picaresque Saint* (1960), *The Poetry of Hart Crane* (1967), and *Edith Wharton: A Biography* (1975).

SHERMAN PAUL is Professor of English at the University of Iowa. His books include *Edmund Wilson: A Study of Literary Vocation in Our Time* (1965), *Emerson's Angle of Vision* (1969), *Hart's Bridge* (1973), and *Olson's Push: Origin, Black Mountain, and Recent American Poetry* (1978).

DEREK SAVAGE is the author of *The Personal Principle: Studies in Modern Poetry* (1944) and *The Withered Branch: Six Studies in the Modern Novel* (1950).

ALLEN TATE (1899-1979), poet and critic, taught at various universities and was Professor of English at the University of Minnesota before his retirement. He is the author of *Reactionary Essays on Poetry and Ideas* (1936), *The Forlorn Demon* (1953), and many other works of criticism, biography, and fiction. The most comprehensive volume of his poetry is *Collected Poems 1919-1976* (1977).

JOHN E. UNTERECKER is Professor of English at the University of Hawaii at Manoa. He is the author of *A Reader's Guide to William Butler Yeats* (1959) and *Voyager: A Life of Hart Crane* (1969).

WILLIAM CARLOS WILLIAMS (1883-1963) wrote poetry, criticism and fiction while also pursuing the full-time practice of medicine. His many works include *In the American Grain* (1925) and *Paterson* (1963).

YVOR WINTERS (1900-1968), poet and critic, was Professor of English at Stanford University. His works include *Primitivism and Decadence* (1937) and *In Defense of Reason* (1947).

PHILIP R. YANNELLA is Professor of English at Temple University.

Selected Bibliography

Butterfield, R. W., *The Broken Arc: A Study of Hart Crane.* Edinburgh: Oliver and Boyd, 1969.

Cambon, Glauco, *The Inclusive Flame: Studies in American Poetry.* Bloomington, Indiana: Indiana University Press, 1963.

Coffmann, Stanley K., Jr., "Symbolism in *The Bridge,*" Publication of the Modern Language Association, LXVI (March 1951), 65-77.

Cowley, Malcolm, *Exile's Return.* New York: Compass Books, 1956.

Dembo, L. S., *Hart Crane's Sanskrit Charge: A Study of The Bridge.* Ithaca, New York: Cornell University Press, 1960.

Friedman, Paul, *"The Bridge:* A Study in Symbolism," *Psychoanalytic Quarterly,* 21 (1952), 49-80.

Hazo, Samuel John, *Hart Crane: An Introduction and Interpretation.* New York: Barnes and Noble, 1963.

Herman, Barbara, "The Lanaguage of Hart Crane," *Sewanee Review,* 58 (January-March 1950), 52-67.

Hoffman, Frederick J., "The Text: Hart Crane's *The Bridge:* The Crisis in Experiment," in *The Twenties* (New York: The Viking Press, 1955), pp. 223-239.

Horton, Philip, *Hart Crane: The Life of an American Poet.* New York: W. W. Norton and Co., Inc., 1937.

Kramer, Maurice, "Six Voyages of a Derelict Seer," *Sewanee Review,* 73 (July-September 1965), 410-423.

Leavis, F. R., "Hart Crane From This Side," *Scrutiny,* 7 (March 1939), 443-446.

Leibowitz, Herbert A., *Hart Crane: An Introduction to the Poetry.* New York: Columbia University Press, 1968.

Lewis, R. W. B., *The Poetry of Hart Crane: A Critical Study*. Princeton, New Jersey: Princeton University Press, 1967.

Lewis, Thomas S. W., ed., *Letters of Hart Crane and His Family*. New York: Columbia University Press, 1974.

Munson, Gorham B., "Hart Crane: Young Titan in the Sacred Wood," in *Destinations: A Canvass of American Literature Since 1900* (New York: J. H. Sears, 1928).

Parkinson, Thomas F., ed., *Hart Crane and Yvor Winters: Their Literary Correspondence*. Berkeley, California: University of California Press, 1978.

Paul, Sherman, *Hart's Bridge*. Urbana, Illinois: University of Illinois Press, 1972.

Pearce, Roy Harvey, *The Continuity of American Poetry*. Princeton, New Jersey: Princeton University Press, 1961.

Perry, Robert L., *The Shared Vision of Waldo Frank and Hart Crane*. University of Nebraska Studies, New Series, 33. Lincoln, Nebraska: University of Nebraska Press, 1966.

Quinn, Sister M. Bernetta, *The Metamorphic Tradition in Modern Poetry*. New Brunswick, New Jersey: Rutgers University Press, 1955.

Quinn, Vincent Gerard, *Hart Crane*. New York, Twayne Publishers, 1963.

Ramsey, Warren, "Crane and Laforgue," *Sewanee Review*, 58 (July-September 1950), 439-449.

Riddel, Joseph, "Hart Crane's Poetics of Failure," English Literary History, Vol. 33, No. 4 (December 1966), 472-496.

Schwartz, Joseph, compiler, *Hart Crane: An Annotated Critical Bibliography*. New York: D. Lewis, 1970.

Slote, Bernice, "Views of *The Bridge*," in *Start with the Sun: Studies in the Whitman Tradition*, by James E. Miller, Jr., Karl Shapiro, and Bernice Slote (Lincoln, Nebraska: University of Nebraska Press, 1960), pp. 137-165.

Spears, Monroe K., *Hart Crane*. University of Minnesota Pamphlets on American Writers, No. 47. Minneapolis: University of Minnesota Press, 1965.

Tate, Allen, "Hart Crane," in *Reactionary Essays on Poetry and Ideas* (New York: Charles Scribner's Sons, 1936), pp. 26-42.

Unterecker, John E., *Voyager: A Life of Hart Crane.* New York: Farrar, Straus and Giroux, 1969.

Vogler, Thomas A., *Preludes to Vision: The Epic Venture in Blake, Wordsworth, Keats* and *Hart Crane.* Berkeley, California: University of California Press, 1971.

Waggoner, Hyatt H., "Hart Crane: Beyond All Sesames of Science," in *The Heel of Elohim: Science and Values in Modern American Poetry* (Norman, Oklahoma: University of Oklahoma Press, 1950), pp. 155-192.

Weber, Brom, *Hart Crane: A Biographical and Critical Study.* New York: Bodley Press, 1948.

———, ed., *The Letters of Hart Crane 1916-1932.* Berkeley, California: University of California Press, 1965.

Willingham, John R., " 'Three Songs' of Hart Crane's *The Bridge:* A Reconsideration," *American Literature,* 27 (March 1955), 62-68.

Winters, Yvor, "The Significance of *The Bridge,* by Hart Crane, or What are We to Think of Professor X?," in *In Defense of Reason* (New York: The Swallow Press, 1947), pp. 577-603.

Index